Performance Measurement in Local Sustainability Policy

Local officials are responsible for a number of important tasks that have a significant impact on the quality of life of most Americans. Arguably, the policy choices made by local governments in the United States more directly impact individual well-being than do the choices made at any other level of government. From zoning decisions to the creation of parks and the maintenance of sidewalks and trails, local governments are largely responsible for direct services to the public and can provide the necessary tools and skills to create an attractive and vibrant community. And yet one area of significant importance for both individuals and for the country as a whole, local sustainability, is a relatively new policy area for many American municipalities. For example, how many local governments are adopting sustainability policies and plans? How are those initiatives performing? Without an honest and robust examination of both the effectiveness and the efficiency of local sustainability policies, the success of the entire sustainability movement in the United States is uncertain. This book provides readers with a comprehensive understanding of what constitutes local sustainability and why it matters.

Focusing closely on environmental initiatives, economic development issues, and social equity concerns, each chapter offers both an account of the sustainability policies being adopted and a close exploration of the performance measurement activities of cities in that policy area. Readers are introduced to the metrics that American cities are using to measure the performance of their sustainability efforts, as well as benchmarks and comparison statistics that may be used to develop and evaluate the performance assessment efforts in their own sustainability programs. Students of public administration, urban planning, and political science – as well as public officials – will find this book useful to understand the complexity of sustainability and local government.

Susan M. Opp is Associate Professor at Colorado State University, USA.

Samantha L. Mosier is Assistant Professor at East Carolina University, USA.

Jeffery L. Osgood, Jr. is Professor of Public Policy and Administration and Senior Vice Provost at West Chester University of Pennsylvania, USA.

With,
Mark W. Davis is Assistant Professor of Public Policy and Administration and Chair of the Sustainability Advisory Council at West Chester University of Pennsylvania, USA.

"This is one of the few books in the policy field that presents both the practitioner perspective as well as the academic literature on these issues, drawing on fascinating examples that document the multiple values at play. This volume not only focuses on the substance of the policy, but is also effective for classroom use."

—**Beryl A. Radin,** *Georgetown University, USA*

PUBLIC ADMINISTRATION AND PUBLIC POLICY SERIES

A Comprehensive Publication Program

EDITOR-IN-CHIEF

DAVID H. ROSENBLOOM

Distinguished Professor of Public Administration
American University, Washington, DC

Founding Editor

JACK RABIN

RECENTLY PUBLISHED BOOKS

Performance Measurement in Local Sustainability Policy, Susan M. Opp, Samantha L. Mosier, and Jeffery L. Osgood, Jr., with Mark W. Davis

The Practice of International Development, edited by Jerrold Keilson and Michael Gubser

The Nonprofit Human Resource Management Handbook: From Theory to Practice, Edited by Jessica E. Sowa and Jessica K. A. Word

Cost and Optimization in Government: An Introduction to Cost Accounting, Operations Management, and Quality Control, Second edition, by Aman Khan

The Constitutional School of American Public Administration, edited by Stephanie P. Newbold and David H. Rosenbloom

Contracting for Services in State and Local Government Agencies, second edition, William Sims Curry

Democracy and Civil Society in a Global Era, Scott Nicholas Romaniuk and Marguerite Marlin

Development and the Politics of Human Rights, Scott Nicholas Romaniuk and Marguerite Marlin

Public Administration and Policy in the Caribbean, Indianna D. Minto-Coy and Evan Berman

Sustainable Development and Human Security in Africa: Governance as the Missing Link, Louis A. Picard, Terry F. Buss, Taylor B. Seybolt, and Macrina C. Lelei

Information and Communication Technologies in Public Administration: Innovations from Developed Countries, Christopher G. Reddick and Leonidas Anthopoulos

Creating Public Value in Practice: Advancing the Common Good in a Multi-Sector, Shared-Power, No-One-Wholly-in-Charge World, edited by John M. Bryson, Barbara C. Crosby, and Laura Bloomberg

Digital Divides: The New Challenges and Opportunities of e-Inclusion, Kim Andreasson

Living Legends and Full Agency: Implications of Repealing the Combat Exclusion Policy, G.L.A. Harris

Performance Measurement in Local Sustainability Policy

Susan M. Opp, Samantha L. Mosier, and Jeffery L. Osgood, Jr.
With Mark W. Davis

NEW YORK AND LONDON

First published 2018
by Routledge
711 Third Avenue, New York, NY 10017

and by Routledge
2 Park Square, Milton Park, Abingdon, Oxon, OX14 4RN

Routledge is an imprint of the Taylor & Francis Group, an informa business

Library of Congress Cataloging-in-Publication Data
A catalog record for this book has been requested

ISBN: 978-0-8153-7305-6 (hbk)
ISBN: 978-1-351-24427-5 (ebk)

Typeset in Sabon
by codeMantra

Printed in the United Kingdom
by Henry Ling Limited

Dedicated to Drs. Beryl Radin, Paul Posner, Stan Meiburg, and all the great pracademics that have provided us with the inspiration in all that we do. You are our inspiration. Thank you.

Contents

About the Authors

Susan M. Opp, PhD, is currently an Associate Professor at Colorado State University in Fort Collins, Colorado. Dr. Opp is a pracademic who focuses on questions of local sustainability, economic development, and urban affairs in her research, teaching, and community service activities. Since receiving her PhD in 2007 from the University of Louisville, Dr. Opp has served as the director of a Network of Schools of Public Policy, Affairs, and Administration (NASPAA)-accredited Master of Public Administration (MPA) program, graduate programs coordinator, internship director, and a variety of other public service-related work. Her research has appeared in a number of academic and professional outlets including *Urban Affairs Review, Journal of Urban Affairs, Economic Development Quarterly,* and *Local Environment,* to name a few. She is also the author or editor of two other books—including one printed as part of the American Society for Public Administration (ASPA) series on public administration and policy in (2013). She had the distinct pleasure of being one of the inaugural APSA "Pracademic Fellows" at the Environmental Protection Agency in 2016—thanks, in part, to the efforts of Dr. Beryl Radin.

Samantha L. Mosier, PhD, is an Assistant Professor at East Carolina University. She received her PhD from Colorado State University in 2014. Dr. Mosier's work focuses on public policy and implementation questions in local sustainability initiatives, including university-community partnerships, and food and agriculture policy, with an emphasis in sustainable production and labeling regulations. She is author of *Creating Organic Standards in U.S. States* and has had her research appear in other outlets including *Environment and Planning C: Politics and Space, Environmental Management, Food Policy,* and the *Public Administration Review*'s Speak Your Mind Symposium. In addition, Dr. Mosier is active in her community, previously serving on the Greene County (MO) Extension Council, the Park Board of Willard (MO), and working on community-based program and policy evaluations.

Jeffery L. Osgood, Jr., PhD, is Professor of Public Policy and Administration and currently serves as Senior Vice Provost at West Chester University of Pennsylvania. He served as founding chair of the department and successfully led the Master of Public Administration program through the accreditation process. Additionally, he was responsible for the development of the Doctor of Public Administration, the university's first research doctorate. Dr. Osgood's research focuses on local government and economic development. His most recent book (2017) is entitled *Participatory Budgeting in the United States: A Guide for Local Governments*, published in the ASPA Public Administration and Public Policy series by Routledge/Taylor and Francis.

With,

Mark W. Davis, PhD, is currently an Assistant Professor of Public Policy and Administration and Chair of the Sustainability Advisory Council at West Chester University of Pennsylvania. Dr. Davis's research includes public sector performance measurement, urban politics, environmental and sustainability policy, and collaborative governance. His research has been published in a number of outlets including *Policy Studies Journal* and the Program for the Advancement of Research on Conflict and Collaboration (E-PARCC, Syracuse University). His teaching in public affairs is at the graduate level and includes budgeting, management, and his personal favorite American Public Policy. Dr. Davis completed his PhD studies at the University of Colorado Denver in the School of Public Affairs where he was a NSF IGERT Researcher in Sustainable Urban Infrastructure Systems and his Master of Public Affairs from Indiana University School of Public and Environmental Affairs. Dr. Davis is comfortable both in the academic and practitioner worlds. Prior to moving into academia full time, Dr. Davis worked as an environmental professional in the fields of integrated solid waste management, water supply and water treatment, and wastewater collection and treatment in a variety of management-level positions. In his spare time, Dr. Davis is an avid bicyclist.

Figures and Tables

Figures

Tables

Contributors

Jennifer L. Collins is the Assistance and Outreach Manager at the Indiana Department of Environmental Management's (IDEM) Office of Program Support. She has worked with IDEM for 15 years where she served as the Pollution Prevention Branch Chief, a Section Chief in the Air Compliance Branch, and as an Air Compliance Inspector. She has a BS in Public Affairs with a concentration in Environmental Science from Indiana University School of Public and Environmental Affairs.

Delaware Regional Valley Planning Commission has served the Greater Philadelphia region for more than 50 years. DVRPC works to foster regional cooperation in a nine-county, two-state area. City, county, and state representatives work together to address key issues, including transportation, land use, environmental protection, and economic development. DVRPC serves as the regional planning agency for the nine-county, bistate, Greater Philadelphia Area, providing guidance and assistance to build a sustainable and livable region. DVRPC provides services to member governments and others through planning analysis, data collection, and mapping services. DVRPC was formed by an Interstate Compact through legislation passed by the Pennsylvania Legislature in 1965, as reenacted and amended in 1967, and by the New Jersey Legislature in a series of conforming acts passed between 1966 and 1974.

David D'Onofrio completed a dual master's degree in urban planning and atmospheric science from Georgia Tech in May 2009. David is a principle planner with the Transportation Access and Mobility Group at the Atlanta Regional Commission (ARC). D'Onofrio's work focuses on air quality, climate change, and transportation. His work includes near-road emissions exposure, transportation conformity, climate resiliency, and emissions calculations for transportation projects. D'Onofrio also works on regional policy, helping to develop ARC's Atlanta Region's Plan Policy Framework and the project evaluation methods used by the agency to allocate transportation funding.

Vanessa M. Fenley currently works as a consultant, primarily in a program management and evaluation capacity on projects related to affordable housing, homelessness, and poverty. Prior to this work, she held positions as the Executive Director of Homeward 2020, a nonprofit initiative dedicated to making homelessness rare, short-lived, and nonrecurring in Fort Collins, Colorado, and as the Director of the Office of Drug Strategy and Drug Strategy Commission for the City and County of Denver. She has held seats with various boards and commissions, including the Neighbor to Neighbor Board of Directors, the Outreach Fort Collins Board of Directors, the Colorado Balance of State Continuum of Care Governing Board, the Denver Crime Prevention and Control Commission, and the Liver Health Connection Board of Directors. Vanessa will receive her PhD in Public Affairs from the University of Colorado Denver in Fall 2017. She received her Master of Arts degree in Sociology from the University of Kansas and her Bachelor of Science degree in Sociology and Organizational Communication from Missouri State University.

Dr. Jairo H. Garcia is the Director of Climate Policies and Renewables in the City of Atlanta. Dr. Garcia develops innovative policies and educational programs to make Atlanta a top-tier sustainable city and reduce its carbon footprint. In 2017, Dr. Garcia received the Individual Climate Leadership Award by the EPA for his leadership both in addressing climate change and engaging organization, peers, and partners. Dr. Garcia worked as a research assistant for the Earth Institute at Columbia University in New York City, and his teaching experience includes two teaching assistant positions at Columbia University, a faculty adjunct and thesis advisor position at Concordia University, and an instructor position for the UCLA Extension program in Global Sustainability. Dr. Garcia holds an engineering degree, an MSc in Management of Information Technologies, an MSc in Sustainability Management, and a doctoral degree in Educational Technology and Sustainability.

Kolbe Krzyzanowski is an analyst in the Economic Development Department of the City of Kansas City and has previously worked as a consultant with the other development organizations such as the Economic Development Corporation of Kansas City. Kolbe has a master's degree in economics from the University of Missouri–Kansas City with an emphasis on economic development. Kolbe's work has focused primarily on the use and development of data for use in public policy decision-making and the evaluation of development transactions between government agencies and private developers. A large emphasis of this work has been on converting transactional data over many years and separate development projects into a workable set of data to aid in the public development process. Kolbe lives in his hometown of Kansas City, MO, with his wife, Alia. He is a voting member of the World Science Fiction Society, and when not working in the real world of economic development, he spends his time reading and writing speculative fiction.

Eric Roche began working with the City of Kansas City, MO, as a Cookingham-Noll Management Fellow in 2013. In his current role, he serves as Chief Data Officer with the City Manager's Office of Performance Management. Eric's role focuses on using data to uncover relationships, communicate ideas, and improve performance within and across all city departments. Eric also oversees the city's open data suite. Open data initiatives include OpenData KC, KCSTAT Performance Management Dashboards, and Open Budget. He works closely with a variety of institutions to further the use of data in city government, including the Harvard Civic Analytics Network, the University of Kansas, Bloomberg's What Works Cities Initiative, the Sunlight Foundation, GovEX at Johns Hopkins University, the Behavioral Insights Team, Code for America, and the Applied Data Analytics Program. Eric received his undergraduate degree in political science with a minor in economics from Colorado State University and his masters in Public Administration from the University of Kansas. Eric lives in Kansas City, MO, with his lovely wife, Stephanie. You can reach Eric by email at Eric.Roche@kcmo.org, online at linkedin.com/in/ericroche, or via Twitter @KansasCityEric.

Kirsten C. Silveira serves as a Process Improvement Specialist II in the City of Fort Collins, CO—working to empower a citywide culture of creative problem-solving and shared leadership. She is passionate about public service and believes change is only sustainable when coupled with employee empowerment. Kirsten began her local government career in Baltimore City's Bureau of the Budget and Management Research, where she managed the City's public safety portfolio of $570M, served as a leader in the City's Outcome Budgeting process, and transformed the way Baltimore engaged the community around budget decisions. In 2016, Kirsten took on the role Government Innovations Analyst, where she managed Baltimore's Lean Government and Innovation Fund programs, supporting City agencies in process improvement and managing a revolving loan fund used for one-time investments that lead to improved results, increased revenue, and/or reduced operating costs for the City. Kirsten received the Medallion for Meritorious Service Award from Mayor Stephanie Rawlings-Blake for her public service to Baltimore residents through commitment to ensuring the quality and efficiency of City services with innovation and process improvement. Prior to returning to Colorado, Kirsten served as the Director of Continuous Improvement for Baltimore Mayor Catherine E. Pugh. Kirsten holds a BA in political science from Colorado State University and a Master of Public Administration from the Edwin O. Stene School of Public Affairs and Administration at the University of Kansas.

Denise Smith has worked in several different capacities for the Town of Silver City since 2010, starting as the Neighborhood Program Coordinator in the Office of Sustainability, advancing to Water Conservation Planner, then becoming the Director of the Office of Sustainability. The Office of Sustainability was enveloped into the Community Development Department in 2017, and Ms. Smith's current title is Sustainability Planner/Trails Coordinator. Ms. Smith is working toward sustainability in the Town by increasing recycling and water conservation, coordinating trail construction and maintenance, and facilitating solar installation on town-owned buildings, local businesses, and other governmental offices. With a love for grant writing, she has helped bring a variety of grant funding into the Town from state, federal, and nonprofit sources. She serves on the Board of the Southwest New Mexico Green Chamber and is the chair of the Mayor's Recycling Advisory Committee. Ms. Smith was previously employed for over 23 years as a Wildlife Biologist and Program Manager for four different federal agencies.

Acknowledgments

We would like to acknowledge and thank the significant investment in time, energy, resources, and support that made this book project possible. First, and perhaps most obviously, we would like to thank Routledge Press for creating and sustaining a venue where academics and practitioners can work together for the betterment of public service and society. The series on Public Administration and Public Policy has been a valuable resource for many working in the public service during these challenging times, and we are eternally grateful for the opportunity to contribute to such a valuable series. A sincere and special thank you is due to Misha Kydd and Laura Stearns. Both have been a pleasure to work with and we want to express our heartfelt thanks to both of them for all the support, patience, and good humor they have shown us over the past year and a half. Last but not least, we all three would like to give a resounding thank you to the hardworking and dedicated public servants that contributed case studies to this book. These public servants often go thankless in their day-to-day jobs, and their willingness to share their stories has added an invaluable dimension to this book. We are truly indebted to them for their true dedication to public service.

Each of us would like to offer our own brief separate thanks. Susan Opp would like to extend her personal appreciation to her family for their endless patience with long work nights, missed activities, and overall distraction over the course of this book project. She would also like to recognize the pracademic role model she seeks to be like in her work—Dr. Beryl Radin. Thank you, Dr. Radin, for providing an exceptional role model for all pracademics.

Samantha Mosier extends much gratitude and thanks to her family for the continual support for her professional endeavors. She deeply appreciates their ability to know when it is time to take a break from working and detach instead. In addition, Samantha is very thankful to her coworkers at Missouri State University for being supportive and a great group of people to work with every semester. Finally, an extensive amount of gratitude is given to Susan Opp, a lifelong mentor and friend.

Jeff Osgood extends a debt of gratitude to Susan and Samantha for their extensive efforts and work on this manuscript. He is in awe of their dedication and fortitude in seeing this project through. Jeff is also extremely grateful for Mark Davis's work in the end, which rounded out the remaining parts of the volume. These three individuals represent the best of collegiality and friendship. Jeff would like to thank Kellen Kane for his contributions as a research assistant and Jared Stufft for his amazing work as a statistical assistant.

Part I

Introduction to Local Sustainability Policy

1 Introduction to Local Sustainability and Performance Measurement

Local officials are responsible for a number of important tasks that have a significant impact on the quality of life of most Americans. Arguably, the policy choices made by local governments in the United States have more of a direct impact on individual well-being than do the choices made at any other level of government. From zoning decisions to the creation of parks and the maintenance of sidewalks and trails, local governments are largely responsible for direct services to the public and can provide the necessary tools and skills to create an attractive and vibrant community. This book tackles one area of significant importance for both individuals and for the country as a whole: local sustainability efforts. Emphasis on developing sustainability initiatives at the local level is a relatively new policy area for many American municipalities.

Chapters in this book provide readers with an in-depth examination of local sustainability initiatives with an added focus on the performance measurement activities surrounding these policies. In essence, this volume provides evidence and examples of how cities can pursue sustainability policies and how they might begin to assess the progression toward particular desired goals and outcomes.

Faced with a relative absence of significant federal or state action on sustainability, local efforts represent the front line for these important initiatives. Federal action on sustainability has largely stagnated since the 1980s and 1990s because of growing divides in Congress and increasing pressures to use the court system to resolve disputes; moreover, state efforts have largely consisted of patchwork initiatives (Fischer, 2010; Klyza & Sousa, 2013; Mazmanian & Kraft, 2009). As a result, local governments have rapidly emerged as the policy leaders in adopting sustainability initiatives across the United States. Given the close relationship between sustainability and the quality of life for city residents, it is important to understand the landscape of these sustainability efforts. For example, how many local governments are adopting sustainability policies and plans? What is the area content focus of those policies and plans? Furthermore, given the increasing scarcity of resources coupled with the politically charged nature of environmental issues in the United States, it is also necessary to consider the performance of these local policies. Without an honest and robust examination of both the effectiveness and the efficiency of local sustainability policies, the success of the entire sustainability movement in the United States is uncertain.

This book covers a range of subjects related to sustainability, and readers will gain a comprehensive understanding of what constitutes local sustainability and why it matters. The nature of sustainability as a topic and practice is complex and presents significant difficulties in balancing competing needs. This book focuses closely on local sustainability policy covering everything from environmental initiatives, economic development issues, and social equity concerns. Each chapter delves into major aspects of sustainability and provides readers with both an accounting of the policies being adopted and also a look into the performance measurement activities of cities in that policy area. Finally, readers will also be introduced to the metrics that American cities are using to measure the performance of their sustainability efforts. From the discussion of performance metrics, this book also provides readers with some potential benchmarks and comparison statistics that may be used to develop and evaluate the performance assessment efforts in their own sustainability programs. Students of public administration, urban planning, and political science will find this book useful as they begin to understand the complexity of sustainability and local government. Public officials will find this book useful as they begin to approach their own challenges with sustainability.

This first chapter provides readers with the necessary background information on this topic so that each chapter that follows will be contextualized in the larger frame of local government and local policymaking for sustainability. This first chapter introduces readers to local government administration, sustainability, and performance measurement. Chapter 2 of this book reports on the overall findings of a 2016 survey of municipalities concerning their policy and performance activities in sustainability. This second chapter provides important contextual information so that the entire landscape of sustainability is understood by the reader. The remaining chapters of this book, or Part II, focus on specific major policy areas commonly found under the larger sustainability umbrella. The book concludes with a final chapter reporting the overall lessons learned and directions for future research and policymaking in local sustainability initiatives.

Local Policymaking in the United States: Fragmentation and Demands > Resources

Local governments in the United States face a difficult working environment marked by infinite demands and scarce resources. To exacerbate this challenging environment, local governments are increasingly being tasked with responsibilities that were previously left to the states or to the federal government. As England, Pelissero, and Morgan (2017) say in their authoritative book on managing urban America, "...cities now operate largely in an intergovernmental milieu best described as 'fend for yourself' federalism" (p. 3). To be sure, local governments are responsible for some of the most important, highly visible, and impactful functions in society. At the same time, local governments face serious revenue raising and policymaking constraints due to a complex legal and economic structure (England et al., 2017; Peterson, 1981). The policy and programmatic choices that a local government makes can be expected to have a significant impact on the quality of life for all of residents living within that community. The legal environment and economic realities of local governments, both of which are not entirely within their control, create challenges for even the most skilled local official. These legal and economic constraints ultimately shape, and sometimes drive, the policy choices that local governments make every day.

Legal Environment of American Local Governments

The legal environment of American local governments is complicated and ever-evolving. The level of autonomy that an individual local government possesses varies based upon both the state that they are located in and also how they are legally defined under that state's laws. There is no such thing as a "one size fits all" when it comes to understanding the powers, constraints, and responsibilities of local governments across the United States. Each local government faces a unique legal structure that ultimately impacts their ability to pursue various initiatives.

The most visible and well-known dimension of local autonomy is related to a local government's status as either a Dillon's Rule (sometimes called a general law or statutory city) or a home rule government. "Dillon's Rule has been a guiding doctrine in the constitutional relations between state and local government for more than a century" (Grumm & Murphy, 1974, p. 120). In simplest terms, Dillon's Rule is the legal doctrine that declares local governments to be instruments of their respective states whereby they only possess the powers delegated to them by the state (England et al., 2017). In some cases, and in some cities, states retain significant centralized control over local governments, and in other cases they do not. Over the course of the last century most states opted to create a legal path, known as home rule, for local governments to obtain greater autonomy over their own affairs. Although the specific requirements and actual process to become a home rule city vary, it is generally the case that a home rule city will have greater autonomy to pursue policies and to manage the day-to-day activities of their community than will their non-home rule counterparts.

In addition to the state-local delegated authority concerns, a large body of court rulings has added to the complexity of local policymaking.

For example, the land-use planning activities of local governments are frequently subject to legal challenges whereby a court ruling can influence the policy choices of a local government (Salkin, 2017). One such area that has a lengthy history of court challenges is that of the regulation of sexually oriented businesses (SOBs). Local policy choices related to the regulation or the restriction of the location of these types of businesses are significantly constrained by a multitude of court rulings including, but not limited to, the 1986 Supreme Court decision on "Renton v Playtime Theatres" (MRSC, 2016). Although SOB regulation has some of the most extensive legal challenge history of all local land-use planning efforts, other areas face similar legal complexity and ongoing challenges. Most recently, cities have struggled with developing policies to limit or to reduce panhandling in their communities (see, for example, DeMillo, 2017; Palazzolo, 2017). Ultimately, American local governments operate in a highly fragmented and complex legal environment whereby officials must navigate a diverse set of rules, restrictions, demands, and mandates while also providing important services and protections to their community members. Being a local government administrator, policymaker, or researcher is no easy feat in this complex legal environment.

Economic Constraints

In addition to the legal complexity surrounding local policymaking activities, economic realities also pose challenges for local governments. As American cities face a growing set of responsibilities, they also face dwindling financial support from higher levels of government. For example, according to the 2012 census of governments, intergovernmental transfers to local governments decreased by 3.1 percent between 2011 and 2012 (US Census Bureau, 2012). Furthermore, "...cities continue to struggle to keep expenditures from outpacing revenues" (England et al., 2017, p. 313). In the quest to provide residents with needed services while also pursuing a high quality of life, local administrators often search for ways to raise additional revenue. Unfortunately, the fragmented nature of local governance makes raising revenue in a fair, equitable, and beneficial way a very difficult challenge that has led to many perverse outcomes in the past.

As Paul Peterson (1981) said in his groundbreaking book on local government, "...cities seek to improve their market position, their attractiveness as a locale for economic activity" (p. 22). Peterson's book set the stage for several decades of research into the fundamental limitations of local policymaking and the relative importance of economic interests to local policy choices (Opp, Osgood, & Rugeley, 2014). This vein of research relies on a fundamental assumption that local governments are constrained and are in a position where they must search for ways to increase the economic activity and revenues within their jurisdictions.

Furthermore, a concern with mobile capital (both in terms of business activity and in terms of taxpaying individuals) is thought to compel cities to compete amongst one another for finite sources of revenue and economic activity available to cities in the United States. This body of research has demonstrated that local governments often turn to economic development policy to provide jobs to residents and to grow revenue sources for the government (Osgood, Opp, & Bernotsky, 2012). Peterson's (1981) inspiration, Charles Tiebout (1956), pointed out that individuals and businesses "vote with their feet" and choose to locate in the community that provides the services they demand at the price they are willing to pay. It is this mobile nature of people and capital that provides an incentive for local governments to pursue policies that they hope will capture sources of revenue.

Research related to local economic development policy has routinely demonstrated that local efforts directed at attracting and retaining mobile capital do not fare as well as expected and sometimes even create poor outcomes for cities and their residents (Banzhaf & Walsh, 2005; Opp et al., 2014). At minimum, much of the evidence related to local economic development demonstrates that local policies seeking to attract mobile capital through financial incentives do not produce the economic benefits expected (Koven & Lyons, 2010; Osgood, Opp, & Bernotsky, 2012). Furthermore, "...targeted tax incentives and financial assistance—as currently practiced—are more likely to harm growth and income inequality" (Goetz, Partridge, Rickman, & Mujumdar, 2010, p. 428). Even with the overwhelming evidence that these incentive-based policies are not beneficial and that they tend to exacerbate interlocal competition, they are still the "go-to" method used to attract mobile capital (Osgood et al., 2012).

In addition to the attention paid to pursuing mobile capital, local governments may also struggle to engage in even the most basic form of redistributive policy: "...local governments have incentives to avoid redistributive policies because they offer few benefits and higher costs for those that cities wish to attract" (Craw, 2006, p. 361). It is thought, although somewhat contested in research, that the cities that choose to pursue redistributive policies will be rewarded with an influx of people that do not contribute to, and instead actually reduce, local revenues. At the same time, it is feared that investment into redistributive policy may actually prompt taxpaying residents to leave the city in favor of a city without these types of efforts and expenditures. To be sure, the economic realities of a limited and declining revenue stream, interjurisdictional competition for mobile and finite capital, and the fundamental need to balance local service demands with financial constraints make a local government official's job exceedingly difficult. By some measures it is surprising that sustainability efforts, particularly with the lack of a central focus on attracting mobile capital, have become so common in American cities. However, as a point of caution, the remaining chapters of this book demonstrate that although these policies are numerous, many of the cities that engage in sustainability policymaking do so in a very limited and selective way. This limited pursuit of sustainability may actually recreate many of the problems found with traditional developmental policies and makes understanding the performance of them very important and timely.

Local Sustainability: What Is It and Why Does It Matter?

The most commonly used definition for sustainability originated in the 1987 Bruntland Report *Our Common Future* where it was declared, "Sustainable development is development that meets the needs of the present without compromising the ability of future generations to meet their own needs" (Brundtland, Khalio, & Agnelli, 1987). In the years since this report was published, many American cities embraced the concept and developed their own similar definition. Even though sustainability and sustainable development are often conflated, there is an important distinction between the two. Sustainable development, while more well known, is generally a narrower concept than is sustainability. Sustainable development is typically focused on the relationship and tensions between economic development and environmental protection (Heberle & Opp, 2008). Sustainability, on the other hand, is most often conceived as a more comprehensive concept that attempts to balance three larger competing concerns—the so-called three E's: Economic development, Environmental protection, and social Equity (Opp & Saunders, 2013; Portney, 2013). Proponents of sustainability argue that if a community or society falls short on one of these three E's, long-term sustainability and well-being will be impossible (Opp & Saunders, 2013). In the most simple terms, the goal of sustainability is to ensure that the earth's environment and resources are able to sustain life while also ensuring that economic and social needs are met (Portney, 2013). When compared to Europe, the United States has been laggard in pursuing sustainability (Slavin, 2011). To date, the federal government has been very slow to adopt policies related to sustainability. Furthermore, state governments have been very uneven in their participation in sustainability policy development with just a few states emerging as leaders. Most of the policy activity related to sustainability in the United States has taken place in local governments.

A growing body of research has documented and studied the various sustainability efforts of American cities (see, for example, Opp & Osgood, 2013; Opp & Saunders, 2013; Portney, 2013). Some of the major findings of this research include an understanding of the types of cities that are more likely to adopt sustainability policies (Opp et al., 2014), the ways that economic development and environmental protection can work in tandem (Opp & Osgood, 2013; Osgood, Opp, & DeMasters, 2016), and also some of the unintended consequences resulting from the pursuit of local sustainability policies (Opp, 2016; Opp & Saunders, 2013). To date, we know that wealthier central cities located in the western part of the United States are more likely to adopt sustainability policies (Opp & Saunders, 2013). We also know that the presence of co-benefits increases the likelihood that a sustainability policy will be adopted (Opp & Mosier, 2017). Finally, research has also provided evidence that the social equity dimension of sustainability is largely absent from these local policy efforts (Opp & Saunders, 2013; Saha, 2009).

Why Do We Care about Sustainability?

If we believe that sustainability is an important goal for the future of the United States and the world, these local policy efforts are of significant importance. The political environment surrounding climate change and environmental science has detracted from a core feature of sustainability: quality of life. Although 97 percent of scientists studying climate change concur that humans are likely causing a warming trend that will have significant consequences for the Earth and for humans (Cook et al., 2016), very little political consensus or policy movement exists in the United States on this issue. Nonetheless, sustainability doesn't have to be about consensus or even about climate change. Sustainability is fundamentally about quality of life. At the most basic level, sustainability policies either create or protect things that contribute to a better quality of life for all Americans. What is important to recognize and understand is that each of the three E's of sustainability has, at their core, the ability to improve the quality of life for all people. More will be said on each of the three E's in the text that follows.

Sustainability: Environment

Environmental protection is certainly the most well known of the three dimensions of sustainability. In fact, to some people, the word sustainability is synonymous with environmental protection (Opp & Saunders, 2013). Environmental sustainability, at the most basic level, is about protecting and preserving the natural environment and the resources contained there. Policies that can be categorized under this dimension of sustainability will generally focus on reducing pollution, conserving natural resources, and sometimes preserving or protecting a species. Environmental sustainability policies can be both regulatory and non-regulatory and are not without significant political challenges across the United States.

Much of the federal-level policy directed at environmental protection comes in the form of command-and-control regulation (La Porte & Opp,

2016; Mazmanian & Kraft, 2009). The regulatory instruments used to protect or to preserve the environment are usually politically contentious and have been historically blamed for reducing the economic competitiveness of the United States (Porter & van der Linde, 1995). Policies such as the Clean Water Act (CWA) and the Clean Air Act (CAA) are key examples of regulatory environmental policies where standards are set and compliance is compelled by threat of penalty. To be sure, although imperfect, these policies have succeeded in improving and extending the lives of many Americans by providing cleaner air to breathe, protecting the fish we eat, reducing the contaminants in the water we drink, and simply increasing the overall health of our natural environment (Adler, Landman, & Cameron, 1993). The benefits of this type of regulation are shared widely and have clear relevance to human health and quality of life. You only have to look as far as Flint, Michigan, to see the human impacts that can come from environmental problems and policy failure (Bellinger, 2016).

Environmental policies at all levels of government can also be non-regulatory and incentive driven (Mazmanian & Kraft, 2009). These types of policies and programs rely on economic incentives to achieve various environmental goals. For example, in the past 20–30 years, all 50 states created a voluntary incentive-driven program directed at encouraging developers to clean up and to redevelop contaminated properties known as brownfields (Opp, 2009). The presence of a brownfield in a community has been shown to directly impact the quality of life of residents through depressed property values, human health impacts, physical hazards, and a reduced level of economic investment due to the stigma associated with these properties (Opp and Hollis, 2005). By using economic incentives, states have been able to encourage the remediation and redevelopment of brownfields and ultimately improve the quality of life of Americans. Furthermore, the redevelopment of these properties likely produces economic benefits for the community as well, further supporting the importance of these types of environmental policy efforts.

Sustainability: Economic

Historically, it was believed that governments must choose between economic development *or* environmental protection, but that doing both was an impossible feat (Opp & Osgood, 2013). At the same time, many have argued that the regulatory environmental protection efforts, although well intentioned, have reduced economic competitiveness (Hempel, 2009; Osgood et al., 2016). It is only recently that the synergies between the natural environment and economic development have been widely studied and accepted to be a possibility for local governments (Leigh & Blakey, 2016; Opp & Osgood, 2013).

Historically, economic development focused on achieving **growth** (Heberle & Opp, 2008; Leigh & Blakely, 2016). Growth in wealth, jobs, production levels, income, and profits are all common metrics used to judge the success of economic policies (Koven & Lyons, 2010; Leigh & Blakely, 2016). However, over the course of the latter half of the twentieth century, it became increasingly clear that natural resources were both important and needed to sustain life and to continue to thrive economically (Hopwood, Mellor, & O'Brien, 2005). Unfettered and uncontrolled economic development has resulted in overuse and exploitation of many of America's natural resources. Eventually, the extended overuse and exploitation result in irreversible damage rendering a resource useless or unavailable for any purpose. To be sure, significantly reducing and/or eliminating important natural resources will have a profound impact on the economic well-being of society. In simple terms, sustainable economic development seeks to balance the tensions that exist between environmental protection and economic development.

Sustainability: Social Equity

Chapter 8 of this book goes into great detail on the topic of social equity. However, in this chapter, it is useful to highlight the broader reasons that social equity is included and considered in sustainability discussions. Social equity, also termed social sustainability, is generally related to a complex set of questions about exactly *who* is receiving the benefits of public investment and exactly *who* is suffering negative consequences of policy choices. Significant income inequality at any scale is known to create perverse outcomes for all individuals in a community and for society in general. For example, poverty is correlated with increased rates of crime, obesity, poor health outcomes, environmental degradation, and many other negative society-wide conditions. The negative aspects of poverty do not just impact those actually living in poverty—rather they impact all of society and reduce overall quality of life for all Americans. For example, crime rates can deter investment into a community and ultimately reduce opportunities for all area residents. Furthermore, increased crime will likely translate into increased resource needs for policing efforts—something that every taxpayer must contribute to. Additionally, obesity and health problems impose significant costs on the public health system in the United States—again, something that everyone will be forced to contribute to (Holzer, Whitmore Schanzenbach, Duncan, & Ludwig, 2008). The distribution of both the *bads* and the *goods* of public investment is not just a moral issue, but is also an environmental and economic issue impacting the quality of life for all Americans and must be considered in any book concerned with sustainability.

At this point in this introductory chapter, it should be clear that sustainability is a complex and multidimensional topic. Sustainability is not just an abstract idealistic goal; rather it is an important set of considerations needed to ensure that Americans can maintain and improve their quality of life for generations to come. Even though it can be argued that local governments are not the appropriate or the ideal level of government to engage in these types of policies, it seems that this is the reality we must contend with. Given the growing prevalence of local sustainability policies in the United States, it is an important time to begin to assess accountability of these efforts. Given the difficult economic and political environment, accountability for effectiveness and efficiency is necessary if we are to continue to invest in these types of efforts. Furthermore, given the emerging evidence showing that local governments are being selective in which policies they choose to adopt, it is imperative that we recognize any shortcomings and unintended consequences that may exist in these policies so that we can alter the path we are on if needed.

Performance Measurement: An Introduction

Accountability and efficiency are central concepts in the study of public policy and public administration. In fact, concern over these two concepts frequently prompt elected officials at all levels of government to embark on a quest to *fix* what they call a broken and wasteful government. In the recent past, concerns over accountability and efficiency instigated two visible federal reform initiatives directed at fixing the federal bureaucracy (Radin, 2006). States and local governments also often engage in a number of initiatives targeted at improving the efficiency and accountability of their programs, policies, agencies, and services (Ammons, 1995; Radin, 2006). As Wilson (1989) so aptly pointed out, "No politician ever lost votes by denouncing bureaucracy" (p. 235).

Performance measurement has been frequently identified as an important and necessary task for communities interested in improving efficiency, process, and accountability in the public sector (Ammons, 2002; Berman & Wang, 2002). "Performance measurement provides a real-time assessment of what a program or policy is doing, what resources it is using, and what it has accomplished recently" (Berman & Wang, 2012, p. 61). To some degree, all levels of government have engaged in performance measurement with local governments leading the way. "...[M]ost U.S. local governments have been active in the development and use of data and performance measurement techniques for several decades" (Melkers & Willoughby, 2005, p. 180).

Much of the literature and research on performance measurement is "...of the 'how to do it' variety" (Radin, 2006, p. 5). For example, a number of technical resources exist to assist interested communities with the process of measuring the performance of their policies and programs. These resources include books that provide an overview of performance measurement as a technique (Ammons, 1995), books that provide a primer for the use of data to evaluate the performance of public programs (Berman & Wang, 2012), resources for setting benchmarks in performance measurement (North Carolina Benchmarking Project, 2016), and a variety of certification and rating programs that seek to provide targets to gauge an individual community's progress in a specific policy area (for one example, see *Star Communities*). Even though most of the literature makes a case for why the public sector should be engaging in performance measurement, it is important to note that not all experts agree on the value of participating in this type of evaluation and raise legitimate concerns over the potential misuse of the process and its findings (Radin, 2006). Nonetheless, given the political and financial challenges surrounding sustainability, as well as the very real consequences that can come from failure or misuse, the performance and eventual success of these efforts is of grave importance. While this book will not be able to ascertain how successful the sustainability programs across the country are in achieving their goals, this book will be able to present a robust resource on what cities are doing, what metrics they are collecting, and ultimately what they perceive to be the biggest challenges for achieving success in this policy area. Furthermore, this book will also provide a resource for cities seeking to identify comparison measures for their own performance measurement activities for sustainability policies and programs.

Performance Measurement: Outputs and Outcomes

Simply stated, performance measurement is the use of data and evidence to determine the effectiveness and the efficiency of a specific public policy, public program, public process, or public agency (Ammons, 1995; Radin, 2006). Performance measurement in local governments tends to be concerned with two major categories of data collection: output and outcome (Ammons, 1995). Output measures can be used to gauge efficiency and productivity, whereas outcome measures can be used to gauge overall effectiveness. Table 1.1 highlights the different measures and provides examples of each.

Output measures are also sometimes called workload measures (Ammons, 2015). Measures of output tend to not mean much when taken as individual data points as they are simply counts of a product or a service delivered (Radin, 2006). Output measures can, however, provide insights when they are taken in combination with other measures or when they are collected over a specified time period for trend assessment. For example, an output measure of interest to sustainability efforts might be the number of zoning variances granted by the planning department for sustainable development. If a city collected this measure on a monthly or a quarterly basis, the measure becomes more useful to assess trends in this specific area. Presumably, more zoning variances

Table 1.1 Performance Measures and Benchmarking

	Output	*Outcome*	*Benchmarking*
Description	Data that provide a "count" of services or products provided. Output measures do not mean much when taken alone; however, these measures can be combined with other metrics to produce an overall efficiency or productivity measure	Outcome measures focus on the effectiveness of a public program, process, or agency. These measures identify the impact/effect derived from a public program	Benchmarking is the process of setting a target or goal for a program. Targets/goals can come from professional organizations, aspirational internal goals, or from peer communities
Examples	1 Numbers of trees planted 2 Dollars spent on purchasing trees 3 Hours of labor planting trees 4 Cost of labor for tree maintenance	1 Percentage reduction in greenhouse gas (GHG) emissions over a specified period of time 2 Percentage change in automobile commuting over a specified period of time	1 Reduce GHG emissions to 20% of 2005 levels 2 50% reduction in automobile commuting between the hours of 7am –7pm, M–F
Efficiency/ productivity measure	Numbers of trees planted divided by dollars spent planting and maintain trees = a cost per tree. *Tracking this measure over a specified time period (monthly, annually, etc.) can provide an indication of trends*	Total cost per ton of GHG emissions reduced through reduced automobile commuting	

being granted over time would be considered a positive sign for a goal of increasing sustainable development within the community. Additionally, output measures can be used in conjunction with other output or outcome measures to provide insights about process or program efficiency. For example, comparing a measure combining the average time a developer waits to receive a decision on a zoning variance application with the number of variances processed within a given time period can provide insights into the time efficiency of the local planning review process. A city could identify both targets for success and problem areas for improvement through these combined measures.

Outcome measures usually consist of data that represent the effectiveness of a policy or a program. For example, assessing local efforts on reducing single-rider automobile commuting might involve an outcome measure identifying the percentage of single-rider automobile commuting occurring over a specified time period. It is common for local governments to collect data at various intervals ranging from short- to longer-term timelines. Outcome measures can provide insights into what a specific program may have accomplished and can usually be useful as a stand-alone metric. However, these outcome measures can, and most often should, be enhanced by providing some sort of contextual information related to local conditions, goals, or benchmarks. Simply reporting a decline does not immediately imply that the program or policy was successful in achieving a defined goal. It could be the case that this particular community suffered a significant population decline over the past year that actually contributed to a measured reduction in commuting—making the program less effective than it may look at first glance. If this was the case, it would not be possible to declare this program successful and is a pitfall that local officials must be concerned with. Furthermore, without a benchmark for success or a predetermined target goal, communities run the risk of declaring success with any outcome obtained regardless of whether or not it is a *significant* outcome. These are the typical areas where local officials run into challenges. For politically motivated officials, it can be difficult to resist the urge to declare success when a measure shows improvement. However, for these measures to be valid, it is imperative that the participants engage in a complete analysis that will include other explanatory information and a critical and honest assessment of the program.

Benchmarks can provide useful insights to local governments pursuing sustainability. Benchmarking is defined as "...the comparison of performance statistics with professional standards and the performance results of respected municipalities" (Ammons, 2015, p. 16). Each substantive chapter in this book provides sample metrics and goals for each policy as identified in cities across the United States. Although these specific metrics may not be a perfect comparison to another city, they can provide a good starting place to assess the relative performance of a particular sustainability effort.

Related to the local engagement in performance measurement is the emergence of performance dashboards and open data initiatives. Borrowing at least partially from the private sector, many cities have developed robust open data policies with visually appealing performance dashboards. These performance dashboards provide citizens, community members, and interested observers with a method to easily and quickly see how a city is doing in key policy areas. In general, these dashboards are closely related to an overall local performance measurement effort and seek to provide accurate and consistent information on city services, provide targets or benchmarks to compare the current statistics to, and provide an opportunity for transparency (Edwards & Thomas, 2005). A quick search for local performance dashboard yields hundreds of cities that purport to have adopted these outward facing portals to illustrate the current performance status of the city.

Conclusion

Local sustainability policy is a complex and multifaceted area to study. Additionally, the local efforts at achieving sustainability likely represent the best hope for a sustainable future in the United States. To date, we have some insights about what types of cities are engaging in this policy area—but we know very little about the successes or failures of these policies. In fact, we know very little about whether cities are even assessing their performance in this area. This book provides the first in-depth examination of local sustainability efforts that also provides insights into the performance measurement activities being conducted in this area by cities across the country. Each of the substantive chapters also provides readers with the unique insights of a practitioner working in this area. A range of geographic locations and city sizes are represented in the chapters of this book. Cities of all size across the country will find important and useful insights in the pages that follow.

References

Adler, R. W., Landman, J. C., & Cameron, D. M. (1993). *The clean water act 20 years later.* Washington, DC: Island Press.

Ammons, D. N. (Ed.). (1995). *Accountability for performance: Measurement and monitoring in local government.* Washington, DC: International City County Management Assn.

Ammons, D. N. (2002). Performance measurement and managerial thinking. *Public Performance & Management Review*, *25*(4), 344–347.

Ammons, D. (2015). *Municipal benchmarks: Assessing local performance and establishing community standards.* New York: Routledge.

Banzhaf, H. S., & Walsh, R. P. (2006). Do people vote with their feet? An empirical test of environmental gentrification. Available at: www.economics.ucr.edu/workshop/papers/RandallWalsh.pdf. Retrieved December 5, 2017.

Bellinger, D. C. (2016). Lead contamination in Flint—An abject failure to protect public health. *New England Journal of Medicine*, *374*(12), 1101–1103.

Berman, E., & Wang, X. (2012). *Essential statistics for public managers and policy analysts.* Los Angeles, CA: CQ Press.

Brundtland, G. H., Khalio, M., & Agnelli, S. (1987). Towards sustainable development. *World Commission on Environment and Development (ed.), Our Common Future. Oxford*, 43–65. Available at: www.un-documents.net/our-common-future.pdf. Retrieved December 5, 2017.

Cook, J., Oreskes, N., Doran, P. T., Anderegg, W. R., Verheggen, B., Maibach, E. W., & Nuccitelli, D. (2016). Consensus on consensus: A synthesis of consensus estimates on human-caused global warming. *Environmental Research Letters, 11*(4), 048002.

Craw, M. (2006). Overcoming city limits: Vertical and horizontal models of local redistributive policy making. *Social Science Quarterly, 87*(2), 361–379.

DeMillo, A. (2017). *Federal lawsuit seeks to overturn Arkansas panhandling law.* August 7, 2017. Us News and World Report. Available at: www.usnews.com/news/best-states/arkansas/articles/2017-08-07/federal-lawsuit-seeks-to-overturn-arkansas-panhandling-law. Retrieved September 3, 2017.

Edwards, D., & Thomas, J. C. (2005). Developing a municipal performance-measurement system: Reflections on the Atlanta Dashboard. *Public Administration Review, 65*(3), 369–376.

England, R. E., Pelissero, J. P., & Morgan, D. R. (2017). *Managing Urban America.* Thousand Oaks, CA: CQ Press.

Fischer, D. (2010). Local governments lead efforts to combat climate change. *Scientific American.* Available at: www.scientificamerican.com/article/local-governments-lead-efforts-to-combat-climate-change/

Goetz, S. J., Partridge, M. D., Rickman, D. S., & Majumdar, S. (2011). Sharing the gains of local economic growth: Race-to-the-top versus race-to-the-bottom economic development. *Environment and Planning C: Government and Policy, 29*(3), 428–456.

Grumm, J. G., & Murphy, R. D. (1974). Dillon's rule reconsidered. *The Annals of the American Academy of Political and Social Science, 416*(1), 120–132.

Heberle, L. C., & Opp, S. M. (2008). *Local sustainable urban development in a globalized world.* Aldershot, UK: Ashgate.

Hempel, L. (2009). Conceptual and analytical challenges in building sustainable communities. In D. A. Mazmanian & M. E. Kraft (Eds.), *Toward sustainable communities: Transition and transformations in environmental policy* (pp. 43–74). Cambridge, MA: MIT Press.

Klyza, C. M., & Sousa, D. J. (2013). *American environmental policy, beyond gridlock.* Cambridge, MA: MIT Press.

La Porte, T. M., & Opp, S. M. (2016). APSA pracademic fellowship: The third epoch: A pracademic view of the EPA's office of policy. *PS: Political Science & Politics, 49*(4), 923–926.

Leigh, N. G., & Blakely, E. J. (2016). *Planning local economic development: Theory and practice.* Thousand Oaks, CA: Sage Publications.

Holzer, H. J., Whitmore Schanzenbach, D., Duncan, G. J., & Ludwig, J. (2008). The economic costs of childhood poverty in the United States. *Journal of Children and Poverty, 14*(1), 41–61.

Hopwood, B., Mellor, M., & O'Brien, G. (2005). Sustainable development: Mapping different approaches. *Sustainable Development, 13*(1), 38–52.

Koven, S., & Lyons, T. (2010). *Economic development: Strategies for state and local practice.* Washington, DC: International City/County Management Association.

Mazmanian, D. A., & Kraft, M. E. (Eds.). (2009). *Toward sustainable communities: Transition and transformations in environmental policy.* Cambridge, MA: MIT Press.

Mazmanian, D. A., & Kraft, M. E. (2013). *Towards sustainable communities: Transition and transformations in environmental policy.* Cambridge, MA: MIT Press.

Melkers, J., & Willoughby, K. (2005). Models of performance-measurement use in local governments: Understanding budgeting, communication, and lasting effects. *Public Administration Review*, *65*(2), 180–190.

MRSC. (2016). Adult entertainment regulation. Available at: http://mrsc.org/Home/Explore-Topics/Legal/Regulation/Adult-Entertainment-Regulation.aspx. Retrieved May 2, 2017.

North Carolina Benchmarking Project. (2016). "North Carolina Benchmarking Project: Overview" Available at: www.sog.unc.edu/resources/microsites/north-carolina-benchmarking-project

Opp, S. M. (2009). ENVIRONMENTAL REVIEW: Experiences of the States in Brownfield Redevelopment. *Environmental Practice*, *11*(4), 270–284.

Opp, S. M. (2017). The forgotten pillar: a definition for the measurement of social sustainability in American cities. *Local Environment*, *22*(3), 286–305.

Opp, S., & Hollis, S. (2005). *Contaminated properties: History, regulations, and resources for community members. Practice Guide# 9.* Southeast Regional Environmental Finance Center EPA Region 4.

Opp, S. M., & Mosier, S. L. (2017). Counting money: Cities love climate policies if they generate local benefits. *Public Administration Review Speak your Mind*. Available at: https://publicadministrationreview.org/climate-change-symposium-local-climate-change-policy/

Opp, S. M., & Osgood Jr, J. L. (2013). *Local economic development and the environment: Finding common ground*. Boca Raton, FL: CRC Press.

Opp, S. M., Osgood Jr, J. L., & Rugeley, C. R. (2014). City limits in a postrecessionary world: Explaining the pursuit of developmental policies after the great recession. *State and Local Government Review*, *46*(4), 236–248.

Opp, S. M., & Saunders, K. L. (2013). Pillar talk: Local sustainability initiatives and policies in the United States—Finding evidence of the "three E's": Economic development, environmental protection, and social equity. *Urban Affairs Review*, *49*(5), 678–717.

Osgood Jr, J. L., Opp, S. M., & Bernotsky, R. L. (2012). Yesterday's gains versus today's realties: Lessons from 10 years of economic development practice. *Economic Development Quarterly*, *26*(4), 334–350.

Osgood, J. L., Opp, S. M., & DeMasters, M. (2016). Exploring the intersection of local economic development and environmental policy. *Journal of Urban Affairs*, *39*(2), 260–276.

Palazzolo, J. (2017). As panhandling laws are overturned, cities change policies. *Wall Street Journal*. August 8, 2017. Available at: www.wsj.com/articles/as-panhandling-laws-are-overturned-cities-change-policies-1502204399. Retrieved September 14, 2017.

Peterson, P. E. (1981). *City limits*. Chicago, IL: University of Chicago Press.

Porter, M. E., & Van der Linde, C. (1994). Toward a new conception of the environment-competitiveness relationship. *Journal of Economic Perspectives*, *9*(4), 97–118.

Portney, K. E. (2013). Local sustainability policies and programs as economic development: Is the new economic development sustainable development? *Cityscape*, *15*(1), 45–62.

Radin, B. (2006). *Challenging the performance movement: Accountability, complexity, and democratic values*. Washington, DC: Georgetown University Press.

Saha, D. (2009). Empirical research on local government sustainability efforts in the USA: Gaps in the current literature. *Local Environment*, *14*(1), 17–30.
Salkin, P. (2017). Law of the land: A blog on land use law and zoning. Available at: https://lawoftheland.wordpress.com/. Retrieved July 13, 2017.
Slavin, M. I. (2011). The rise of the urban sustainability movement in America. In *Sustainability in America's cities* (pp. 1–19). Washington DC: Island Press/ Center for Resource Economics.
Tiebout, C. M. (1956). A pure theory of local expenditures. *Journal of Political Economy*, *64*(5), 416–424.
U.S. Census Bureau. (2012). Census of governments. Available at: www.census.gov/govs/cog/. Retrieved January 14, 2017.

2 Sustainability and Performance Measurement Overview

As discussed in Chapter 1, pursuing sustainability requires that communities consider the three interrelated dimensions of environmental protection, economic development, and social equity. While previous research has provided some insights into the types of cities and policies being adopted across these three areas, much remains unknown. Of significant consequence is the absence of information on how, or even if, cities are measuring the performance of their sustainability efforts. As cities emerge as the most important participant in the effort to achieve sustainability in the United States, it is of vital importance that cities be prepared to assess the successes, failures, and consequences of these policies. This chapter summarizes the overall findings of a survey distributed by the authors to study sustainability policy adoption and the related performance measurement activities of American cities. Using this newly collected survey data, this chapter explores the following three topics:

1 Using a comprehensive definition of the "Three E's" framework of sustainability, what policies are cities adopting?
2 What are the policy goals for the three E's of sustainability policy across cities (what are cities trying to accomplish)?
3 What methods do these cities employ to measure the effectiveness and the efficiency of these policies (what information do they collect)?

This chapter provides cities and researchers with a broad view of sustainability policy adoption and performance measurement as reported by the participants of the 2016 survey. Each of the remaining chapters of this book will delve more in depth into the specific areas of sustainability; however, this chapter provides the overall findings and trends to provide a comprehensive picture of this topic in the United States.

Survey Methods

Previous surveys have worked to identify sustainability policy adoption in American cities (see, for example, Opp, Osgood, & Rugeley, 2014;

Opp & Saunders, 2013; Swann, 2015; Wang, Hawkins, & Berman, 2014). Unfortunately, previous survey instruments on this subject have been incomplete and have missed important dimensions of sustainability—usually focusing on one or two of the three dimensions of sustainability. Additionally, previous surveys have tended to focus primarily on larger cities and have mostly ignored smaller communities in the United Sates. This is particularly problematic given the fact that the distribution of population across cities in the United States is largely skewed to mid- and small-sized cities. Much of the research on local sustainability policy has not be representative of the average American city.

In order for this book to provide a comprehensive accounting of engagement in sustainability and the related performance measurement activities, it is necessary to collect new data to supplement the older data derived from larger cities. The primary source of information used throughout this book originated from an original survey conducted using Qualtrics over a seven-week period from June to August 2016. Respondents received an initial email solicitation on June 27, 2016 with four follow-up reminders sent in July and August.[1] Survey solicitations were sent to elected officials and civil servants representing 2,109 U.S. municipalities. The municipalities selected for this survey were initially identified based upon their participation in the 2010 International City/County Management Association (ICMA) sustainability survey, which provides one of the largest existing snapshots of sustainability activities at the local level. The list of cities was further refined to add additional cities known to be active in sustainability policymaking based upon other research in this area and to also try to get a more representative sample of cities to study. The most common respondents were city managers and sustainability directors. Two graduate research assistants updated and collected contact information for city officials with the authors refining the contact list.[2] A total of 460 individuals responded to the survey with 276 fully completing the survey, representing a completed survey response rate of approximately 13% of all the cities solicited. Responses were received from cities in 44 states with a larger percentage of respondents from California (9.1%), Pennsylvania (8.7%), and Texas (6.2%) (see Table 2.1).

A large percentage of the cities (64.5%) responding to this survey are council-manager forms of government with populations of 25,000 residents or less (67%). The sample is similar to the population sample found in the original 2010 ICMA sustainability survey and also compares favorably to the overall U.S. statistics (see Table 2.1). Even with the relatively small sample size, the similarity in characteristics to the overall United States provides assurance that the results of this survey are of value to understand how American cities are engaging in this policy area. Additionally, as mentioned briefly earlier, one particular benefit of this study's population sample is the responding size of

Table 2.1 Sample Characteristics

	2010 ICMA Survey Population	*2016 Survey Sample*	*U.S. Overall*
Council-manager form of government	62.10%	64.50%	59%
Other form of government	37.90%	35.50%	41%
Percent white	85%	82%	77.10%
Median household income	$56,258	$59,951	$53,482
Median home value	$229,901	$220,044	$175,500
Poverty	12.60%	14.38%	13.50%
Population less than 25,000	76%	67.40%	93%

Sources: NLC (2007); ICMA (2011); U.S. Census.

communities. In particular, much less is known about sustainability policy and performance measurement in smaller communities, even though smaller communities make up a larger portion of American cities than do the large cities that are usually studied. With two-thirds of respondents in this study coming from communities with populations of 25,000 or less, the results of this research shed some light on an understudied area of local sustainability policy. Most studies on local sustainability policy development and performance measurement have predominantly focused on larger cities (for example, see Portney, 2013, 2014; Slavin, 2011). Given the fact that 93% of the cities in the United States have populations under 25,000, small- to midsized communities are an important and often overlooked population to understand.

The survey asked respondents a series of closed- and open-ended questions regarding the nature of their city's sustainability policies and programs as well as questions concerning the city's sustainability goals and related performance measurement activities. The first half of the survey focused on the identification of overall sustainability goals as well as existing policies and programs in the broader areas of organizational greening, energy and resource conservation, transportation, pollution prevention and air quality, smart growth/economic development, and social equity/sustainability. These categories are consistent with past research in this area (see, for example, Opp & Saunders, 2013) and represent all three dimensions of sustainability. This survey instrument is designed to be more comprehensive than previous surveys on sustainability so that a full account of what is occurring in American cities can be adequately assessed. Therefore, this survey explicitly asks about a far wider swath of possible policies than have previously been reported on. This is especially true for the social equity/social sustainability section where a comprehensive definition derived from previous research on social sustainability was utilized in order to more fully capture the social equity policies that might be present within a given community (see, for example, Agyeman, Bullard, & Evans, 2003; Opp, 2017). The inclusion of social equity and sustainability policies provides a more accurate assessment of local sustainability efforts.

The second half of the survey focused on the metrics currently utilized by cities to assess performance in each policy area. Cities were able to preselect from lists of common measurements in each policy area and also had the ability to identify alternative or other measurements used in assessment. Cities were also asked to provide links if a city's performance measurement documents, activities, or additional information was publicly available so that we could glean additional insights into some of these measurement efforts. Performance metric questions were not displayed if the respondent indicated that no performance or evaluative metrics were currently in place. Demographic information was collected from each community at the end of the survey. The following sections of this chapter will highlight the overall findings from this survey before the remaining chapters turn to specific policy areas of sustainability.

Sustainability Policy and Evaluation—The Survey Results

What Policies Are Cities Adopting and What Are Their Stated Goals?

Although each chapter of this book will document the specific policy areas in greater detail, Table 2.2 provides the overall view of city engagement in sustainability policies and programs. The table is organized by the overall area of sustainability mentioned before. Similar to past research in this area, there is evidence that cities are engaging in the easier and less expensive policies with an emphasis on the policies that have economic co-benefit potential. For example, a full 82.6% of the sample cities report upgrades to efficiency lighting in public buildings, and 62% of the sample cities report conducting energy audits of public buildings. Changes in lighting and energy audits provide opportunities to reduce energy usage as well as GHG emissions in a community—both are important for sustainability. However, at the same time, upgrades to energy efficient lights and audits would also work to reduce energy expenses for a community (likely an important economic co-benefit). Policies such as targeted GHG reduction goals and environmental justice programs, while also important sustainability efforts, are not as widely reported with only 13.8% reporting a GHG reduction goal and only 5.1% reporting having an environmental justice program.

Table 2.2 Reported Sustainability Policies

Smart Growth/ Sustainable Economic Development	*Transportation*	*Pollution Prevention*	*Energy/Resource Conservation/ Efficiency*	*Organizational and Administrative Initiatives*	*Social Sustainability/ Equity*
N = 13	*N = 24*	*N = 15*	*N = 21*	*N = 14*	*N = 26*
1 Brownfields Program (25.4%)	1 Incentives for public employees to use multi-modal/alt transport (11.6%)	1 Single-stream recycling (48.2%)	1 Energy audits of government buildings (62%)	1 Established a formal sustainability policy/plan (28.6%)	1 Gentrification prevention policy ([illegible].9%)
2 Downtown revitalization (62%)	2 Free or reduced passes for public transit for public employees (10.1%)	2 E-waste recycling (35.5%)	2 Purchased fuel efficient or hybrid vehicles (41.7%)	2 Established a formal sustainability department (10.1%)	2 Housing affordability policy (34.11%)
3 Mainstreet program (37%)	3 Parking policies to reduce single-occupancy commuting (3.6%)	3 Curbside recycling (72.8%)	3 Purchased compressed natural gas vehicles (13.8%)	3 Established a formal social sustainability department (2.2%)	3 Workforce housing program (21%)
4 Infill policy (34.8%)	4 Telecommuting options for public employees (10.9%)	4 Hazardous waste recycling (41.7%)	4 Installed energy management systems in government buildings (44.9%)	4 Provided a budget or dedicated staff to the sustainability efforts (23.9%)	4 Homelessness prevention or reduction policy (13.1%)

5 Open space preservation (43.1%)	5 Compressed work week option for public employees (17.4%)	5 Zero-waste initiative (5.8%)	5 Upgraded lighting in public buildings for efficiency (82.6%)	5 Formal partnerships with other sustainability groups in the community (29.7%)	5 Housing for the elderly (25.7%)
6 Farmland preservation (12.7%)	6 Incentives for citizen use of alternative transit (5.1%)	6 Construction/ demolition recycling (19.6%)	6 Installed solar panels on government buildings/ property (28.6%)	6 Organization makes purchasing and/ or contracting decisions based upon sustainability goals (31.2%)	6 Housing for the disabled (13%)
7 Mixed use development policy (51.4%)	7 Intelligent transport systems (6.2%)	7 Composting program (31.9%)	7 Upgraded traffic signals to improve efficiency (46.7%)	7 Resolution stating policy goals on the environment (28.3%)	7 Veteran housing (10.9%)
8 Density allowances for sustainable economic development (29.3%)	8 Partnership with car share (4%)	8 Disposable water bottle restrictions (4.7%)	8 Upgraded streetlights to improve efficiency (65.9%)	8 Resolution stating policy goals on the economy (21%)	8 At-risk housing policy (4.3%)
9 Parking variances for sustainable economic development (27.9%)	9 Reserved Parking for residents (12%)	9 Water bottle reuse policy/ incentive (4%)	9 Use of permeable pavement for new infrastructure (24.3%)	9 Resolution stating policy goals on social justice (11.2%)	9 Equitable development strategy (4.0%)
10 Park and recreation development (64.9%)	10 Bike share/library (10.9%)	10 Restrictions/ fees grocery bags (7.2%)	10 Established green purchasing requirements (18.1%)	10 Resolution stating policy goals on climate change (13%)	10 Local incentive for low-income housing (18.5%)

(*Continued*)

Smart Growth/ Sustainable Economic Development	*Transportation*	*Pollution Prevention*	*Energy/Resource Conservation/ Efficiency*	*Organizational and Administrative Initiatives*	*Social Sustainability/ Equity*
N = 13	*N = 24*	*N = 15*	*N = 21*	*N = 14*	*N = 26*
11 Business assistance for childcare support (8%)	11 Incentives to employers for subsidizing mass transit (4.7%)	11 Established a baseline GHG emission level (18.8%)	11 Energy efficiency or renewable energy incentives for homeowners (21.4%)	11 Resolution stating policy goals on energy conservation (28.6%)	11 Foreclosure prevention policy (6.9%)
12 Asset-based economic development (6.5%)	12 Transit-oriented development (17.4%)	12 Established a GHG reduction goal (13.8%)	12 Energy efficiency or renewable energy incentives for businesses (13.4%)	12 Resolution stating policy goals on green jobs (4.7%)	12 Other Housing Program (2.5%)
13 Historic preservation policy (47.8%)	13 Regulations on idling at Railroad crossings (0.7%)	13 Carbon credit market participation policy (1.8%)	13 Weatherization incentives for homeowners or local businesses (13.4%)	13 Resolution stating policy goals on housing for all income groups (27.2%)	13 Locally funded income-support program (0.7%)
	14 Creation of a hotline for idling offenses (1.1%)	14 Urban forest policy (22.1%)	14 Tiered energy price system (5.4%)	14 Resolution stating policy goals on public transit (18.8%)	14 Higher than state/ fed minimum wage requirement (4.3%)
	15 Noise pollution policies from traffic (15.9%)	15 Carbon footprint education policy (8%)	15 Tiered water price system (21.7%)		15 Other income program (1.4%)
	In the last five years improved or developed		16 Use of grey water or reclaimed water systems (15.6%)		16 Local food processing (5.4%)

1 Biking infrastructure (72.1%)	17 Limits on impervious surfaces for new development (40.6%)	17 Local food production (15.9%)
2 Walking infrastructure (79%)	18 Incentives for permeable pavement in private businesses (6.5%)	18 Community Supported Agriculture program (15.6%)
3 Commuter rail (4%)	19 Low-impact development policies (21.4%)	19 Shared kitchens (4.3%)
4 Other mass transit (16.3%)	20 Energy audits homeowners (13.4%)	20 Local food in schools (9.8%)
5 Trolley or streetcar system (4.7%)	21 Energy audits for businesses (13%)	21 Healthy food access program (14.9%)
6 Green car preferred parking (9.4%)		22 Community gardens (47.5%)
7 Carpool lanes (1.8%)		23 Food Co-op support (6.9%)
8 Green vehicle lanes (0.7%)		24 Farmers' market policy (52.9%)
9 Bus rapid transit (12%)		25 Environmental justice program (5.1%)
		26 Special health concern policy (19.6%)

Collapsing the individual policies into larger policy area groupings is instructive. Table 2.3 provides an overview of the average adoption rate for each major policy area studied. As can be seen in this table, the average adoption rate across all of the policies is 19.7%. Smart growth/sustainable economic development policies enjoy the highest rate of adoption at 32.4%. Energy and resource conservation policies come in second with 23.1%. Pollution prevention is a close third with 22.4%. Transportation, social sustainability, and organizational initiatives report the lowest average adoption rates for these cities.

In addition to asking for an inventory of sustainability policies, the survey also asked cities to identify priority areas for their sustainability efforts and to also indicate on a scale of 1–5 (with 5 being the highest priority) to rank these sustainability goals (see Table 2.4). Two areas emerged as being top priorities for most cities in this sample: infrastructure and the economy. Over half of the cities in the sample indicate that developing local infrastructure was their top sustainability priority with an additional 32.2% citing it as the second highest priority. The economy also tops the priority list with 46.4% of the cities selecting it as

Table 2.3 Average Adoption Percent for Each Area of Sustainability

	Average Adoption Rate for Sample (%)	*Average Adoption Rate for Cities That Also Use Performance Measurement (%)*
Social sustainability	15.6	20.6
Smart growth/economic development	32.4	39.8
Pollution prevention	22.4	29.2
Organizational	15.8	24.1
Transportation	13.8	18.5
Energy and resource conservation	23.1	26.2
Overall	19.7	25.2

Table 2.4 Priorities for Sustainability

Priority Level	*Housing (%)*	*Climate Change (%)*	*Local Food (%)*	*Economy (%)*	*Infrastructure (%)*	*Human Health (%)*	*Preserving the Environment (%)*	*Social Equity (%)*
5 (Highest)	25	10.9	8.7	46.4	52.2	16.7	25.4	10.1
4	29.7	13	25	28.6	32.2	30.4	34.1	21.4
3	22.8	25	25.7	14.9	8	28.3	26.4	33.7
2	12	23.9	23.2	2.9	5.1	18.5	9.1	19.6
1 (Lowest)	9.1	26.1	16.7	3.3	1.4	5.4	3.3	14.5
No response	1.4	1.1	0.7	4	1.1	0.7	1.8	0.7

their top priority. Interestingly, the preservation and protection of the environment was only selected as a top priority by 25.4% of the cities. Similarly, climate change and social justice/equity were also not common top priorities among these cities, with only 10.9% and 10.1% of the cities indicating those are among their top priorities. Even when focusing on sustainability efforts of the city, it appears that basic concerns over the economy and infrastructure outpace concerns with the protection of the environment or the pursuit of social equity. This is a concerning indicator given the importance of these local efforts for the overall pursuit of sustainability in the United States. This finding also highlights some of the most likely reasons that the policies and programs with clear co-benefits are the ones that enjoy higher adoption rates.

Performance Measurement Activities

Approximately 38.5% of the cities responding to this survey indicate they routinely evaluate or measure the performance of one or more of their sustainability policies. The communities in this survey report utilizing a variety of measures to assess the performance of their efforts. Not surprisingly, metrics that are freely available and easily identifiable are most often utilized. For example, among the most commonly reported measures collected are basic census data on home values, population density, and poverty levels—all information freely available and that does not require a specific level of expertise within the community. Moving beyond the census data metrics, the next most commonly reported measures include various performance data related to infrastructure development like miles of bike lanes or walking trails developed, numbers of trees planted, and acres of community gardens located in the city. Most of these measurements are predominantly output-based rather than outcome-based assessments of sustainability, leaving us with questions about the progress being made toward sustainability in these cities.

In addition to asking cities about the metrics that they use to measure the performance of these policies, they were also asked to identify what areas they are struggling to make progress in and then to also identify the top reasons they believe they are having this difficulty. Across all policies areas, with the exception of social sustainability, the most commonly cited reason for struggling to achieve programmatic success is a simple lack of resources (Table 2.5). In terms of social sustainability, however, lack of resources was a close second choice behind "lack of political support" for the top reason for not being able to achieve success in that policy area. Resource constraints are often a challenge for local governments when needing to balance investment decisions across a multitude of critical policy areas. Policies geared toward sustainability may often be pursued, particularly when co-benefits are available, in order to maximize returns on resource investments. Conservation, pollution

Table 2.5 Reported Causes for Struggle Ranked by Programmatic Area (Cities That Measure Performance)

		Lack of Resources (%)	*Human Capital Constraints (%)*	*Infrastructure (%)*	*Geographic Constraints (%)*	*Lack of Political Support (%)*	*Lack of Citizen Support (%)*	*Regulatory Environment Too Strict (%)*
Energy and resource conservation	Ranked 1st	23.8	7.4	2.6	1.3	1.0	5.1	3.8
	Ranked 2nd	11.9	11.1	5.3	1.3	4.8	2.6	1.3
	Ranked 3rd	3.6	1.2	0.0	1.3	1.9	7.7	6.4
Pollution prevention	Ranked 1st	19.2	3.9	2.7	5.3	3.9	7.6	3.9
	Ranked 2nd	6.4	6.6	0.0	5.3	3.9	5.1	5.2
	Ranked 3rd	5.1	1.3	0.0	2.7	5.2	6.3	1.3
Organizational initiatives	Ranked 1st	23.3	12.2	2.6	0.0	7.3	3.8	0.0
	Ranked 2nd	12.8	15.9	2.6	1.3	4.9	5.1	1.3
	Ranked 3rd	5.8	2.4	2.6	2.7	7.3	2.5	3.9
Smart growth	Ranked 1st	10.3	1.9	1.4	0.0	7.6	3.8	2.7
	Ranked 2nd	3.8	2.9	5.4	1.3	1.3	3.8	2.7
	Ranked 3rd	2.6	1.9	0.0	0.0	3.8	6.3	0.0
Social sustainability	Ranked 1st	11.4	9.0	1.3	0.0	11.7	3.2	0.0
	Ranked 2nd	6.7	9.0	0.0	1.3	3.9	3.2	0.0
	Ranked 3rd	2.9	1.3	0.0	0.0	2.6	2.1	3.9
Transportation	Ranked 1st	34.9	2.6	1.9	8.0	6.5	2.6	0.0
	Ranked 2nd	9.6	2.6	13.3	1.3	5.2	3.8	0.0
	Ranked 3rd	1.2	2.6	3.8	5.3	0.0	2.6	3.8

prevention, smart growth, transportation, and organization initiatives are policy areas where it is more readily apparent how co-benefits may be received. However, social sustainability may not appear to have the same co-benefit potential or return on resource investment. As such, it is not surprising to see lacking political support as a primary barrier as compared to other sustainability policy areas.

Human Capital Constraints

Moving beyond the common concern about a lack of resources, it is instructive to explore the other frequently reported problems across each policy area. Human capital constraints were frequently cited as a secondary concern for achieving organizational, social sustainability, and energy and resource conservation goals. For organizational efforts in sustainability (internally focused on the city—see Chapter 9), 12.2% of the sample reported this as their top barrier to achieving success with another 15.9% indicating that it was the second most important reason they were having difficulty achieving success in this area. A total of 19.7% of cities reported human capital challenges as one of their top three barriers to achieving programmatic success in the area of energy and resource conservation. For social sustainability, human resource constraints were the third overall most common barrier to success, with 19.3% of the cities reporting this as one of their top three barriers. Identifying human capital constraints as a common reason for lack of success in sustainability provides some clues about ways that the pursuit of sustainability might be able to be improved in the future. Although these human capital constraints could be a function of understaffing in a city government (and therefore a secondary problem related to resource availability), it could also indicate a lack of training or knowledge necessary to achieve these types of sustainability goals through proper management and policy implementation techniques. Faculty and program directors of Masters of Public Administration (MPA) programs can contribute to the improvement of human capital by providing necessary curriculum and training opportunities for current and future public servants.

Infrastructure and Geographic Constraints

Infrastructure is a commonly identified barrier to programmatic success in transportation policies with almost 19% of cities indicating this is one of their top three barriers to success. This could also potentially be a function of resource limitations. Sustainable transportation policies usually require investment into mass transit and alternative transit infrastructure. If a community is struggling with resource availability, it could be manifesting as an inability to invest in the needed infrastructure to pursue transportation options. Given the fragmentation and resource constraints that local governments face, this is an area that the federal Department of Transportation (DOT) can potentially contribute to improvement. The DOT provides billions in federal transportation dollars to maintain and improve transportation infrastructure across the country. Increasing the emphasis on sustainable transportation infrastructure could perhaps assist local governments in reducing this barrier to success.

In both transportation and pollution prevention policy areas, geographic constraints were reported as common secondary problems to achieving success. While resource constraints were overwhelmingly reported as the most common problem for transportation policy success, 8% of the cities indicate that geographic constraints were their top reason for a lack of success. In total, 14.6% of cities had geographic constraints as a top-three problem. For pollution prevention, the percentage of cities ranking it as a top-three problem was slightly less at 13.3% of the respondents. This barrier reflects some of the concerns with local government fragmentation. It could be that cities find it challenging to coordinate efforts on pollution reduction or transportation infrastructure with neighboring communities. Solutions to this problem area will require collaborative efforts and perhaps assistance from an outside entity. One such possibility could stem from area universities that have academic programs focused on public deliberation. One such example is the Colorado State University's Center for Public Deliberation (cpd.colostate.edu). These deliberation-focused centers can potentially provide an important resource to get community members talking about the issue in a fact-based and nonemotional way.

Lack of Political or Citizen Support

The final area of interest related to barriers to success is the lack of political or citizen support. Two policy areas emerge as struggling with this barrier: smart growth and social sustainability. For smart growth policy, lack of political support and lack of citizen support fall into second place with almost 12% of the cities reporting each of these as one of their top reasons for lack of success. However, when it comes to social equity policies, the lack of political support is the top barrier to success with almost 12% of the cities ranking this as their top barrier.

The lack of political or citizen support for these two policy areas suggests that more education and information might be needed for the community to better understand these policies and the importance of them. Social equity, to be sure, is a commonly misunderstood issue and can be construed as something that it is not. Furthermore, some of the smart growth policies may be met with resistance from those who do not view density or mixed income as a desirable goal to be pursued in cities. For these policy areas, it is important that administrators, future public servants, and those teaching the future public servants more clearly explain the purposes and expected benefits of this type of effort.

Overall Lessons

The responses to this survey confirm several important findings from previous research. First and foremost, cities are still more likely to adopt the easy and low-cost sustainability policies that also have the potential for economic co-benefits. For example, policies that can work to save the city revenue in the form of a reduction in energy costs emerge as some of the most adopted policies across cities. Given the comprehensive approach to sustainability that this survey took, we can be more confident that cities are, in fact, engaging in these easier policies at the expense of the more aggressive or ambitious sustainability policies. This trend may be perceived as particularly troubling as cities may not be actually taking sustainability seriously by pursuing the higher impact, but more difficult and expensive, policies needed to move the sustainability effort ahead in the United States. Co-benefits, revenue savings, and easy-to-implement policies still dominate the sustainability movement in local governments. If sustainability efforts in cities are what America will rely on for combating climate change and improving the quality of life for residents, then we have a long way to go to really meet these demands.

As a secondary finding and confirmation, social equity, even when broadly defined, is still lagging behind the other two dimensions of sustainability in adoption rates. An emphasis on economic and environmental concerns remains dominant in local sustainability discussions. Equity considerations may be embedded within broader quality of life concerns in both domains, but the results of this survey leave room for skepticism. In particular, the range of social sustainability indicators included within this survey offered a range of both economic and environmental considerations for how minorities and marginalized groups are integrated into overall local sustainability efforts. If social equity is an integral part of achieving sustainability, then we would expect to see policies and indicators to specifically capture this dynamic beyond macro-level assessments of economic and environmental conditions within the community.

Beyond confirming previous research, this survey also shows that most cities do not routinely collect information to measure the efficiency or the effectiveness of their sustainability initiatives. In fact, as an example, of the cities with adopted GHG reduction goals less than half of them actually measure the progress or the performance of that policy with any metric—even the freely available ones. Adequately assessing and capturing GHG reduction may be challenging depending on the metrics used and the ability of the city to calculate a beneficial performance indicator. There is no consistent measurement approach for each individual sustainability indicator, and certain cities may lack the capacity to develop and utilize performance indicators (see Portney, 2013). As such, this survey demonstrates that of the cities that do collect information to gauge the performance of these policies, most of them are only collecting freely available census data. While census data may provide some important indicators for sustainability, they are not nearly comprehensive enough to adequately gauge the progress, if any, that a community's sustainability policies and programs are making. Moreover, as Portney (2014, p. 299) indicates, freely available data from the Census Bureau may not "be of much programmatic use" as these data do not capture important elements of achieving success. If cities are seeking to truly address sustainability concerns, improving the overall quality and utilization of performance metrics is paramount—particularly in areas where communities are able to take action. This factor might be even more important for social sustainability concerns, as readily available census data may inadequately reflect equity and justice concerns.

This survey also outlined a number of potential challenges for cities seeking to achieve success with their sustainability efforts. As demonstrated by the results, resource barriers pose a real challenge for evaluating these sustainability initiatives as well as achieving success. Other causes for lack of success may be reflective of an overall lack of resources but also point to area-specific challenges to achieving sustainability goals. Nevertheless, if the future of sustainability rests with local efforts, more must be done to establish a balanced sustainability policy portfolio and adequately evaluate these policies and programs. Sustainability policies have the potential to combat climate change and to improve the quality of life in American cities. However, without a clear evaluation and assessment of the successes, consequences, and progress on these policies—, success is not going to be easy or achievable in the near term. Much of the sustainable cities literature documents various policies cities are adopting to address sustainability concerns. However, none of that literature adequately documents the successes or failures of these policies. Without attention to the evaluation of these policies, it is unclear whether these city efforts are succeeding in achieving their goals and addressing environmental sustainability.

The remaining chapters of this book will delve into each of these major policy areas. Chapter 3 focuses on the sustainable transportation policies and programs. Policies such as alternative transportation infrastructure, mass transit development, and other policies meant to reduce GHG emissions from transportation will be discussed alongside the performance measurement efforts in this area. Chapter 4 of this book delves into pollution prevention policies across cities. The policies contained in Chapter 4 represent some of the purest environmental programs discussed in this book. Chapter 5 broadens out to explore energy and resource conservation efforts in American cities. This chapter highlights efforts that span economic, environmental, and equity concerns. Chapter 6 focuses on sustainable economic development policies like brownfield redevelopment and tax increment financing (TIF) efforts. This chapter has strong connections to the material found in Chapter 7. Chapter 7 discusses smart growth and land-use planning efforts. Of all the chapters in this book, this chapter strikes the clearest balance of the "Three E's" of sustainability. Chapter 8 is the most abstract of the content in this book and brings the discussion of social equity into focus so that the importance of the policy area can be understood and appreciated. Chapter 9 finishes up the last remaining policy area by discussing and explaining organizationally focused policies. This chapter provides a deep look at how cities are engaging in internal efforts at sustainability. Chapter 10 completes this book with conclusions and lessons learned.

Notes

1 Additional solicitations were sent on June 29 and July 18 to city officials whose initial or reminder emails either bounced or were no longer active. Retirements, resignations, and termination were the most common observed cause for failed email solicitation.
2 The authors extend gratitude to Jerry Kendall and Gabrielle Hane for their work.

References

Agyeman, J., Bullard, R. D., & Evans, B. (Eds.). (2003). *Just sustainabilities: Development in an unequal world*. Cambridge, MA: MIT press.

Opp, S. M. (2017). The forgotten pillar: A definition for the measurement of social sustainability in American cities. *Local Environment*, 22(3), 286–305.

Opp, S. M., Osgood, J. L., & Rugeley, C. R. (2014). Explaining the adoption and implementation of local environmental policies in the United States. *Journal of Urban Affairs*, *36*(5), 854–875.

Opp, S. M., & Saunders, K. L. (2013). Pillar talk: Local sustainability initiatives and policies in the United States—Finding evidence of the "three E's": Economic development, environmental protection, and social equity. *Urban Affairs Review*, *49*(5), 678–717. doi:10.1177/1078087412469344.

Portney, K. E. (2013). *Taking sustainable cities seriously: Economic development, the environment, and quality of life in American cities*. Cambridge, MA: MIT Press.

Portney, K. E. (2014). Developing sustainable cities indicators. In D. Mazmanian and H. Blanco (Eds.), *Elgar companion to sustainable cities* (pp. 283–301). Cheltenham, UK: Edward Elgar.

Slavin, M. I. (2011). *Sustainability in America's cities*. Washington DC: Island Press/Center for Resource Economics.

Wang, X., Hawkins, C., & Berman, E. (2014). Financing sustainability and stakeholder engagement: Evidence from US cities. *Urban Affairs Review*, *50*(6), 806–834.

Part II

Measuring Efficiency and Effectiveness in Sustainability

3 Transportation Sustainability

Transportation can create tremendous challenges to cities in their quest to achieve local goals. At their core, transportation policies are key drivers behind community activities and can determine economic productivity, environmental performance, and social equity within a community. Two key transportation challenges that American cities currently face are the personal automobile and infrastructure. Americans predominantly rely on personal automobiles to commute with a singular passenger vehicle emitting about 4.7 metric tons of carbon dioxide annually (EPA, 2016). Automobiles are the primary commuting choice for many Americans due to the overall convenience and poor alternative or public transit options including walking, biking, light rail, streetcars, or buses. As a result of this reality, communities may be plagued with traffic congestion, poor air quality, urban sprawl, increased infrastructure expenditures, and a host of negative public health concerns such as increased stress and fatigue—all related to their transportation options and infrastructure.

This chapter details the various policies, programs, and initiatives adopted by local governments in the United States to achieve a sustainable transportation system both efficiently and effectively. This chapter starts with an overview of what sustainable transportation encompasses and details some of the underlying consequences of traditional transportation planning. Next, sustainable transportation policies adopted by cities are discussed, followed by an evaluation of the performance measurement and management techniques used. The chapter concludes with a case study on sustainable transportation efforts in Atlanta, Georgia, as detailed by two practitioners working in this area.

What Is Sustainable Transportation?

Sustainable transportation has been defined and approached in a number of different ways. The University of Winnipeg's Centre for Sustainable Transportation (2002) provides one of the most comprehensive definitions and identifies three components to sustainable transportation, which include the following:

- Allows the basic access needs of individuals and societies to be met safely and in a manner consistent with human and ecosystem health, and with equity within and between generations.
- Is affordable, operates efficiently, offers choice of transport mode, and supports a vibrant economy.
- Limits emissions and waste within the planet's ability to absorb them, minimizes consumption of nonrenewable resources, limits consumption of renewable resources to the sustainable yield level, reuses and recycles its components, and minimizes the use of land and the production of noise.

The Centre's definition mirrors the three pillars of sustainability discussed in Chapter 1 and also clearly identifies numerous departures from traditional transportation planning and policies. The traditional approach, also referenced as the "business as usual" model, follows a unimodality linear planning process whereby faster automobile transport options are the end goal to achieving economic prosperity (Litman & Burwell, 2006; Schiller, Brunn, & Kentworthy, 2010). In essence, this model encourages a shift away from walking and biking modalities, which are perceived as slower and less efficient, to the automobile, which is seen as providing faster and better mobility (Figure 3.1). Economic concerns are valued, and environmental and social issues are largely ignored. In contrast to the traditional system, sustainable transportation systems rely on a multimodality approach that is not solely reliant on the

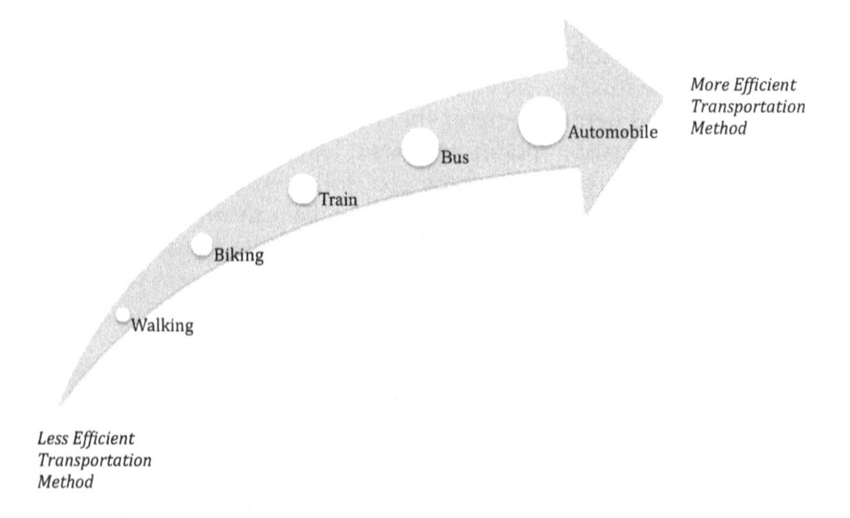

Figure 3.1 Business as Usual Linear Transportation Planning Model.
Source: Partially adapted from Litman, and Burwell (2006).

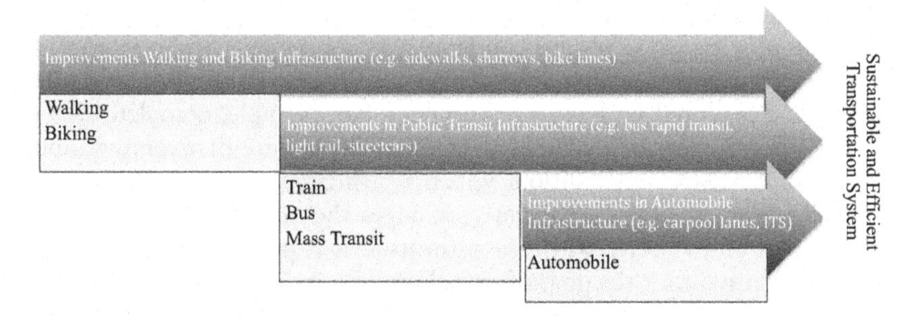

Figure 3.2 Sustainability-Based Transportation Planning Model.

personal automobile for economic prosperity (Figure 3.2). Instead, emphasis is also placed on other modalities that can address environmental and equity concerns while maintaining economic development goals (see Chapter 6 for more about sustainable economic development).

According to Schiller et al. (2010), sustainable transportation arose from three main and interrelated sources. First, the reliance on the automobile in planning was counterproductive in achieving an efficient transportation system. Conventional planning led to expansive highway systems that created urban sprawl and, in some cases, destroyed entire communities by either physically demolishing neighborhoods or by removing economic opportunities. In turn, pollution, maintenance costs, and traffic congestion all increased for most cities. Moreover, community inequities may have arisen from this conventional transportation planning. There is evidence to suggest that minority and low-income residents have not shared the same economic advantages and are also exposed to more negative externalities as compared to their white and upper- to middle-class counterparts in automobile-dependent transportation systems (see, for example, Bullard, Johnson, & Torres, 2004; Semuels, 2016). Nevertheless, reliance on just automobiles for transport has created inefficiencies for transportation systems and has prevented economic prosperity from reaching its maximum potential.

Second, some cities and related research demonstrate the numerous benefits to be gained from multimodality transportation systems. Aside from increasing economic activity, multimodality systems can improve public health and environmental quality by reducing automobile traffic. Air quality, traffic-related injuries, and personal mental health (e.g. stress of commuting, noise pollution) can all improve through a multimodality transportation system. In turn, rising quality of life can impact local economic development activities and productivity. Finally, a rising emphasis on sustainability and the environment after the release of the 1987 Brundtland Commission report *Our Common Future* led to a heightened awareness of environmental and intergenerational justice concerns for transportation planners and policymakers.

Today, a sustainable transportation system is one that balances economic, environmental, and equity concerns during the policy development and planning process. Several contemporary movements and concepts to improve transportation systems to be more efficient, sustainable, and safe have been explored by local governments. For example, complete street policies began emerging around the turn of the twenty-first century, and the Complete Streets Coalition, which is affiliated with Smart Growth America (see Chapter 7), currently manages the initiative. According to Zehngebot and Peiser (2014), the term itself was in reference to "a new policy initiative with the goal of ensuring the same rights and safe access for all users of streets, including pedestrians, bicyclists, motorists, and transit rides of all ages and abilities". As policies have emerged in various communities, there has been a significant variation in what a complete street looks like in rural, suburban, and urban communities. However, safety and the creation of livable communities, which address equity and public health concerns, is a shared key goal (Smart Growth America, ND).

Transit oriented development (TOD) is another transit-based policy initiative, emerging in the mid-twentieth century, which aims for a "mixed-use community that encourages people to live near transit services and to decrease their dependence on driving" (Still, 2002). A number of institutes and organizations define TOD as development that pursues mixed-use communities (e.g. live, work, and play in the same neighborhood) with close walkable access to high-quality public transportation (*for more information, see* Reconnecting America, ND; Transit Oriented Development Institute, ND). TOD emerged as many communities faced challenges with community development and suburban sprawl. Environmentalists backed TOD planning to protect open spaces, coastal regions, and promote high-density and sustainable communities (Carlton, 2007). Today, key components to TOD planning include a focus on the pedestrian, mixed-use and high-density neighborhoods, and high-quality public transit options.

Intelligent transportation systems (ITSs) also emerged in the twentieth century as continued reliance on the automobile led to suburban sprawl and the limits to "surface transportation" were realized (ITS JPO, 2016). As noted by the Intelligent Transportation Systems Joint Program Office (ITS JPO), many lack proper knowledge of ITS but benefit from the operational system that "encompass a broad range of wireless and wireline communications-based information electronics technologies" (ITS JPO, ND, 2016). Historically, a number of technological applications have been used in ITS management including navigation and mapping technologies, loop detectors, dynamic message signs, ramp management, automated traffic surveillance and control systems, fuel-efficient traffic signal management, automation, vehicle-based safety applications (e.g. self-braking and blind-spot warnings), and electronic vehicle license plate recognition systems. While ITS was not conceived to directly address environmental or sustainability concerns, the system can lead to better environmental conditions by minimizing some of the inefficiencies in current transportation systems that lead to congestion, poor air quality, and general public health and safety concerns.

One final and very recent concept in sustainable transportation efforts is the naked streets movement. Perhaps more popular in Europe than the United States, the naked streets movement seeks to remove transportation signage, including traffic lights, to reduce over stimulation of the senses (Bain, Gray, & Rodgers, 2012). Instead, environmental cues and additions are used to improve safety and efficiency of multimodality transportation systems. The naked streets concept is perhaps better suited for transit systems where all modality modes travel at similar speeds.

Complete Streets, the naked streets movement, TOD, and ITSs are just some examples of initiatives and movements currently altering transportation planning and policy development globally. Each incorporates key policy dimensions that encompass and embody sustainable transportation but does so through various techniques and approaches to infrastructure, community behavior, and pollution control and energy reduction. In the section that follows, specific policies and initiatives adopted by American cities are detailed.

What Policies Have Cities Adopted to Create a Sustainable Transportation System?

In our 2016 survey, cities were asked a series of questions about adopting infrastructure, community behavior, and pollution control policies. The survey included a range of questions that incorporated sustainable transportation trends and policies as identified by the U.S. Department of Energy, the Federal Transit Administration (FTA), the National Center for Sustainable Transportation, and the International City/County Management Association (ICMA). Moreover, established city sustainability plans were assessed for various elements of measuring transportation policy performance. Table 3.1 lists the policies and programs included in the survey with the percentage of cities self-reporting the adoption of the policy and measuring policy performance. As follows, each category of sustainable transportation policies is discussed further.

Sustainable Infrastructure Transportation Policies

Infrastructure policies in transportation focus on the development and improvement of transport modalities. Modalities can include walking, biking, rail, buses, streetcars, and the automobile. The physical element to transportation requires careful planning for how each modality method can be executed within a community. This can encompass roadways (with appropriate lanes for automobiles, buses, bikes, and streetcars), sidewalks, recreation trails, railways, capital assets (including buses and streetcars), and

Table 3.1 Sustainable Transportation Policies

Policy Area	*Policies and Programs*	*% of Cities Reporting Policy/ Program*	*% of Cities Reporting Performance Measurement*[a]	*% of Cities Reporting Performance Linked to Budget*[a]
Infrastructure	Biking improvements	72.1	14 (10.14)	4.52 (3.26)
	Walking improvements	78.99	10.55 (8.33)	4.59 (3.62)
	Commuter rail improvements	3.99	27.27 (1.09)	–
	Mass transit improvements	16.3	26.67 (4.35)	4.44 (<1)
	Trolley improvements	4.71	53.85 (2.54)	7.69 (<1)
	Reserved parking areas for residents in certain parts of the community	11.96	15.15 (1.81)	3.03 (<1)
	Green car preferred parking space	9.42	3.85 (<1)	–
	Carpool lanes	1.81	40 (<1)	–
	Green vehicle lanes	<1	50 (<1)	–
	Bus rapid transit improvement	11.9	21.21 (2.54)	–
Community behavior	Incentives for citizen use of multimodal/alternative transport methods	5.07	21.43 (1.09)	–
	Incentives to encourage private employers to subsidize mass transit costs for employees	4.71	15.38 (<1)	–
	City Partnership/agreement with Zipcar or other car sharing service	3.99	54.55 (2.17)	–
	Bike share/library programs	10.87	23.33 (2.54)	–
	ITSs	6.16	29.41 (1.81)	5.88 (<1)
	TOD initiatives	17.39	14.89 (2.54)	2.13 (<1)
	Others	2.89	12.5 (<1)	–
Energy management and pollution control	Use of permeable pavement for new public infrastructure	24.28	14.93 (3.62)	4.48 (1.09)
	Incentives for businesses to use permeable pavement	6.52	22.22 (1.45)	5.56 (<1)
	Upgraded streetlights to improve efficiency	65.94	19.23 (12.68)	10.44 (6.88)
	Upgraded traffic signals to improve efficiency	46.74	24.81 (11.59)	6.98 (3.26)
	Regulations restricting idling at railroad crossings	<1	–	–
	Regulations restricting idling in other parts of the community	10.87	10 (1.09)	3.33 (<1)
	Creation of a hotline to report offenses	1.08	33.33 (<1)	–
	Policies directed at noise pollution from traffic noise (bus, car, etc.)	15.94	11.36 (3.29)	4.55 (1.65)
	Policies directed at noise pollution from aircraft	5.07	28.57 (10.35)	7.14 (2.59)

[a]Reported as the following: % of cities with reported policy (% of all cities surveyed).

parking and storage facilities. In addition, as discussed fully in Chapter 9, the greening of city operations and rules can also lead to regulations for better energy-efficient and ecological sound infrastructure applications including the purchasing of fuel-efficient vehicles and the use of LED traffic and streetlights on city streets. In essence, infrastructure policies encompass the physical requirements necessary for transportation systems and, in turn, will also determine and shape behavioral and pollution control policies.

As stated previously, traditional transportation planning relies heavily on the automobile to create faster and more efficient movement of people and goods across a specific geographic area. Therefore, most infrastructure policies are designed around the automobile to accommodate for an expansive roadway system. However, increasing the level of sustainability for transportation systems requires improving and expanding non-automobile infrastructure. In our 2016 survey, city respondents were asked about the nature of infrastructure improvements (Table 3.1). Nearly 79% of all cities identified improvements in walking infrastructure, and approximately 72% reported biking infrastructure improvements. This is similar to the 2010 ICMA survey where 61.4% of local governments report the addition of biking and walking trails, and 24.5% of cities also reported the widening of sidewalks in the previous five years. The most commonly reported improvements in the 2016 survey include the addition and improvement of new biking and walking pathways and upgrading or expanding existing sidewalks. Of the cities opting to elaborate on their improvements, 67% indicated expanding or improving biking and walking trails and upgrading sidewalks to maintain community connectivity and to improve ADA access and compliance. In some cases, pathway development and expansion were multimodal (e.g. pathways not specific to just walking or biking, sharrows[1]) and encompassed widening of sidewalks to permit multiuse. There was also significant variation in the type of primary use between commuting versus recreational purposes and type of pathways (e.g. improved/unimproved and detached/street). A total of 28% of cities did specifically indicate current or near-future development and improvements of dedicated bike lanes on streets.

Other significant walking and biking improvements include improved safety efforts of intersections (8.3% reporting) that included reduced automobile speeds, development of over-and underpasses, car-free zones, and more efficient and clearly marked intersection signage. Several communities cited a Complete Streets policy, which aims "to balance safety and convenience for everyone using the road", when specifically referencing improvements to intersections (Smart Growth America, ND). Other notable but less commonly self-reported walking and biking infrastructure improvements include the development of biking parking/storage facilities (7.24%) and requiring sidewalks in new development (3.62%). This is surprising considering the high report rates in the 2010 ICMA survey by cities. However, respondents may not have elected to offer this information in the 2016 survey and were not prompted with a list of specific improvements. Respondents were able to elaborate on the nature of their infrastructure improvements and each varied considerably in depth. To that extent, some communities even noted specific aesthetic, community improvement, and pet-friendly upgrades to walking infrastructure such as library stations, pet-leash holders and hydration stations, and planting of trees for shade along paths.

Comparatively, public transit and automobile-based modalities received far less reported improvements in cities when compared to biking and walking. For cars, the highest reported improvement was the creation of reserved parking for residents in certain neighborhoods (11.96%) followed by preferred parking spaces for green cars (9.42%), carpool lanes (1.81%), and green vehicles lanes (<1%). Mass transit system improvements were more common than auto improvements. Mass transit improvements were reported by 16.3% with specific bus rapid transit improvements following close behind at 11.9% of cities reporting. Trolley and commuter rail improvements were reported by less than 5% of communities. The low reported improvements of trolley and commuter rail systems are not surprising; in 2010, only 7.2% of ICMA survey respondents indicated a current rail or streetcar system. In the expansion of services, 10.1% of cities self-reported an expansion of bus, light rail, and trolley services. For one community, the nature of expanded bus services coincided with the termination of the public school bus system for high school students, who were then expected to ride the bus to and from school.

In terms of performance measurement, most cities adopting sustainable infrastructure policies do not assess or measure the performance of their transportation policies and programs. Moreover, even fewer cities actively link performance metrics to the budget. Carpool lanes, trolley/streetcar improvements, and green vehicle lanes received the highest self-reported performance measurement assessment by cities with adopted policies with reported performance ranging from 40% to 53.85%. While the total number of cities adopting these policies is very low, communities that have pursued these policies are tracking performance. For the remaining categories, approximately 10%–25% of cities reported measuring performance of transportation policies. A little over a quarter of all cities with commuter rail and mass transit improvements report performance tracking in each category, and one-sixth of communities with improvements in bus rapid transit track performance measures. Of surprise is the low-performance measurement of biking and walking modality policies and initiatives. Less than 15% of cities with reported biking and walking improvements track performance in either category, and less than 5% of cities linked performance to the budget in each category. This highlights the reality that over 80% of all communities with improvements in this area do not track the performance of the policies adopted to improve walking and biking infrastructure.

Sustainable Community Behavior Transportation Policies

A second set of transportation policies is geared toward community commuting behavior. In addition to making physical modifications and improvements, cities can also enact a series of incentives, initiatives, and programs that alter behavior in such a way to reduce congestion, particularly during peak periods, and increase overall system efficiency. The first challenge in increasing the use of public transit and non-automobile-based commuting is improvement of infrastructure and services. Infrastructure improvements, like those noted before, are just one primary step to achieving sustainable and multimodality transport systems. The second challenge to achieving a sustainable transport system is behavioral. Personal automobile use is often seen as advantageous compared to other modes of transportation and becomes habit forming. The automobile is perceived as faster means of travel with the added benefits of comfort, safety, cleanliness, flexibility in scheduling and geographic reach, carrying capacity, and general psychological feelings of superiority (Chowdhury & Ceder, 2016; Currie & Delbosc, 2013; Diekstra & Kroon, 1994; Gray, 1992; Redman, Friman, Garling, & Hartig, 2013; Volinski & Page, 2006). Overcoming the automobile dependency, when other options are available, is dependent on using a set of behavioral modification and incentive-based policies.

Changing individual-level behavior in transportation decisions is deeply dependent on understanding human psychology and decision-making. To simplify, human behavior can be modified through positive or negative reinforcement (a carrot vs. stick phenomenon). Positive reinforcement policies may include offering incentives or subsidies for individuals to use public transportation or walk/bike to their destination. In the 2016 survey, 5% of cities reported using incentives for citizens to use multimodal or alternative transportation methods (Table 3.1). For example, the city of Telluride, Colorado, offers free transit throughout the year via shuttle and aerial tramway, which connects with the nearby community of Mountain Village, and also participates in a regional cost-share program with two other local governments to provide free or reduced-fare transit for local residents and visitors alike. Some local governments went even further (approximately 4.71%) by offering incentives to private companies, universities, and school districts to subsidize the cost of commuting for employees using mass transit. As in the case of Telluride, free transit opportunities provide an incentive for local residents to use public transportation instead of their own personal vehicle. In similar vein, city employees can also be incentivized to use public transit. Chapter 9, which focuses on the greening of city operations and includes government employee management, elaborates upon city employee transportation incentives further.

Another method to alter transportation behavior is through ride sharing service partnerships or agreements. Almost 4% of cities reported in

2016 developing a partnership or agreement of Zipcar or other car sharing services. This does not encompass the regulatory permission of such companies as Uber or Lyft to operate within the community. Rather these types of policies discourage personal automobile possession and use by providing residents and visitors the opportunity to use a vehicle temporarily or as needed. More popular than car sharing, nearly 11% of cities reporting bike share and library programs. Bike share, or sometimes known as a bike library, programs are similar to car sharing services. Patrons pay a fee for temporary use of a bicycle. In some communities, patrons have the option of purchasing a longer-term subscription to utilize a local bike library over the course of a week, month, or year.

Finally, modification of transportation behavior can be achieved through a system-wide overhaul and monitoring efforts. Approximately 6% of cities adopted an ITS. The ITS is meant to increase efficiency and safety by utilizing technology to monitor and to evaluate transit conditions. Such a system can be used in both urban and suburban communities to monitor a range of transportation modalities. For example, roadside message boards are commonly adopted as part of ITSs where the automobile is a primary transport method. Message boards can provide weather alerts, accident delays, and communicate information about travel times and alternative routes in real time.

Communities may also go one step further in systematic behavior modification by implementing a TOD initiative, and 17.3% of the sample did so. The FTA defines TOD as creating "compact, mixed-use communities near transit where people enjoy easy access to jobs and services" (FTA, ND). TOD can truly revitalize communities by providing comprehensive overhaul of community planning and design through appropriate land use near major transit corridors. A TOD initiative may include mixed-use zoning, neighborhood revitalization, creation of affordable housing supply, increasing pedestrian and cyclist safety, and targeted efforts to increase ridership through public transit systems. A key goal is to improve quality of life for all residents by decreasing the distance and time commuting thereby leading to less congestion and fewer negative environmental impacts. A TOD system, if properly executed, increases connectivity in a community and can increase equity within a community by providing access to leisurely and economic opportunities to all residents. Chapter 8 discusses the element of social equity in sustainable communities further and details the element of geographic opportunities.

Performance measurements for community transportation behavior policies are utilized by cities at about the same rate as infrastructure policies. Over half of the cities with development car sharing partnerships or agreements actively measure performance, but not one of those cities linked performance to the budget for that effort. Only 23% of cities with bike share programs indicate performance tracking of the program itself. A third of communities with ITSs tracked performance compared to approximately 15% of cities with TOD initiatives. Finally, policies intended to incentive multimodal transportation received low rates of performance tracking with 15.38% of cities tracking performance of private employer incentive policies and 21.43% of cities tracking citizen incentive policies.

Sustainable Transportation Pollution Control and Energy Policies

As a final category, cities may enact a series of specific pollution control policies either as stand-alone measures or as part of infrastructure and behavioral policies. Of the cities surveyed in 2016, 24.28% indicated use of permeable pavement for new public infrastructure projects, but only 6.52% of cities have developed policies to incentivize businesses to use permeable pavement for projects. Performance tracking is on average with other transportation policies at 14.93% of cities tracking public infrastructure permeable pavement performance and 22.22% of cities tracking performance of incentives for businesses to use permeable pavement.

When used, permeable pavement allows rainwater or snowmelt to seep through the pavement and filters pollutants from water systems (EPA, 2017). The utilization of permeable pavement in infrastructure projects is an easily incorporated policy and mandate for most cities that can reduce overall development and maintenance costs over time. For example, the City of Toledo, Ohio, adopted permeable pavement requirements as part of the city's pollution prevention and good housekeeping requirements. In turn, the city has incorporated permeable pavement as part of a major roadway infrastructure greening project that would improve storm drainage while simultaneously beautifying the roadway.[2] Similarly, the City of Santa Monica, California, also utilized permeable surface requirements into an alleyway capital improvement project and has adopted pervious pavement requirements into the city's code of ordinances.[3] Both cities also extend incentives to businesses to use permeable pavement for projects as well, with the City of Santa Monica offering a suggested list of paving products detailing type, cost, and companies offering installation services.

Another pollution and energy reduction method centers on the use of energy-efficient bulbs for streetlights and traffic lights. Traffic lights are key to managing traffic flows, whereas streetlights can increase safety and economic activity at night. The cost of operating traffic lights and streetlights can be high, particularly if using inefficient light bulbs. LEDs are considered a gold standard but are expensive to integrate into existing systems initially. Larger cities, including Los Angeles and Seattle, have reportedly spent millions to upgrade existing streetlights to LED bulbs (Office of Energy Efficiency and Renewable Energy, ND).

A similar cost also applies to traffic lights. While some international cities may be moving towards the naked streets concept by removing traffic lights and signage (see Bain et al., 2012), a majority of U.S. cities are still utilizing traffic lights to manage intersection traffic. Reducing use of inefficient lights on roadways can reduce spending on energy cost. Of the cities surveyed, approximately two-thirds have upgraded streetlights to be more efficient, and almost half increased the efficiency on traffic signals. However, only 19.23% and 24.81% of those same cities measure performance in each respective category.

Reduction of idling time is another pollution control measure that specifically targets emissions and air quality, especially during weather extremes such as very hot or cold weather (EPA, 2008). It is estimated the 30 million tons of carbon dioxide and 6 billion gallons of fuel are wasted annually from idling vehicles (DOE, 2015). In 2016, almost 11% of cities report restriction in idling within the community for residents and businesses, with a tenth of those cities tracking performance and even fewer linking performance to the budget. Only 1% of these cities had a hotline to report idling time offenses. For some cities, there are idling restrictions required by state law. Twenty-seven states and the District of Columbia currently have enacted idling restrictions (Clean Cities, ND). State laws do, in many instances, apply to unattended idling or idling of non-personal use of vehicles including commercial heavy-, medium-, and light-duty vehicles.

As a final set of transportation pollution policies, cities may also enact noise pollution regulations. Currently, only 5% of cities had policies addressing aircraft noise pollution, and nearly 16% had policies regulating noise pollution for ground traffic. More cities tracked the performance of aircraft noise pollution policies compared to ground traffic noise pollution policies. Noise pollution policies have less to do with traditional environmental pollutants and are geared more toward public health concerns in particular. Title IV of the Clean Air Act includes provisions toward reducing unwanted or disturbing sounds that can lead to stress, high blood pressure, hearing loss, and sleep disruption among health problems (EPA, ND). Noise pollution laws go above and beyond just establishing noise ordinances to include restrictions on appropriate hours of emitting noises, excessive noise, and require appropriate insulation to reduce noise.

The results of the 2016 survey show that cities are pursuing a wide range of sustainable transportation policies, albeit with overall adoption totals averaging less than 20% of all cities surveyed across most policy categories. Two infrastructure policy areas, biking and walking infrastructure improvements, buck the trend with approximately three-quarters of cities committing to development and improvement of bike lanes, sharrows, sidewalks, and pathways. Commitment to improving these traditionally "less efficient" modalities may serve as an initial step for many communities in improving transit and recreation opportunities.

Performance Measurement in Sustainable Transportation—Common Metrics and Barriers to Success

Collectively, cities do not typically measure the performance of their transportation policies. As discussed previously and outlined in Table 3.1, an overwhelming percentage of cities do not measure the performance of transportation policies adopted. One policy, idling restrictions, did not have **any** city reporting performance measurement of that policy. Remaining policies all had at least a few cities reporting performance measurement for each transportation-focused policy with trolley and car sharing services receiving the largest percentage of cities measuring performance. The table also shows that even fewer cities actually link performance directly to the budget. Eleven policy areas, including railroad idling restrictions, did not receive any self-reporting for performance linkage to the budget. Of those policy areas where performance is linked to the budget, the overall number of cities is still low. Biking and walking improvements, the two most popular forms of infrastructure policies, only average 4.5% of cities linking performance to the budget in each category.

Common Transportation Performance Measurements

The survey distributed to city officials provided a list of a number of the more common performance metrics for transportation policies and also offered the opportunity to expand upon other measurements used by the city. Many of the performance measurements used for sustainable transportation policies are more output focused rather than outcome focused. Specifically, tracking the number of miles, facilities, personal autos, or noise complaints are simple metrics tracking frequency rather than direct policy impact or goal successes. Table 3.2 outlines the frequency in self-reported use of each commonly used metric among all cities surveyed. In addition, the table outlines some performance benchmarks used by cities. As evident, few cities actually use the measurements included in the survey but even fewer communities (1.09%) identified additional or other measurements used to assess the performance of their transportation policies. The most frequently used measurements are associated with walking and biking infrastructure improvements. Communities will often track the number of miles of walkways and bike lanes developed or targeted for development soon. For example, Palm Springs, California, developed a bike route plan that identified several types of bike lanes and pathways to be developed with goals for the length of miles and budget needed to develop each mile on average.[4]

Table 3.2 Sustainable Transportation Performance Metrics

Performance Metrics	*% of Cities Reporting*	*Sample Benchmark*
Number personal of autos in community (per capita or otherwise)	All cities—3.26% Cities with ITS or TOD initiatives—16.66%	Lakewood, CO: Reduce trips to work by single-occupant vehicles from a 2007 baseline of 75% to 65% by 2025
Miles of high-capacity public transit	All cities—4.71% Cities with Bus Rapid Transitor commuter rail improvements—34.21%	Atlanta, GA: Expand MARTA Blue Line from Indiana Creek station to I-20 and Stonecrest Mall; BRT expansion from Five Points station to Stonecrest Mall
Miles of light passenger public transit	All cities—2.9% Cities with mass transit or trolley improvements—15.09%	Denton, TX: Increase public transit ridership within the city above the 2011 2.4 million ride baseline
Miles of bicycle paths and/or lanes	All cities—20.29% Cities with bicycle infrastructure improvement—28.14%	Palm Springs, CA Bike Plan: Create 28.11 miles of buffered bike lanes
Miles of walking trails	All cities—17.75% Cities with walking infrastructure improvement—22.37%	Atlanta, GA: Develop 33 miles of walking/multiuse trails near the Beltline corridor by 2030
Measures of sidewalks in community	All cities—14.86% Cities with walking infrastructure improvement—18.72%	Atlanta, GA: Construct 900 miles of new sidewalks adjacent to roadways
Number of transportation facilities (i.e. bus stops, train stations, etc.)	All cities—9.78%	Atlanta, GA: Have bike share stations installed in disconnected and low-income neighborhoods Santa Monica, CA: Construct 300 smart charging stations by 2022
Percentage of commuters using a travel mode to work other than a personal vehicle	All cities—5.8%	Atlanta, GA: Increase biking by 15% by 2020 Nashville, TN: Increase biking and pedestrian transportation to 7% by 2020, 12% by 2030, and 30% by 2050
Number of noise complaints from traffic	All cities—3.26% Cities reporting noise pollution policies—100%	N/A
Other measures	All cities—1.09%	Atlanta, GA: Reduce VMT and increase alternative fuel vehicles to achieve a total reduction of 374,846 mTCO2e by 2020 Atlanta, GA: By 2020 have all citizens lie within .5 mile of a bikeway network

Challenges and Barriers in Sustainable Transportation Policy Success

Cities identified a number of barriers to achieving progress and success in their transportation policy initiatives. Lack of resources was the most frequently cited barrier with nearly 35% of all cities ranking it as a first-order challenge (see Chapter 2, Table 2.5). Other barriers to sustainable transportation efforts include general geographic constraints and infrastructure limitations. The barriers cited by cities are reflective of the physical and fiscal restraints many communities face. Existing infrastructure and planning designs are often hard to alter, particularly in cases where the personal automobile is the primary transportation method. Moreover, the sheer cost associated with capital improvement projects may deter investments into sustainable transportation policies. Effective transportation planning can require years of fiscal savings and planning for a project to be executed.

Concept in Action: Sustainable Transportation Policies in Atlanta, Georgia

Transportation is a policy area that is at the heart of economic activity of a community and can also dictate quality of life and environmental health. Cities pursuing sustainable transportation policies must alter planning and policy adoption away from traditional and unimodality planning, which focus predominantly on the personal automobile, toward transportation systems that use multiple modalities for the movement of people and goods. The evidence from this chapter suggests cities are engaging in a wide variety of sustainable transportation policies and even returning emphasis to walking and biking modalities, which were once considered inefficient transportation modes. The performance measurements and benchmarks outlined in Table 3.2 provide a guiding framework for cities on how to start measuring transportation policy efforts.

The following case study highlights how Atlanta, Georgia, a city and metropolitan area with significant suburban sprawl and one of the longest commutes in the county, has worked to improve the sustainability of its transportation system. Dealing with causes and effects of transportation is a transboundary issue and requires cities to reorient how they may approach sustainability efforts. Coordination within a metro region to deal with transboundary issues is a new direction for most cities pursuing sustainability initiatives (Portney, 2013). As is evident by the case, transportation planning and policy development is closely intertwined with smart growth, economic development goals, and equity considerations. The City of Atlanta, in coordination with other regional organizations, has worked to reenvision how Atlantans commute in order to keep the city economically competitive and moving. This has involved comprehensive planning by the City of Atlanta, as well as relying on a host of other transportation policies geared toward biking and walking modalities, TOD, improvements in public transit, and efforts to reassess neighborhood planning.

Dr. Jairo Garcia, the Director of Climate Policies and Renewables for the City of Atlanta, and David D'Onofrio, Principal Planner of Air Quality and Climate Change for the Atlanta Regional Commission, provide a historical context for why changes to Atlanta's transportation system were needed and how the city is managing to achieve success in creating a more sustainable transportation system. While not all communities are the size of the Atlanta metro area, there are plenty of lessons derived from one of America's largest cities.

A MULTIFACETED APPROACH TO A SUSTAINABLE TRANSPORTATION SYSTEM: REVERSING TRANSPORTATION TRENDS IN ATLANTA, GA

By: Jairo H. Garcia, PhD, and David D'Onofrio

Developing comprehensive and sound transportation policies in one of America's largest cities has required extensive planning and coordination among key city, regional, and state stakeholders. As the capital of the state of Georgia, Atlanta is a sprawling metropolitan region of the state and a significant economic powerhouse. The tale of sustainable transportation policies in Atlanta follows a familiar historical path of many American cities, but the policies to correct years of automobile dependency are more complex than the average American city.

Transportation has played a significant role in the City of Atlanta since its inception. The city was once a focal point for railroad lines at the foothills of the Appalachian Mountains. Recognized as a major terminal for railroads, the city's founders named the town Terminus in 1837. That name wouldn't last, and in 1847 the name Atlanta was officially adopted.

Atlanta was pivotal for confederate troop transportation during the Civil War, a key reason for its destruction. Postwar reconstruction happened quickly and by 1889 the city had restored railroads extending in every cardinal direction. At that time, the city began the introduction of electric streetcars for local and regional travel.

For the first part of the twentieth century, streetcars were the main transportation system in Atlanta. By the 1920s, Atlanta's regional population was estimated to be 600,000 and streetcar ridership peaked at approximately 97 million trips per year. However, by 1937, electric trackless trolleys were introduced to the city, replacing streetcars.

Post-World War II, Americans' dependency on cars began, and by 1946 Georgia prepared a highway and transportation plan for Atlanta called the Lochner Plan. The primary goal of which was to accommodate car needs. Beyond freeways, the Lochner Plan included the increase of parking in downtown Atlanta, which swelled from roughly 15,000 spaces in the 1940s to over 95,000 spaces today. Freeways and parking spaces displaced many historic and minority-occupied properties in central Atlanta.

Between the 1950s and the 1990s, few places in America saw the extent of suburbanization more than Atlanta. City population stagnated as suburban population boomed. Jobs relocated from downtown into communities outside of the city where major freeways and arterials met. Today, the lack of a comprehensive regional transit system results in 78% of city residents driving to work, whereas 97% of all regional trips are done by car. Razing neighborhoods and buildings for freeways and parking usage disconnected the city where it was once linked. Consequences of suburbanization included poor air quality, a high carbon footprint, and blight in many of Atlanta's historic neighborhoods.

Today, Atlanta has become the city with the longest distance commute in the entire United States and one of the top 10 cities with the worst traffic (Caldwell, 2016; Kneebone & Holmes, 2015). Atlantans waste an average of 40 hours per year and lose roughly $1,522 in fuel and productivity sitting in traffic. Loss in productivity and air pollution has motivated many companies and residents to relocate from the suburbs to areas in the city closer to public transit. Atlantans have recognized that walkable communities and high-density developments increase economic growth, while contributing to a sustainable environment.

Four different bodies govern transportation planning and policy efforts for the metro Atlanta region: The *City of Atlanta Transportation Planning Division* at the local level; the *Atlanta Regional Commission* (ARC) and the *Metropolitan Atlanta Rapid Transit Authority* (MARTA) at the regional level; and the *Georgia Regional Transportation Authority* (GRTA) at the state level. Each governing body contributes to the overall vision for sustainable transportation in the Atlanta metro. The four organizations work on the areas of public planning, policy, and investments, and focus on primarily alternative transportation and better land use. A critical focus of these organizations is to transform Atlanta from being the poster child for urban sprawl into a region that is embracing twenty-first-century clean transportation options.

The City of Atlanta Transportation Planning Division

The Transportation Planning Division of the City of Atlanta Office of Planning and Community Development leads and coordinates transportation planning efforts within the City of Atlanta. The division also coordinates project development activities with other regional and state organizations in planning, designing, and implementing transportation facilities and services (City of Atlanta, ND1). The City of Atlanta has developed two plans specifically addressing transportation within the city—the Climate Action Plan and the Transportation Plan. In addition, the city has also developed particular project programming geared toward improving bicycling throughout the city.

City of Atlanta Climate Action Plan

Fossil fuel vehicles produce one-third of the 9 million metric tons of greenhouse gas emissions yearly within the City of Atlanta limits. In 2015, the City of Atlanta Office of Sustainability, in collaboration with the city's Transportation Planning Division, ARC, and 35 more stakeholders, developed The *Atlanta Climate Action Plan*. The plan proposes reducing *Vehicle Miles Traveled* (VMT) through programs and policies that allow and promote alternative transportation modes.[5] Alternative transportation modes, in this case, include bicycles and encouraging telecommuting and compressed work weeks.

The City of Atlanta Transportation Plan

The 2017 *Comprehensive Atlanta Transportation Plan* developed by the City of Atlanta Transportation Planning Division reiterates the need for fully functional roadways through the adoption and implementation of a Complete Streets Program. This initiative is dedicated to improving street and roadway design standards to promote health, safety, livability, and sustainability in the city. With a combination of street design, zoning standards, and sustainable green infrastructure, Atlanta will be able to provide accessible and safe commuting alternatives and sustainable traffic management. Atlantans have the ability to learn more about the city's effort and provide direct feedback to city officials at www.atlantastransportationplan.com/. The website features the transportation plan and provides up-to-date information about projects and future plans.

Cycling in Atlanta

A key focus of transportation planning for Atlanta centers on improving bicycle modalities. Atlanta's City Council has followed up with funds for bicycle projects, and in 2015 the city hired its first Chief Bicycle Officer with the support of the Atlanta Falcons Youth Foundation and the Atlanta Bicycle Coalition. In June 2016, Atlanta launched its bike share program, Relay. Beginning with just 100 bikes at 10 stations, the system expanded to 500 bikes at 70 stations in 2017. The 2017 *Comprehensive Atlanta Transportation Plan* proposed the addition of more than 200 miles of bike lanes within the city limits.

The Atlanta Regional Commission

ARC is the state-designated regional planning and intergovernmental coordination agency for the 10-county Atlanta region. ARC is also the federally designated Metropolitan Planning Organization (MPO) for a broader 20-county portion of the region. The agency's responsibilities include preparing a Regional Transportation Plan and allocating federal transportation funds in the Transportation Improvement Program. Since 1947, ARC and its predecessor agencies have helped focus the region's leadership, attention, and resources on critical issues including land use and transportation planning. A key plan, the Atlanta Region's Plan, is developed and executed by ARC. In 2016, ARC's board approved the latest *Atlanta Region's Plan.*[6] This plan consists of investments and programs needed to ensure metro Atlanta's future. The plan focuses on promoting world-class infrastructure, healthy livable communities, and a competitive economy including an $85.1 billion investment in the region's transportation system through the year 2040. Nearly two-thirds of the funds will be allocated to maintain existing infrastructure. Approximately $28 billion will be spent to expand the region's transportation network, and $3.1 billion of the plan's budget is designated to the expansion of new transit projects and to improve low-carbon mobility by creating more walkable communities, mixed-use centers, and corridors that provide better access to jobs and services.

The Metropolitan Atlanta Rapid Transit Authority

The MARTA is the principal public transportation operator in the Atlanta metropolitan area. MARTA operates rail, bus, and paratransit services in Clayton, DeKalb, and Fulton Counties. The MARTA rail system consists of 48 miles of track and 38 rail stations. It also operates a network of over 550 buses that navigate along 1,439 miles of streets in the metro area. The system's paratransit service, developed under the Americans with Disabilities Act, is a complementary service for customers unable to ride or disembark from the regular service. MARTA is the ninth largest rapid transit system in the United States, transporting more than half a million people every weekday (MARTA, ND).

MARTA was created by an act of the Georgia General Assembly in 1965. Originally envisioned to operate in the region's central five metropolitan counties, MARTA's reach was limited due to hostility from suburban communities, which did not embrace the inherent value of public transportation. Through regional popular referenda to levy a one-cent sales tax to pay for operations and capital, MARTA was authorized to initially serve Fulton and DeKalb Counties only. Gradually, opposition toward MARTA lessened across the region based on its economic and quality of life impacts. In 2014, Clayton County voted to join the system overwhelmingly with a 74% favorable vote.

Georgia's Transportation Funding Act of 2015, although primarily focused on raising money for more statewide roadway construction, recognized the need for public transit and allowed cities and counties to increase sales taxes to allocate additional resources through *Transportation Special-Purpose Local-Option Sales Taxes* (T-SPLOST) for a period of five years at a time. The Act also allowed a one-time bonding through the *State Roads and Tollway Authority* (SRTA) in the amount of $75 million to fund transit capital projects.

In 2016, Georgia Senate Bill 369 authorized the City of Atlanta to place a referendum before the voters for an additional half penny sales tax for MARTA. Residents overwhelmingly supported both the TSPLOST and the MARTA referenda, allowing the city to invest in improving transit and transportation infrastructure (City of Atlanta, ND2). The half-penny sales tax for MARTA will generate approximately $2.5 billion over the next 40 years, allowing MARTA to make major investments in transit infrastructure including: expanded light rail and streetcar service, new infill MARTA stations, and new or improved bus service in the City of Atlanta. Other MARTA jurisdictions may consider holding additional referenda over the coming years. Today, MARTA is still the largest transit system in the country that does not receive dedicated funding from its state government.

The Georgia Regional Transportation Authority

The GRTA's core responsibilities are reducing congestion and improving mobility through transportation performance management and operating regional commuter transit, including 27 express bus routes between 12 metro Atlanta counties and major employment centers.

GRTA was created by an act of the Georgia state government in 1999 as a response to the Atlanta region being out of conformity with federal transportation air quality requirements (Paget-Seekins, 2014). This conformity lapse limited the use of federal transportation funds. GRTA's role was to help coordinate transportation and land-use planning in the region. The authority works closes with ARC to approve Developments of Regional Impact (DRIs). DRIs evaluate proposed developments for their effect on the surrounding transportation infrastructure and identify options to mitigate current and future mobility impacts. GRTA also approves ARC's Transportation Improvement Program on behalf of the governor (GRTA, ND).

Collaborative Efforts

In addition to efforts pursued by the four central transportation organizations described before, there have also been efforts by citizens and local governments in the metro area to improve transportation. The lack of a comprehensive and effective transportation system in the Atlanta region has motived citizens and local governments to develop alternative solutions. These local solutions are igniting collaborative efforts at the local, regional, and state level. Some of these solutions, like the Atlanta BeltLine, have been recognized nationally and internationally for being innovative in their approach to urban development and mobility.

The Atlanta BeltLine

The Atlanta BeltLine is a 22-mile loop of pedestrian-friendly and rail transit corridor being constructed over an abandoned railway system around the core of Atlanta. This sustainable redevelopment project includes approximately 3,000 acres of underutilized land along the corridor, making it available to public and private redevelopment opportunities including 28,000 new and 5,600 affordable housing, and up to $20 billion in total projected economic development. Once completed in 2030, the Atlanta BeltLine will connect more than 45 neighborhoods and will cost around $4.8 billion.

Funding for the project comes from a combination of government grants and partnership. The Atlanta Public Schools, the City of Atlanta, and Fulton County agreed to forego future property tax revenue increases on properties in the BeltLine Tax Allocation District over the next 25 years and dedicate them to the project (Atlanta Beltline, 2017). Additional funds were appropriated when Atlanta voters supported the 2016 Tax for Transportation purposes (i.e. T-SPLOST).[7] This tax is expected to generate approximately $300 million over a five-year time span in which $66 million is allocated solely for the BeltLine. Funds from the 0.4% sales tax will help to purchase the last portions to complete the 22-mile BeltLine loop.

The Atlanta BeltLine has received numerous recognitions such as the *EPA's Overall Excellence Award for Smart Growth*, the *Best Environmental Rehabilitation Project in the World* from the International Real Estate Federation, a recognition by the *International Economic Development Council* (IEDC), and in 2016 it received the *Envision Gold Award* from the *Institute for Sustainable Infrastructure.*

The New Atlanta Streetcar

The new Atlanta Streetcar is the result of a collaborative effort among the City of Atlanta, MARTA, the Atlanta Downtown Improvement District, and the U.S. Department of Transportation. The goal was to interconnect touristic and historic sites downtown with MARTA and eventually the BeltLine, and serve as a comprehensive last-mile connection for city transit needs. The system opened for service in December 2014 with a 2.7-mile loop serving 12 stops in downtown Atlanta with access to MARTA rail. The city estimates that up to $2.5 billion in economic development opportunities exists on over 80 acres of underutilized land and 30 vacant buildings along the initial route.

Funding for the Atlanta Streetcar showcases the diversity of partnerships supporting transit in the city. In addition to a Federal Transportation Investment Generating Economic Recovery (TIGER) II grant, the City of Atlanta, the Atlanta Downtown Improvement District, and the ARC all contributed money toward the development and operations of the new Atlanta Streetcar. In June 2017, the City of Atlanta announced that MARTA will operate the Atlanta Streetcar (Green, 2017). The streetcar will tap into the transit's $2.5 billion 2016 T-SPLOST expansion approved by Atlanta's voters. The plan includes the expansion of the Atlanta Streetcar to the BeltLine and to MARTA stations.

Transit-Oriented Development

MARTA, the City of Atlanta, and ARC are increasing their efforts to support transit through the implementation of comprehensive TOD. TODs are pedestrian-friendly, mixed-use communities adjacent to transit infrastructure. These communities reduce car dependency by providing residents and workers easy access to transit and multiuse development (ARC, 2017). Investing in TODs improves ridership on transit and maximizes the community's investment in local development and rail infrastructure. For Atlanta, reducing dependency on the automobiles for transportation and revitalizing communities can be achieved through TOD.

The first Atlanta TOD was developed in the 1990s when BellSouth Corp, now part of AT&T, constructed a one-million-square-foot office building adjacent to MARTA's Lindbergh station, located near the I-15 and GA-400 junction in the central Atlanta metro area. The development also included apartments, shopping centers, and MARTA's new headquarters. A second development shortly followed at the Medical Center station, location in northern Atlanta near the Emory Saint Joseph's Hospital and Northside Hospital along I-285 (e.g. the Perimeter) and GA-400 intersection. The success of these pilot projects encouraged MARTA to create TOD guidelines and policies that would provide the agency with a framework for future projects (MARTA, 2010). To date, 36 out of 38 MARTA stations are part of ARC's Livable Centers Initiative (LCI) program, which allocates federal money to communities implementing best practices in land use, alternative transportation, and TOD.

Conclusion: Challenges in Sustainable Transportation Planning

The historical perception of transit as a social service or congestion relief has not produced effective results in Atlanta but instead has created obstacles in the funding of a comprehensive regional transit system. Framing transit in terms of economic development, accessibility, and sustainable communities has been more effective as the Atlanta BeltLine and the 2016 T-SPLOST approved by the City of Atlanta voters have demonstrated. Many companies in the suburbs are relocating closer to public transit, and many cities in the region are recognizing that walkable communities and high-density developments increase economic growth, while contributing to a sustainable environment.

Approaching transit as a mechanism to increase economic activities, accessibility, and sustainable communities, instead of approaching transit as a social service or congestion relief, has brought renewed development and funding for the implementation of alternative transportation systems to the Atlanta region. The city's planning and allocation of funds for transportation improvements will ensure a competitive economy and consistent mobility options. Atlanta is predicted to have continued growth by adopting Complete Streets policies and offering Atlantans other means of travel, whether it be the BeltLine, MARTA, streetcar, or bicycle, which ensures the commitment to livable communities, environmental sustainability, and smart growth. Atlanta's continued focus on reducing dependency on automobiles will lead the way in reducing greenhouse gas emissions, combating global climate change, and creating a sustainable future.

Notes

1 A sharrow typically refers to street lanes that bicyclists and motorists can use. This shared lane is often marked with white-colored double chevron over top of a bicycle symbol on the street itself.
2 See presentation of Toledo, Ohio's greening infrastructure from 2015 at www.tmacog.org/Environment/Environmental_Council/2015/09_Day_Green_Infrastructure_Presentation.pdf.
3 For more information about Santa Monica's permeable pavement efforts, see www.epa.gov/sites/production/files/2015-12/documents/nps-ordinanceuments-santa-monica-ur.pdf and www.smgov.net/uploadedFiles/Departments/OSE/Categories/Landscape/UR_Permeable.pdf.
4 For more information about Palm Springs' bike plan, see www.palmspringsca.gov/home/showdocument?id=30342.
5 The City of Atlanta climate and greenhouse gas plans can be viewed at http://p2catl.com/climate-action/.
6 The regional plan can be found at www.atlantaregionsplan.com.
7 More information about T-SPLOST referendum can be viewed at www.atlantaga.gov/government/mayor-s-office/projects-and-initiatives/tsplost-and-marta-referenda.

References

ARC (Atlanta Regional Commission). (2017). Transit oriented development | Atlanta Regional Commission. Available at: www.atlantaregional.com/land-use/transit-oriented-development.

Atlanta Beltline. (2017). How the Atlanta Beltline is Funded, Atlanta BeltLine Funding Comments. Available at: http://beltline.org/about/the-atlanta-beltline-project/funding/.

Bain, L., Gray, B., & Rodgers, D. (2012). *Living streets: Strategies for crafting public space*. Hoboken, NJ: John Wiley & Sons.

Bullard, R. D., Johnson, G. S., & Torres, A. G. (2004). *Highway robbery: Transportation racism and new routes to equity*. Cambridge, MA: South End Press.

Caldwell, C. (2016). Report: Atlanta traffic is getting worse. *Atlanta Business Chronicle*. Available at: www.bizjournals.com/atlanta/morning_call/2016/03/reportatlanta-traffic-is-getting-worse-top-10.html.

Carlton, I. (2007). *Histories of transit-oriented development: Perspectives on the development of the TOD Concept*. Berkley Institute of Urban and Regional Development Working Paper 2009-02.

The Centre for Sustainable Transportation. (2002). Definition and vision of sustainable transportation. Available at: http://cst.uwinnipeg.ca/documents/Definition_Vision_E.pdf.

Chowdhury, S., & Ceder, A. (2016). Users' willingness to ride an integrated public-transport service: A literature review. *Transport Policy*, *48*, 183–95.

City of Atlanta. (ND1). Transportation division overview. Available at: www.atlantaga.gov/government/departments/planning-community-development/office-of-zoning-development/transportation-division.

City of Atlanta. (ND2). TSPLOST and MARTA Referenda. Available at: www.atlantaga.gov/index.aspx?page=1300.

Clean Cities. (ND). IdleBox toolkit for idling reduction projects. Available at: https://cleancities.energy.gov/technical-assistance/idlebox/.

Currie, G., & Delbosc, A. (2013). Factors influencing young peoples' perceptions of personal safety on public transport. *Journal of Public Transportation*, 16(1), 1–19.

Department of Energy [DOE]. (2015). Idling reduction for personal vehicles. Available at: www.afdc.energy.gov/uploads/publication/idling_personal_vehicles.pdf.

Diekstra, R. F. W., & Kroon, M. C. (1994). Car and behavior: Psychological barriers to fuel efficiency and sustainable transport. Available at: www.iapsc.org.uk/assets/document/0606_Kroon_combined.pdf.

EPA. (ND). Clean Air Act Title IV—Noise Pollution. www.epa.gov/clean-air-act-overview/clean-air-act-title-iv-noise-pollution.

EPA. (2008). *Idling vehicle emissions for passenger cars, light-duty trucks, and heavy-duty trucks*. Office of Transportation and Air Quality EPA420-F-08-025.

EPA. (2016). Greenhouse gas emissions from a typical passenger vehicle. Available at: www.epa.gov/greenvehicles/greenhouse-gas-emissions-typical-passenger-vehicle-0.

EPA. (2017). Soak up the rain: Permeable pavement. Available at: www.epa.gov/soakuptherain/soak-rain-permeable-pavement.

Federal Transit Administration. (ND). Transit-oriented development. Available at: www.transit.dot.gov/TOD.

Gray, G. E. (1992). Perceptions of Public Transportation. In G. Gray and L. A. Hoel (Eds.), *Public transportation*, 2nd ed. Englewood Cliffs, NJ: Prentice Hall.

Green, J. (2017). Atlanta Mayor: MARTA will take over Streetcar, linking system to Beltline. Available at: https://atlanta.curbed.com/2017/6/21/15845650/atlanta-streetcar-marta-take-over-system-beltline.

GRTA. (ND). About: Georgia Regional Transportation Authority. Available at: www.srta.ga.gov/georgia-regional-transportation-authority/.

ITS JPO. (ND). Frequently asked questions about ITS. Available at: www.its.dot.gov/about/faqs.htm.

ITS JPO. (2016). History of Intelligent Transportation Systems (Publication Number FHWA-JPO-16-329). U.S. Department of Transportation Intelligent Transportation Systems Joint Program Office.

Kneebone, E., & Holmes, N. (2015). The growing distance between people and jobs in metropolitan America. *Metropolitan Policy Program at Brookings*. Available at: www.brookings.edu/wp-content/uploads/2016/07/Srvy_JobsProximity.pdf.

Litman, T., & Burwell, D. (2006). Issues in sustainable transportation. *International Journal of Global Environmental Issues*, 6(4), 331–347.

MARTA. (ND). MARTA at a Glance. Available at: www.itsmarta.com/MARTA-at-a-Glance.aspx.

MARTA. (2010). MARTA transit-oriented development guidelines. Available at: www.reconnectingamerica.org/assets/Uploads/MARTATODGuidelines-11-2010-Final.pdf.

Office of Energy Efficiency. (ND). Financing guidance for led street lighting programs. Available at: https://energy.gov/eere/ssl/financing-guidance-led-street-lighting-programs.

Paget-Seekins, L. (2014). From transit as a social service to transit as congestion relief: The failure of transit planning in Atlanta. In H. Etienne & B. Faga (Eds.), *Planning Atlanta*. American Planning Association.

Portney, K. E. (2013). *Taking sustainable cities seriously*, 2nd ed. Cambridge, MA: MIT Press.

Reconnecting America. (ND). What is TOD? Available at: http://reconnecting-america.org/what-we-do/what-is-tod/.

Redman, L., Friman, M., Garling, T., & Hartig, T. (2013). Quality attributes of public transport that attract car users: A research review. *Transport Policy*, *25*, 119–127.

Schiller, P. L., Bruun, E. C., & Kentworthy, J. R. (2010). *An introduction to sustainable transportation: Policy, planning and implementation*. London: Earthscan.

Semuels, A. (2016). The role of highways in American poverty. *The Atlantic*. Available at: www.theatlantic.com/business/archive/2016/03/role-of-highways-in-american-poverty/474282/.

Smart Growth American. (ND). What are complete streets? Available at: https://smartgrowthamerica.org/program/national-complete-streets-coalition/what-are-complete-streets/.

Still, T. (2002). Transit-oriented development: Reshaping America's metropolitan landscape. *On Common Ground*, (Winter), 44–47.

Transit Oriented Development Institute. (ND). Benefits of transit oriented development. Available at: www.tod.org.

Volinski, J., & Page, O. (2004). Developing bus transfer facilities for maximum transit agency and community benefit. Report No. BC137–53, prepared by the National Center for Transit Research for Florida Department of Transportation.

Zehngebot, C., & Peiser, R. (2014). Complete streets come of age. *Planning*, May. Available at: www.planning.org/planning/2014/may/completestreets.htm.

4 Pollution Prevention

Pollution prevention is a concept that is simple to understand but more challenging to implement. Pollution prevention is the act of preventing pollution before it is generated rather than managing the pollution after it has been created. When the U.S. Environmental Protection Agency (EPA) uses the term "pollution prevention", the term has a specific and narrow meaning: source reduction of waste (EPA, 2017a; Fryrear, 2002). This chapter utilizes a broader definition of pollution prevention, not limited just to this "reduce" component of the famous mantra of "reduce, reuse, recycle" but to a broader definition inclusive of all three of these components. Whatever terms are used—pollution prevention, waste minimization, source reduction, reuse, recycling, composting, or integrated solid waste management—pollution prevention is a critical environmental component to any municipal sustainability strategy as it helps to minimize the total volume and/or weight of waste to be disposed of, can help to reduce the toxicity of waste prior to disposal, and can improve home and workplace safety as well as enhance both the local and global environment. Pollution prevention is not merely the right thing to do; it is a better way of conducting business for the public sector, the private sector, and individual citizens.

This chapter will first focus on pollution prevention from the perspective of solid waste management and will then further explore the topic from the standpoint of greenhouse gas (GHG) emissions and their related reduction efforts. Beyond the environmental benefits, what are the incentives in favor of pollution prevention? From an economics perspective, there are reduced regulatory costs: municipal solid waste disposal is itself expensive, and hazardous waste disposal even more so. Pollution prevention can also abate liability, can promote a healthier workplace that better protects employees' health and safety and reduces risks, and can lead to lower overall insurance costs. Finally, pollution prevention promotes a positive public image. For municipalities, this includes being a steward of the environment, a good employer, an honorable neighbor, and an upstanding member of (and representation of) the broader municipal community.

Defining Municipal Efforts in Solid Waste Pollution Prevention

This chapter will first discuss pollution prevention from the perspective of solid waste management. One of the most basic municipal services is often solid waste collection. Colloquially called trash collection, garbage collection, or rubbish removal. Solid waste collection is the means by which trash/waste is removed from one location for final disposal at another location. While there are environmental regulations on how solid waste is managed, there are no Federal requirements mandating pollution prevention activities. Despite no clear mandate, trash collection at the municipal level often occurs in conjunction with the additional collection of recyclables—materials bound for recycling rather than disposal—and/or the collection of organics—materials bound for composting rather than disposal (Davis, 2014).

As we see throughout this book, our sustainability performance measurements will be built around the "3Es" of effectiveness, efficiency, and equity. Thus, within this chapter, the 3Rs (reduce, reuse, and recycle) will face our key performance measurements, the 3Es (effectiveness, efficiency, and equity). While the use of the mantra "reduce, reuse, and recycle" has become ubiquitous, it is actually built upon EPA's waste management hierarchy. The EPA hierarchy has four distinct levels from most preferred to least preferred (Davis, 2014; EPA, 2017a; Fryrear, 2002). Figure 4.1 outlines the four levels of EPA's waste management hierarchy.

Turning to our 3E performance measurements, we will define each in a trash, recycling, and organics collection context. *Effectiveness* is defined as the successful delivery of collection services. Basically an effective program would mean the production of the service meets the provision goals for that service. It should be noted that cost is not a factor for effectiveness, it is simply a measure of whether the job was well done (Davis, 2014; Dietz, Dolsak, E. Ostrom & Stern, 2002; Oakerson, 1999).

Efficiency takes into account comparative measures. For this chapter, efficiency will be divided into two measures: fiscal efficiency and environmental efficiency. Fiscal efficiency is specific to providing the most service for the least cost. Similarly, environmental efficiency is specific to providing the most service with the smallest environmental footprint (Davis, 2014; McGinnis, 2011; Oakerson, 1999). Both of these will be specifically considered in the municipal waste and recycling collection context.

Finally, this chapter will look at *equity* using Opp's (2017) four dimensional approach to social equity. Opp (2017) defines an equitably sustainable city as a place where "... all people, regardless of race, ethnicity, gender, or income level must have the ability to enjoy equal access to the fruits of public investment while also being able to satisfy their

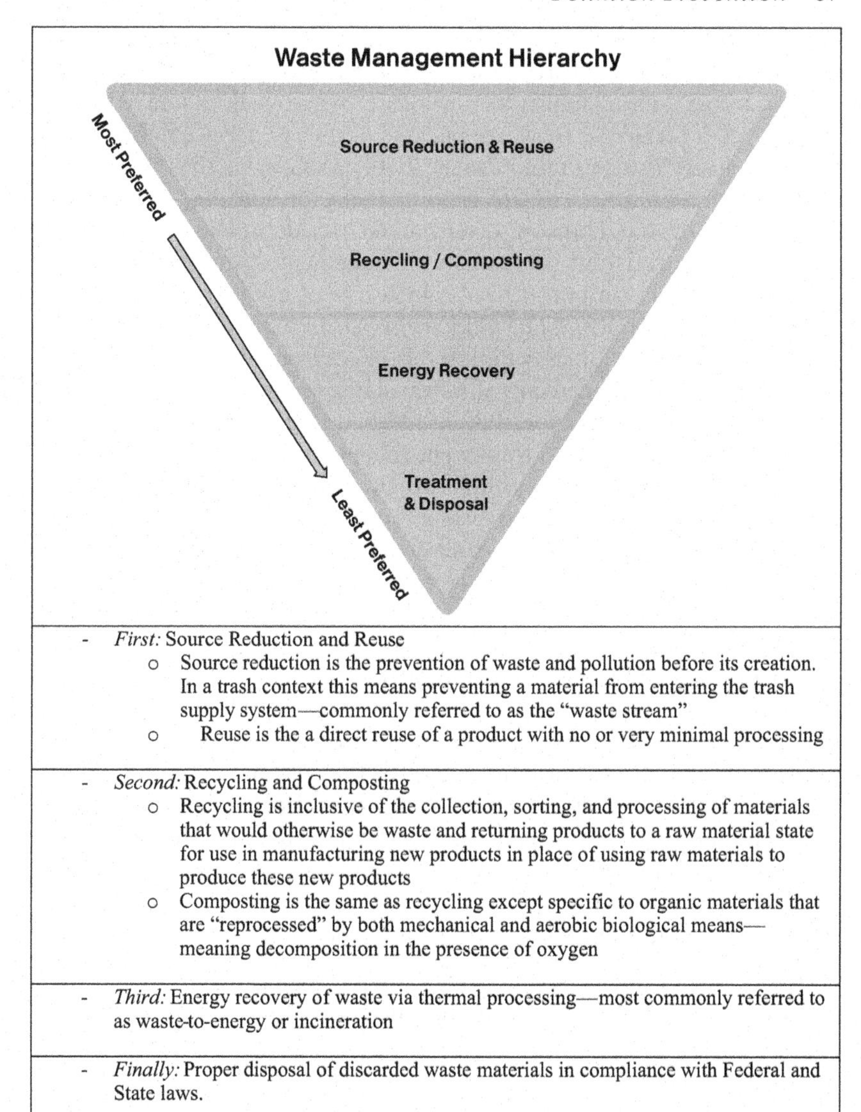

- *First:* Source Reduction and Reuse
  - Source reduction is the prevention of waste and pollution before its creation. In a trash context this means preventing a material from entering the trash supply system—commonly referred to as the "waste stream"
  - Reuse is the a direct reuse of a product with no or very minimal processing
- *Second:* Recycling and Composting
  - Recycling is inclusive of the collection, sorting, and processing of materials that would otherwise be waste and returning products to a raw material state for use in manufacturing new products in place of using raw materials to produce these new products
  - Composting is the same as recycling except specific to organic materials that are "reprocessed" by both mechanical and aerobic biological means—meaning decomposition in the presence of oxygen
- *Third:* Energy recovery of waste via thermal processing—most commonly referred to as waste-to-energy or incineration
- *Finally:* Proper disposal of discarded waste materials in compliance with Federal and State laws.
- Source: EPA 2017a, https://www.epa.gov/smm/sustainable-materials-management-non-hazardous-materials-and-waste -management-hierarchy

Figure 4.1 EPA's Waste Management Hierarchy.

basic human needs" (p. 6). The four dimensions to this social equity approach are as follows

- Equal access and opportunity
- Basic human needs
- Environmental justice
- The value of place: social cohesion and social capital

From a service delivery perspective, *equal access and opportunity* means there is equity in the distribution of service provided across a service area or across a municipality as a whole. If everyone does not receive an equal level of service or there are pockets of uneven service delivery, this service delivery is inequitable (Davis, 2014; McGinnis, 2011; Oakerson, 1999). *Basic human needs* are encompassing of housing, safety, food, and income (Brown, Hanson, Liverman & Merideth, 1987; Opp, 2017). From the perspective of solid waste management, "safety" is certainly inclusive of basic sanitation needs. In terms of *environmental justice,* Ringquist (2006) notes "The evidence is clear that minorities and the poor face disproportionately high levels of environmental risk" (p. 247). For solid waste management, this translates to final disposal facilities being disproportionately located within communities that are least able to afford the fight required to prevent this placement. As a core sustainability component, equity within the environmental justice definition should be thought of as fair treatment and equitable distribution in regard to the environmental costs and benefits borne across the world, the United States, and within local communities. Pollution prevention efforts can therefore be a first line of defense against these environmental inequities heaped upon those who are socioeconomically disadvantaged and/or members of racial/ethnic minorities.

While the *value of place* is the most abstract and challenging to capture, it can be built upon *social cohesion and social capital* among other measures (Opp, 2017; Putnam, 2001). In the solid waste pollution prevention context, proper collection and disposal of waste can certainly enhance value of place—simply think of a tidy and clean street compared to a street cluttered with litter. More abstractly, many communities take pride in their environmental stewardship, and recycling programs and composting programs can be direct manifestations of this pride.

Municipal Solid Waste Management

Utilizing the 3Rs "reduce, reuse, and recycle" mantra, this portion of this chapter will explore solid waste collection methods from the most preferred to the least preferred management option. We will first discuss municipal efforts at reducing solid waste before it is created, next efforts to reuse solid waste will be discussed, then we turn to the recycling and/or composting of remaining solid waste, and finally properly collection and disposal of solid waste not already managed via the 3Rs.

Reduce

When possible, source reduction is viewed as the preferred management strategy (EPA, 2017a; Fryrear, 2002). At the municipal level, this translates to waste that is never "created" in the first place, thus waste that never ends up in a dumpster or at the curb awaiting disposal *or* recycling.

Source reduction (also called waste prevention in the trash context) is always viewed as the most efficient means of waste "management", and the EPA has placed emphasis on source reduction over all other waste management options. "Management", however, is in quotations because the challenge with source reduction (in particular in relation to measuring it) is that we are in fact attempting to quantify and measure a nonevent: the nonproduction of waste. Where it is simple to measure the number of household hazardous waste collection events or the tons of recyclables collected, quantifying the nonevent of source reduction is puzzling from a measurement perspective.

Among respondents to our municipal survey, five activities clearly fell under the banner of reduce. Waste reduction efforts included the following (with percentage of respondents implementing in parenthesis):

- Policies reducing construction/demolition wastes (20%)
- Restrictions or fees on plastic grocery bags (7%)
- Disposable water bottle restrictions (5%)
- Policies restricting other types of materials (e.g. Styrofoam) (8%)
- "Zero Waste" initiatives (6%)

Construction and demolition (C&D) materials comprise a major weight and volume contribution to the waste stream. Somewhere between 20% and 30% of the discards from households and businesses falls into the category of C&D (Apotheker, 2010). These are wastes created during the construction, remodeling, repair, or demolition of structures and include clean dirt and stone; scrap lumber; plaster and gypsum wallboard; roofing materials including shingles; plumbing, heating, and electrical fixtures/parts; brick, concrete, and glass; non-asbestos insulation; and even cardboard *that is specifically from construction projects.* Construction and demolition materials often contain many reusable components. Thus, municipal policies designed to encourage the separation of the reusable component from the waste materials can effectively and efficiently minimize final disposal of these materials. Municipal exchange programs for these materials can also be an equitable and affordable way to provide building materials to those least able to afford them. After the reusable elements have been removed, most remaining residuals are still likely recyclable rather than requiring final disposal.

One way that municipalities have taken control of the source reduction dialog is via ordinances that ban or restrict the use of particular materials. The most popular of these measures has been plastic grocery bag bans and Styrofoam bans (more formally referred to as single-use polystyrene foam packaging). Wagner (2016) documents 146 local ordinances specific to restricting polystyrene and 62 local ordinances specific to restricting plastic grocery bags. California hosts the majority, with 97 of the total number of bans. As noted from our survey, 8% of municipal respondents had adopted polystyrene limits and 7% had adopted plastic grocery bag limits. Often these materials are specifically singled out because they are difficult to recycle and when mixed within other recyclables in curbside programs they create contamination problems.

Zero Waste is both a philosophy and movement that encourages the redesign of our society from a waste management "cradle-to-grave" approach to a sustainable "cradle-to-cradle" or "infinite reuse" approach. From our municipal survey respondents, 6% indicated a Zero Waste initiative of some kind. Two cities clearly leading the Zero Waste movement are San Francisco, California, and Austin, Texas.

San Francisco has an extremely ambitious plan to achieve Zero Waste by 2020. The city defines this as "zero discards to the landfill or high-temperature destruction. Instead, products are designed and used according to the principles of highest and best use" (San Francisco, 2017). The city-specific waste management hierarchy follows EPA's hierarchy but completely eliminates the "proper disposal" option instead ending at "recycle and compost". San Francisco was the first city in the United States to launch a comprehensive citywide food composting program. This program was launched in concert with their three-bin collection system: a blue bin for recyclables, a green bin for organics, and a black bin for residuals.

The City of Austin's Resource Recovery Master Plan (2011) is a model Zero Waste initiative and outlines a comprehensive vision for moving from a sanitation modality to a resource recovery paradigm. The cornerstones of the plan are as follows: a materials management focus, enhanced recycling services for all, expanded organics diversion and composting for both yard wastes and food wastes, and economic development via local green jobs. The plan's vision statement is decisive, "To be the national Zero Waste leader in the transformation from traditional integrated waste collection to sustainable resource recovery" (Austin RRMP, 2011, p. 3), and includes a comprehensive series of sustainability goals and key benchmarks toward the eventual goal of Zero Waste. From the near-term goal of 75% diversion to reuse and recycling by 2020 to the ultimate goals of 95% diversion by 2040 and the "Restorative Economy" by 2050. The waste reduction components of this plan include reducing unnecessary consumption, reducing packaging, giving environmental preferences in purchasing standards, and encouraging durability and reusability (Austin RRMP, 2011).

Both the San Francisco and Austin plans reflect an often-neglected component on the reduce front: organics recycling—more commonly termed composting. As a source reduction technique, the U.S. Composting Council looked into the effectiveness of backyard composting programs across the United States in 1996. Their conclusion was that for an average cost of $12 per ton in education outreach, communities realized approximately $56 per ton in savings from avoided collection and disposal costs for a net benefit of $44 per ton for local communities in avoided costs (U.S. Composting Council, 1996).

Reuse

A formal solid waste-related definition of *reuse* is "the use of a waste in place of a commercial product or reintroducing a waste back into the process as a feedstock. If the waste must be processed before reuse, that is considered recycling rather than reuse" (Fryrear, 2002, p. 341). The practical definition of reuse is simple and logical: reusing something in its original form (most likely multiple times) rather than disposing after a single use. The reuse may be the same as the original usage or may be a completely different use. Whether one is refilling their reusable coffee cup daily at their local coffee shop or reutilizing an old phone book as a doorstop, reuse is simply means using something again.

While our municipal survey did not explicitly indicate any municipal reuse efforts, it must be noted that construction demolition programs and bans on single-use materials implicitly include within them a bias in favor of material reuse. Thus, the corollary to a ban on single-use water bottles is the adoption of reusable water bottles. Banning, restricting, or charging for the use of plastic grocery bags, likewise, fosters the use of reusable grocery bags and totes.

While it is intuitively clear that reuse is effective, efficient, and even equitable—, reuse presents a measurement challenge much like reducing waste. One innovative solution to this quantification problem has been water fountains specifically designed to refill reusable water bottles. Referred to as bottle filling stations, this water fountain feature provides a count of the number of single-use bottles "saved" (by never being used) via this reuse option.

Recycle

A strict definition of *recycling* is "the collection and reprocessing of a waste material to permit its use in replacing virgin materials" (Fryrear, 2002, p. 341). By this definition, recyclables are collected, processed, and then ultimately used as a replacement feedstock, instead of the use of virgin materials, for the production of new products. While most municipalities are active participants in the collection of waste and recyclables, few are actually in the business of reprocessing, thus this section will focus on the collection-related aspects of recycling. Recycling efforts among surveyed municipalities included the following (with percentage of respondents implementing in parenthesis):

- Implemented curbside recycling (73%)
- Implemented single-stream recycling (48%)
- Implemented hazardous waste recycling (42%)
- Implemented E-waste recycling (36%)
- Created composting programs (32%)

Curbside recycling today is collected in one of three manners: (1) most common is the single-stream method, where all recyclables are placed into one single bin; (2) dual-stream recycling is where there are two recycling containers with one dedicated to paper/fiber products and the second dedicated to plastic, glass, and metal containers; (3) finally the increasingly rare "curb sort" option has each material separated into its own container and the recycling collection truck is likewise segregated to keep material separate from one another during transportation and ultimate processing at a material recovery facility.

While curb sort was the standard when most curbside recycling programs were first created in the 1990s, it is moving toward extinction because of its inefficiency and ineffectiveness. The collection process for curb sort is extremely inefficient because when the first of the segregated bins is full the truck must be emptied. It is also very ineffective in that collection rates for curb sort programs generate far less recyclable materials than both single- and dual-stream programs. The one merit of curb sort programs is that for material recovery facilities this method provides the highest quality materials because the separation greatly reduces cross-contamination problems.

The relative merits of single-stream versus dual-stream are largely a matter of perspective. For material recovery facilities that must process recyclables into market-ready feedstock, dual-stream offers a compromise of greater volume collected than curb sort yet with less contamination issues than single-stream. From the collection perspective, the effectiveness and efficiency of single-stream collection is undeniable. First, there is elegance to its simplicity. Operating costs are lower for single-stream programs and collection rates for materials are higher. Unless a municipality is both in the collection and processing business, the merits of single-stream largely win out over dual-stream (Davis, 2014; Kinsella & Gertman, 2007; Morawski, 2010).

Davis (2014) completed a study of the efficiency of recycling systems and found among eight case study cities three key factors improved efficiency: single-stream collection, automated collection, and utilizing natural gas-powered vehicles over diesel-powered vehicles. This efficiency was realized both from a cost perspective and an environmental perspective. Among cities studied, the least cost and smallest environmental footprint option was found to be a combination of these three operation methods. Of the eight case study cites, three cities had fully converted to automated collection, four cities were in the process of converting to automated collection, and only one city was continuing to utilize manual collection. For the three cities fully converted and the four cities in process of conversion, all cited improved efficiency and smaller environmental footprint as reasons for the conversion. The one city that had not converted and had no plans to convert to automated collection, they simply noted their system worked "as is" and there was not a desire to disturb the status quo.

A Michigan study likewise confirmed the finding of single-stream effectiveness and efficiency, noting "A Dual Sort Bi-weekly program has an estimated net cost of approximately 56% higher than the Single Sort Biweekly program and achieves a 27% recovery rate" (RRI et al., 2016). The study also identified an additional measure that enhanced effectiveness and efficiency: "capacity at the curb" (RRI et al., 2016). The study found that when communities moved from small-capacity bins (generally approximately 14 gallons in size) to large-capacity roll-off carts (with capacity ranging from 30 to 96 gallons), the recovery of recyclable materials significantly increased.

In terms of material recovery, single-stream also has the highest recovery rate. However, the "at curb" rate is somewhat dampened due to cross-contamination and subsequent processing loss. However, despite this loss, single-stream recycling programs still send more feedstock materials to recyclable material manufacturers than equivalent-sized dual-stream recycling programs (Morawski, 2010). As noted by Morawski (2010), "Processors tell quite a different story about the effectiveness of single-stream recycling" (p. 22) noting, in particular, that paper recyclers have seen processing costs escalate since the mass adoption of single-stream recycling.

Ironically, the greatest victim in single-stream recycling is also its greatest villain: glass. The problem is glass breakage: the collection, compaction, dumping, and process of mixed recyclables offer a multitude of opportunities for a glass bottle to break. Once glass is broken it becomes more difficult to sort for ultimate recycling (different colors of glass are chemically incompatible with one another for reprocessing into new glass) and the broken glass now becomes a contaminant mixing in with the other recyclables. This contaminant problem is particularly problematic/pronounced for paper recycling (LBA Associates & SERA, 2008; Morawski, 2010).

The City of Grand Rapids, Michigan, offers a model case example for a fully integrated recycling program utilizing single-stream recycling. The program places emphasis on recycling education via their website and direct outreach to citizens. They provide recyclables collection via free-of-charge single stream every other week in concert with their pay-as-you-throw weekly trash collection service and their free-of-charge drop-off composting service. Materials accepted curbside include paper, cardboard/paperboard, glass bottles and jars, plastic containers #1–#7, aluminum and steel cans, HDPE #2 and LDPE #4 plastic grocery bags, and telephone books. This program is a component of the city's sustainability plan that includes over 200 specific targets for environmental sustainability. Solid waste specific targets include the following:

- Increasing participation in recycling
- Increasing the number of households composting

- Recycle or reuse 100% of city-owned equipment and supplies
- Divert waste from solid waste landfill disposal and hazardous waste landfill disposal
- Increase the reuse of construction/demolition materials
- Implement recycling at city parks
- Continue toward full adoption of residential cart service (replacing smaller bins)

All city sustainability measures are actively calculated and tracked by the City's Office of Energy and Sustainability.

E-waste and hazardous waste collection programs are important because they recover some of the most toxic components of the municipal solid waste stream. There is, however, no denying these programs are costly. Communities must balance the operating costs against the environmental benefits—which are indeed significant. While many communities have periodic collection events to recover these materials, a growing number of communities are finding that ongoing collection programs can be far more effective and at a minimum equally financially efficient when compared against collection event style programs. The Monroe County Solid Waste Management District in Bloomington, Indiana, serves as a long-term success story for this type of program and is more fully profiled in Table 4.2 later in this chapter.

Finally, composting programs offer recycling of two additional components in the solid waste stream not captured by more traditional recycling programs: yard debris and food wastes. Composting is a mechanical and biological form of recycling. Organic waste is decomposed by a combination of microorganisms and/or macroorganisms to produce a soil-like substance. This process keeps organics out of the landfill where they contribute to methane generation—a potent GHG. Many cities operate yard waste drop-off locations, and a growing number are offering curbside collection of organics. The most innovative of these programs are further adding food wastes to this composting mix. Large cities like San Francisco are certainly the leaders on this front, but Table 4.2 presents a small community success story as well describing the City of Arvin, CA's model curbside composting program (Layzer, 2014). The San Francisco case also deserves a bit more discussion, as their collection method is very likely the next major evolution for the integrated collection of solid wastes. San Francisco utilizes what is termed the "three-bin" collection method. Single-stream recycling (in San Francisco's case, a blue bin) is paired with a single-stream organics collection (in a green bin), remaining residuals are then placed in a trash bin (a black bin). Many cities beyond San Francisco are finding that transitioning to this collection method is considered to be a cost-effective and efficient option (Layzer, 2014).

A final means to increase the effectiveness, efficiency, and even the equity of recycling and composting programs is to pair them with a pay-as-you-throw pricing system for the collection of trash (also termed united-based pricing or volume-based pricing). Studies by Skumatz and Freeman have demonstrated the effectiveness and efficiency of pay-as-you-throw as a means to reduce waste, increase source reduction, and increase recycling rates. Likewise, it is efficient and generally inexpensive to implement (Skumatz & Freeman 2006; Skumatz, Freeman, D'Souza, & BeMent, 2010). Pay-as-you-throw also more equitably distributes the price of trash collection as people pay based on the volume they place at the curb, not a flat rate. This price signal also encourages, without mandating, recycling. While there are alternative incentive programs to encourage recycling beyond pay-as-you-throw, they have not been found to be as effective or efficient (Skumatz et al., 2010). Pay-as-you-throw is a common feature in the solid waste section of many city sustainability plans nationally—San Francisco, California, and Austin, Texas, being two examples of this that are profiled within this chapter.

Managing Residuals: Proper Collection and Disposal of Municipal Solid Waste

While not explicitly captured within our municipal survey, there are certainly methods to enhance the effectiveness and efficiency of trash collection at the municipal level as well as ensure the more equitable delivery of trash collection services. Most are identical to those previously identified and discussed within the recycling discussion, thus this section is limited only to efficiency, effectiveness, and equity measures beyond those already discussed. Waste disposal is regulated under the Resource Conservation and Recovery Act (RCRA). RCRA became law in 1976 as an amendment to the Solid Waste Disposal Act of 1965. The last amendments of significance to RCRA occurred in 1984. The Hazardous and Solid Waste amendments of 1984 set the environment standard by which both municipal solid waste landfills (RCRA Subtitle D) and hazardous waste landfills (RCRA Subtitle C) are regulated today. Per the EPA, the broadest goals set by RCRA include the following:

- Protect human health and the environment from the hazards posed by waste disposal;
- Conserve energy and natural resources through waste recycling and recovery;
- Reduce or eliminate, as expeditiously as possible, the amount of waste generated, including hazardous waste; and
- Ensure that wastes are managed in a manner that is protective of human health and the environment (EPA, 2017b).

When single-family household trash collection is analyzed at the municipal level, there are essentially four primary means by which garbage is collected in the United States today: free market arrangements, exclusive franchise arrangements operated by a municipality, exclusive franchise

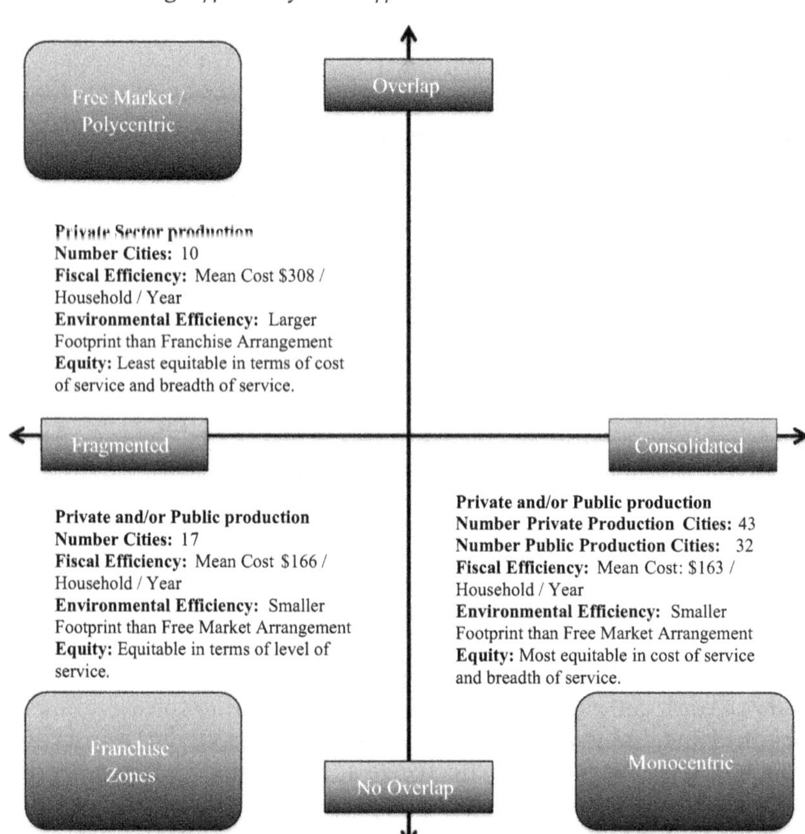

Figure 4.2 Fiscal and Environmental Efficiency and Equity.

arrangements operated by a private sector contractor on behalf of a municipality, and multiple franchise zone arrangement (Davis, 2014). First, let's briefly define each of these, then Figure 4.2 will provide a visual representation of these arrangements.

- Free market arrangement (also termed a polycentric arrangement): A local municipality is not involved in the provision nor the production[1] of trash collection. Multiple private sector service providers deliver trash collection on an individual customer basis. Because of this individual contracting service production is multiple (more than one company is in the market) and overlapping (multiple companies serve the same geographic area).
- Municipal exclusive franchise arrangements (also termed a monocentric arrangement): A local municipality is involved in both the provision and the production of trash collection. The municipality itself provides trash collection. This single municipal provider delivers service to all households.

- Private sector exclusive franchise arrangements (likewise, also termed a monocentric arrangement): A local municipality is involved in the provision of trash collection, but the production of trash collection is delivered by a single private sector contractor via a contractual relationship with the municipality.
- Franchise zones: "This arrangement is non-overlapping yet fragmented. In a *franchise zone* arrangement, citywide there will be multiple service producers and multiple non-overlapping geographic service delivery zones, however within any one given zone there will only be one single service producer" (Davis, 2014, p. 262). These service producers may be municipalities or private sector entities.

In a study of 102 municipalities across the United States representing all four of these trash collection service arrangements, Davis (2014) found that while there was no statistically significant variation in the efficiency, cost effectiveness, or environmental footprint of trash collection between the two exclusive franchise arrangements and the multiple franchise zones arrangement, there was, indeed, a statistically significant demarcation between the free market arrangement cities and the cities utilizing the other three service production models. Free market cities were found to have a higher average customer cost and a larger environmental footprint than the other three service production models (Davis, 2014). This finding would indicate that municipal involvement, in some form, in the provision and production of trash collection leads to a more fiscally and environmentally efficient delivery of the service.

The study also included three equity-based questions. On a within-city basis, all service production models were found to deliver equitable service, which means within a given city residents received an equal level of service. However, on an across-cities basis, the free market arrangement was found to be least equitable in terms of cost of service and breadth of service. Breath of service was defined as the delivery of a combination of trash, recycling, and composting collection. Free market cities were found to be equitable in the delivery of trash and recycling services but inequitable in the delivery of composting services. In essence, this means that free market cities were very unlikely to have curbside compost collection (Davis, 2014).

Greenhouse Gas Reductions

In this era of increasing concern over the consequences associated with climate change, establishing a baseline and then measuring performance via GHG emissions, reductions can be an important performance measurement/monitoring tool. Among our municipal survey respondents, 19% of the cities had established a baseline for GHG emissions, 14% of the cities had established a reduction goal for GHG emissions, 8% of cities had adopted carbon footprint education programs, and 2% of cities had adopted carbon credit and allowance market participation policies. On the carbon mitigation and management front, 22% of cities had adopted urban forest policies.

Full-fledged measurement of GHGs is beyond the scope of both this volume and this chapter. Instead, this section will point out major accepted principals on the measurement of GHGs at the local level and point the reader to additional resources on this topic. There are three key scope areas that should be considered to establish both a GHG baseline and subsequent GHG emission evaluations: (Scope 1) Within municipal boundary emissions, (Scope 2) Within municipal boundary electricity usage, and (Scope 3) Out of boundary energy usage and emissions tied to municipality. This three-scope approach is more fully articulated in writings in a number of studies (see Hillman & Ramaswami, 2009; Kennedy et al., 2009a, 2009b; Ramaswami, Hillman, Janson, Reiner, & Thomas, 2008), and the approach has been utilized as a framework for measurement by a number of cities in their climate action plans including Denver, CO; Fort Collins, CO; Port, OR; Seattle, WA; and Minneapolis, MN. The next three paragraphs more fully articulate what is included within each scope area:

Scope 1: Within Boundary Emissions

Within boundary emissions are exactly what they sound like: fossil fuel combustion occurring within the municipal boundary (e.g. natural gas burnt to heat a house), in boundary emissions tied to waste disposal (e.g. methane emissions from a landfill), in boundary industrial processes (e.g. emissions from a chemical plant), and in boundary agricultural and/or forestry emissions (e.g. nitrous oxide emissions created by agricultural fertilizer application) (Kennedy et al., 2009b).

Scope 2: Within Boundary Energy Usage

Within boundary energy usage must be tied to electricity production occurring outside the municipal boundary. Just because a coal plant powering a city is physically outside the boundary of this municipality does not mean these releases should not be included as a component of the city's total GHG emissions (Kennedy et al., 2009b).

Scope 3: Additional Emissions

These are addition emissions generated outside the municipal boundary but, like the electricity from Scope 2, are tied directly to the city's functionality. This should include emission from foods and materials consumed within the municipal boundary, upstream emissions from fossil fuel usage, out of boundary waste emissions that are from waste generated within the municipal boundary, and a proportion of the to-and-from travel emissions when a traveler ventures from one municipality to another (Kennedy et al., 2009b).

C40 Cities, ICLEI, and EPA WARM

Two organizations dedicated to assisting cities in measuring results, attaining climate action, and fostering GHG mitigation efforts are C40 Cities and the International Council for Local Environmental Initiatives (ICLEI). C40 Cities describes itself as "Created and led by cities, C40 is focused on tackling climate change and driving urban action that reduces greenhouse gas emissions and climate risk, while increasing the health, wellbeing and economic opportunities of urban citizens" (C40 Cities, 2017). ICLEI—Local Governments for Sustainability describes itself as "ICLEI is the leading global network of more than 1,500 cities, towns, and regions committed to building a sustainable future" (ICLEI, 2017). ICLEI provides a suite of assistance to municipalities related to sustainability and climate change, resilience, productivity, equity, and green/smart economic development and growth (ICLEI, 2017).

Finally, the EPA Waste Reduction Model (WARM) is a GHG evaluation model that pairs this chapter's two major topics: municipal solid waste management and estimating GHG emissions. The WARM model allows for the environmental evaluation of a waste stream utilizing GHG emissions as the metric. It allows for a material-by-material comparison of source reduction, recycling, composting, anaerobic digestion, waste-to-energy, and landfilling options. This model can be useful to municipalities as they conduct GHG inventories or as they look to assess the performance of various alternative approaches to their solid waste management (EPA, 2017c).

Monitoring Performance of Source Reduction Focused City Operations

While this chapter has clearly demonstrated strong sustainability practices from our municipal survey participants on both the solid waste management and the GHG reduction front, often linking these measures to quantifiable performance measurements and municipal budgets is a more challenging endeavor. Table 4.1 outlines these practices to performance measurement to budget linkages across the categories of activities outlined throughout this chapter.

Given the challenge of finding clear performance measures, the remainder of this section will be dedicated to looking at various measurement practices. As noted by Cohen et al., "The public sector is a key player in advancing and supporting sustainability metrics, measurement, and reporting. It can play a role in mandating and monitoring various forms of sustainability reporting" (Cohen, Eimicke, & Miller, 2015, p. 172). Some of the performance measurements within this section are advocated by academics and/or nonprofits dedicated to serving municipalities. Others are direct from-the-field efforts being utilized by various municipalities across the United States today.

Table 4.1 Linking Pollution Prevention Program Measures, Performance Measurement, and Municipal Budgets

	Pollution Prevention Program Measures	*Percentage of Municipalities Implementing Pollution Prevention Program (%)*	*Percentage of Municipalities That linked Pollution Prevention Program to Performance Measurements (%)*	*Percentage of Municipalities That linked Performance Measurements to Municipal Budget (%)*
Reduction focused	Policies reducing construction/ demolition materials	20	6	2
	Zero Waste Policy	6	3	0
	Disposable water bottle restrictions	5	1	0
	Restrictions/fees on plastic grocery bags	7	3	0
	Policies restricting other material restrictions (e.g. Styrofoam)	8	2	0
Reuse focused	Disposable water bottle restrictions (by design these encourage the adoption of reusable bottles)	5	1	0
	Restrictions/fees on plastic grocery bags (by design these encourage the adoption of reusable bags and totes)	7	3	0
Recycling focused	Curbside recycling	73	25	7
	Single-stream recycling	48	20	7
	Hazardous waste recycling	42	15	3
	E-waste recycling	36	15	3
	Created composting programs	32	11	4

First, what are the "traditional" solid waste management measurements? Commonly collected solid waste data includes the following:

- Volume and/or weight of waste collected
- Volume of material diverted from the waste stream
- Weight of material diverted from the waste stream
- Number of households served
- Number of setouts serviced per day
- Number of household participating in recycling on a monthly basis
- Number of household participating monthly by each class of material recycled (i.e. glass, plastics, metals, etc.)
- Frequency of participation (i.e. weekly, every two weeks, monthly)
- Route size
- Time to complete route
- Number of containers per truckload (Lund, 2001).

While these measurements can be helpful to solid waste managers, they certainly do not present a complete measurement picture for sustainability practices. For example, Apotheker notes, "Though the U.S. recycling rate has increased fivefold over a 45-year time span [at the time of his paper's publication it was 33.2%], the nation's carbon footprint has doubled in this period" (Apotheker, 2010, p. 14). Likewise, the waste management hierarchy we have utilized throughout this chapter presents three clear sustainability measurement challenges.

First, there is no preference on toxins prevention. Household hazardous waste is 1% of the municipal solid waste stream but represents the majority of the toxicity within this stream. A weight- or volume-only approach to measurement misses the criticality of removing hazardous waste from the waste stream bound for disposal. Second, the hierarchy focuses exclusively on diverting materials from final disposal with an assumption that this is always the most energy efficient outcome. While this is generally the case, there are exceptions and the following examples highlight some exceptions. One means to increase energy efficiency greatly is updating appliances (such as refrigerators) and for buildings installing new energy-efficient windows. If the waste management hierarchy is applied to these examples, reuse would be given preference over their recycling or final disposal—but doing this clearly defeats their energy efficiency gains—when an old inefficient appliance or an old inefficient window is decommissioned, recycling (not reuse) is the best end outcome for these particular items. Chapter 5 of this volume will delve into the topic of energy efficiency. Third, an excessive focus on recycling rates is a misdirected objective. Focusing exclusively on recycling rates sets up a completion between waste prevention and recycling—as waste prevention will actually reduce recycling numbers. Thus, a better approach is the "landfill diversion rate" or the "Zero Waste" approach.

In both these scenarios, waste prevention and recycling work in concert toward the stated goal.

Additionally, recycling rates exaggerate environmental benefits. Recycling rates measure what is collected at the curb. But what is collected at the curb is never 100% recycled. As discussed within the recycling section, particularly in the case of single-stream programs, there is loss due to contamination and/or breakage in the processing of recyclables.

Given the clear limitations laid out, there are two alternative measurement frameworks, one advocated by Apotheker (2010) and one advocated by the nonprofit "The Natural Step" (2017). Apotheker (2010) advocates a four-point approach to making measurements matter. First, have measures that focus on the management of the resource rather than focusing on discards. "Valuing discards by the amount of environmental benefit provided by their end-use, not scrap type, is [a] more accurate [view] of resource utilization" (Apotheker, 2010). Second, adopt a stewardship model that measures responsibility at the point of consumption rather than at the point of discard. An emphasis should be placed on valuing not buying junk in the first place rather than commenting the recycling of junk after its purchase. Third, managing resources not just municipal solid waste discards. Ensure the best end use for products whether they be postconsumer municipal solid waste or all types of pre-consumer/postindustrial scrap, which are materials missed by traditional recycling measurements. Fourth, adopt and then work to attain the sustainable use of resources. "The pertinent question is not what is saved by recycling, but what total resources are actually used by all products" (Apotheker, 2010).

The nonprofit "The Natural Step" advocates the following four steps to measuring sustainability. The first three measures are environmental in nature and the fourth is social equity in nature. First, minimize and eventually eliminate the constant extraction of materials from the Earth's crust (e.g. heavy metals and fossil fuels). Second, eliminate the progressive buildup of chemicals and compounds produced by our society (e.g. environmental endocrine disruptors). Third, minimize and eventually stop the degradation of natural and physical resources (e.g. deforestation and ground water mining and/or contamination). Fourth, end structural barriers that obstruct people from obtaining health, influence, competence, impartiality, and meaning. Finally, "The Natural Step" advocates for what it describes as its ABCD four steps to sustainability planning: Awareness, Baseline data, Compelling vision, and Down to action (The Natural Step, 2017).

Returning to our practitioners in the field, Table 4.2 outlines a sampling of real-world performance metrics and their related sample measures and/or goals related to our topics of solid waste management and GHG emission measurement.

Table 4.2 Performance Measures and Goals for Solid Waste Management and GHG Emissions

	Performance Metrics	*Sample Measures/Goals/Strategies*
Reduction focused	• Policies reducing construction/demolition materials	**Mecklenburg County, North Carolina Strategies:** After reviewing practices utilized around the country, the county developed a set of best management practices for C&D: Mandatory recycling percentage, economic incentives such as fee with rebate for meeting recycling target, C&D disposal bans, mandatory use of certified recycling facilities, require a waste management plan as a component of construction and/or demolition permits.
	• Zero Waste policy	**San Francisco, California Goal:** Achieve Zero Waste by 2020. By that time send nothing to landfills or incineration. Their plan can serve as a model for other communities.
	• Material disposable bans (such as water bottle restrictions, restrictions/fees on plastic grocery bags)	**New York City, New York Strategy:** Largest city in the United States to ban use of single-service Styrofoam containers. **Solana Beach, California Strategy:** Specifically citing beach and ocean degradation, this coastal community has banned via municipal ordinance single-use Styrofoam containers and plastic grocery bags. (90+ municipalities in California have adopted bans on single-use products including Styrofoam containers, plastic grocery bags, and water bottles. Many can serve as models.)
	• Pay-as-you-throw trash collection	**Bloomington, Indiana/Monroe County, Indiana Strategy:** Both city curbside collection and county drop-off collect utilize pay-as-you-throw (volume-based rates) for their trash collection. Both governmental agencies tie their PAYT funds to free up other funding sources to furthering recycling operations.
	• Procurement guidelines as a strategy to prevent waste generation	**Oswego, Oregon Measure and Strategies:** Created procurement guidelines and procedures to support waste prevention/reduction including requests for reduced packaging, preference for durable and repairable goods, hand-dryers rather than paper towels, and ban the purchase of single-use water bottles for use within city organizations. **Orlando, Florida Goal and Benchmark/Strategies:** Via the city's municipal operations sustainability plan, Orlando has set a goal of 100% environmentally preferential purchasing (EPP) and disposal standards by 2030. Initial objectives: 50% of materials purchased follow EPP guidelines by 2017; 50% reduction in paper consumption by 2017; and 60% recycling rate at all city facilities. Benchmarks (with 2010 baseline in parenthesis): Purchasing contracts issued that meet EPP standards (0%); recycled paper purchases (17,000 reams); and number of city store catalog products that meet EPP standards (41 of 131 products).

(*Continued*)

	Performance Metrics	*Sample Measures/Goals/Strategies*
Reuse focused	• Disposable water bottle restrictions (by design these encourage the adoption of reusable bottles)	**Houston Zoo, Texas Measure:** The zoo has banned the sale of single-use water bottles (and single-use plastic bags) within the zoo property and combined this action with sales of reusable water bottles (including recycled aluminum and recycled plastic varieties) in concert with water fountains (many chilled water) throughout the zoo property. During the first year of implementation, the waste from 300,000 single-use bottles was effectively eliminated.
	• Restrictions/fees on plastic grocery bags (by design these encourage the adoption of reusable bags and totes)	**Pittsburgh, Pennsylvania Strategy:** Citing environmental concerns tied to the production of and improper disposal of plastic grocery bags, city enacted an ordinance banning the distribution of single-use plastic bags at retail establishments.
Recycling focused	• Curbside recycling best management practices	**Mecklenburg County, North Carolina Strategies:** After reviewing practices utilized around the country, the county developed a set of best management practices for recycling: (1) Make recycling participation mandatory for residents, (2) pair with a pay-as-you-throw (volume-based pricing) mechanism for trash collection, compost both food waste and yard waste, ban disposal of recyclables and compostable materials from trash containers including a fine mechanism for violations.
	• Single-stream recycling	**City of Grand Rapids, Michigan Measures, Goals, and Strategies**: Offers a model case example for a fully integrated single-stream recycling program. • Strategies: Pairing single-stream recycling with public education and PAYT trash collection. • Measures: Increased participation in recycling, increased number of households composting, diverted waste from landfill disposal, increased reuse of construction/demolition materials, and adoption of newer larger capacity carts over older smaller bins for recycling. - Goals: Each measure has a related goal and these are calculated and tracked by the Office of Energy and Sustainability.
	• "Three-Bin" collection programs: blue bin for recycling, green bin for compost, black bin for residual waste	**San Francisco, California strategy:** This strategy links single-stream recycling with curbside organics collection (combining both food scraps and yard trimmings) and finally a trash bin for remaining residuals. Their website states: "What is trash? Not much! Cat litter, ceramics, and broken glass to name a few. Less of these items placed in the landfill cart the better".

	• Hazardous waste recycling and E-waste recycling	**Monroe County, Indiana Strategy:** This program breaks from the seasonal event strategy of hazardous waste collection and efficiently operates a year-round, permanent facility open to county residents Tuesdays-Saturdays. The multiple awards winning facility is a best-case example. Hazardous materials are collected free of charge and include the following: used motor oil, antifreeze, and oil filters; pesticides and fertilizers, household and automotive batteries; Freon-containing appliances, mercury, pharmaceuticals and sharps, and Universal Wastes. The program has a swap room for usable latex paints. E-waste is collected via a combination of fee-for-service and free of charge. The district charges $20 each for the following items: TVs, computer monitors, laptop computers, and any other item with a screen. The following items are accepted free of charge: cell phone, telephone, fan, radio, curling iron, hair dryer, power tool, speaker, calculator, toaster, toaster oven, computer mouse, keyboard, coffee maker, countertop appliances, among other electronic devices.
	• Creating composting programs	**Arvin, California Model Program:** This small community of fewer than 20,000 is a model as a small community that operates a curbside compostables collection services. The program was initiated after the city faced penalties for falling below California's statewide waste diversion benchmark. For its size, it generates a substantial waste diversion via its organics collection program, diverting 2,210 tons in 2010. This translates to 70 lbs. of food waste and 155 lbs. of yard waste diversion per person per year.
	• Technological innovations	**Olympia, Washington Measure:** One of a growing number of communities offering residents the "Recycling Coach" App for complete recycling information on their smartphone.
Pollution prevention planning	• Zero Waste Goal	**Austin, Texas Goal/Vision Statement:** "To be the national Zero Waste leader in the transformation from traditional integrated waste collection to sustainable resource recovery".
Quantifying GHG reductions	• Model climate action plans including comprehensive measurement and management strategies	**Boulder, CO; Denver, CO; Fort Collins, CO; Portland, OR; Seattle, WA; and Minneapolis, MN:** Climate action plans for these cities are model examples that have utilized the Ramaswami et al./ICLEI measurement and management framework outlined in this chapter for their climate action plans. **Austin, TX; Chicago, IL; Fort Collins, CO; Knoxville, TN; San Diego, CA; Boston, MA; Chicago, IL; New York, NY, Philadelphia, PA; Washington, DC:** 2017 U.S. finalist cities for the C40 Cities awards for their excellence in climate action and climate action planning. C40 Cities cite these cities as model communities.
	• Run city fleet vehicles on 100% renewable sources by 2030	**Orlando, Florida Goal and Benchmark/Strategies:** Via the city's Municipal Operations Sustainability Plan, Orlando has set a 100% renewable goal for their fleet vehicles by 2030. Initial objective: 25% reduction in fossil diesel and gasoline use by 2017. Benchmarks (with 2010 baseline in parenthesis): Alternative fuel capacity vehicles (273 of 2,100); fleet fuel economy (17.8 mpg); diesel consumption (5% biofuel; 865,894 gallons); gasoline consumption (10% biofuel; 1,231,583 gallons); fuel costs ($5.3 million).

Conclusions and Concept in Action

This chapter provided an exploration of the key environmental components of sustainability—primarily via an analysis of municipal waste collection, including source reduction and material reuse options, recycling and composting, and trash collection. These various efforts were analyzed using our sustainability performance measurements of effectiveness, fiscal efficiency or cost effectiveness, and environmental efficiency as a representation of an environmental footprint. This chapter also looked at equity specifically within this solid waste management context. Finally, this chapter closed with sustainability measures tied to GHG emissions and the advantages and disadvantages of various performance measures as well as some examples of model performance measurement efforts being implemented across the United States. Dependable measures are a critical success factor. As noted by Cohen et al., "Performance metrics and measurements systems are critical to successful management strategies, without them, it is impossible to determine what is working and what is not" (Cohen et al., 2015, pp. 169–170). It is the authors' hope that municipal managers, local sustainability professional, and concerned citizens will all come away from this chapter with many ideas toward successfully measuring environmental performance, sustainability performance, and social equity performance within their communities.

This chapter will now close with a concept in related action pollution prevention case study. The Indiana Department of Environmental Management (IDEM) received a federal grant from the U.S. EPA to create a program called the Comprehensive Local Environmental Action Network (CLEAN) Community Challenge. This case study examines the sustainability efforts of Fishers, Indiana, and their approach in measuring the efficiency and effectiveness of their strategies.

CONCEPT IN ACTION: POLLUTION PREVENTION IN A MUNICIPAL SETTING: DEVELOPING A PLAN TO IMPROVE THE QUALITY OF LIFE OF A COMMUNITY

By: Jennifer L. Collins

Indiana Clean Community Challenge

In 2004, the IDEM received a federal grant from the U.S. EPA to create a program called the CLEAN Community Challenge. IDEM believed Indiana CLEAN Community Challenge would increase communication between state and local governments, provide incentives and rewards for effective implementation of pollution prevention techniques, and increase partnerships between local government, business, and citizen organizations all while improving the quality of the environment. In addition, municipalities were facing several environmental issues. These environmental issues included non-attainment status for ozone and particulate matter of 2.5 µm in size (PM 2.5), new storm water requirements, mercury in wastewater, illegal dumping, and open burning. They were also faced with managing their internal operations to maintain compliance with regulatory requirements.

The goals of creating the Indiana CLEAN Community Challenge for the state included the following:

1 Creating a voluntary recognition program for the local government sector;
2 Providing increased state consideration for local concerns through improved communication, planned compliance, and technical assistance efforts;
3 Fostering local government pollution prevention success stories in Indiana;
4 Promoting high-quality environmental project implementation at the local level;
5 Offering valuable rewards in proportion to projects implemented;
6 Improving overall environmental performance and quality of life for Hoosier citizens;
7 Tracking environmental performance associated with Environmental Management System (EMS) implementation;
8 Enjoying cleaner water, improved waste management, reduced toxics; and
9 Encouraging municipalities to develop cross-media EMS plans.

In order to accomplish these goals, IDEM developed a multiagency program to reward municipalities for their voluntary environmental and public outreach achievements. The Indiana CLEAN Community Challenge encourages municipalities and units of local government to take steps to plan, develop, and implement an environmental management system that includes input and support from the community and local businesses. Due to the community and business outreach requirements of the Indiana CLEAN Community Challenge, the implemented EMS is referred to as a Quality of Life Plan.

There are many benefits the Indiana CLEAN Community Challenge provides to municipalities. IDEM recognizes that the agency's priorities may not reflect the priorities of a town or city. The Indiana CLEAN Community Challenge allows each municipality to identify local environmental concerns, determine the most feasible solution, and implement a project with local citizen and business input. Participating municipalities that successfully implement projects that address local environmental issues receive incentives for participating in the CLEAN Community Challenge such as reduced reporting frequencies, advanced notice on inspections, and other financial incentives from various participating state agencies.

Public benefits include a more informed community with regard to environmental and health issues, more energy-efficient and cost-effective local government, and an overall improvement in environmental quality and health for citizens.

Components of the Clean Community Challenge

The CLEAN Community Challenge is a voluntary recognition program that recognizes and rewards Indiana cities, towns, and counties for proactively managing environmental impacts associated with governmental operations. The Challenge is open to all Indiana municipalities including cities, towns, and county levels of government and must include local partners representing citizens and business.

Challenge applicants identify environmental impacts of the municipality's operations, ultimately selecting four environmental priorities to complete during a four-year designation period. Environmental priorities must fall into at least one Environmental Media Category (Figure 4.3).

These environmental priorities are identified through a step-by-step process working with IDEM's CLEAN Program Manager to develop a Quality of Life Plan. A Quality of Life Plan includes

Environmental Media Categories

- Pollution Prevention
- Energy Use
- Water Use
- Water Discharges
- Transportation
- Materials Use
- Air Emissions
- Environmental/Children's Health
- Community Sustainability
- Solid Waste Generation
- Accidental Releases and Emergency Response
- Preservation and Restoration
- Vulnerability and Security Issues

Figure 4.3 Environmental Media Categories.

the following elements: Mission Statement, Responsibilities for the Task Force, Identifying Aspects and Impacts, Prioritizing Aspects, Environmental Goals, Implementation and Operation Procedures, Document Management and Control, Monitoring and Progress Review, Community and Business Outreach, and an Action Plan.

Step 1: The city or town first identifies the municipal departments or operations that they want to include in the scope of their Quality of Life Plan.

Step 2: A CLEAN Community Task Force is identified and a chairperson of that committee is appointed. Typically, the members of this committee are the heads of the departments included in the scope of the Quality of Life Plan and any other community leaders who have a significant role to play in the implementation of the projects.

Step 3: The CLEAN Community Task Force develops the Environmental Policy and Mission Statement for the municipality and obtains commitment from the mayor, town manager, or county commissioners.

Step 4: The CLEAN Community Task Force in conjunction with IDEM then performs an assessment of their operations to determine which operations have significant aspects that have environmental impacts. Environmental priorities selected must fall into at least one Environmental Media Category. A list of ideas is provided to the community.

Step 5: The IDEM CLEAN Program manager leads the committee through a series of ranking exercises to identify the significant aspects that they want to address through their CLEAN Community Challenge participation. The significant aspects can be ranked by legal requirement, regulatory requirement, cost, and any other relevant criteria.

Step 6: For each significant aspect that was selected as a priority to work on during the four-year membership term, a project statement and reduction goal is developed. An Objective and Target are identified. A SMART (Specific, Measureable, Achievable, Relevant, and Timely) project statement is written for each project.

Step 7: The CLEAN Community Task Force determines who will be the champion for each project within the municipalities' operations and who will collect and report the data at the assigned intervals.

Step 8: Each project is broken down into action items and each task is assigned to either a person in the CLEAN Community Task Force or the individual who performs the operation.

Step 9: Baseline data is collected for each of the projects. If the baseline data is not readily available, the CLEAN Community Task

Force sets action items to install metering or a means to collect the data and sets the timeline to complete the baseline data collection.

Step 10: The Quality of Life Plan with the four identified projects is submitted by the municipality with an application to join the CLEAN Community Challenge.

These steps are all part of an Environmental Management System or continuous improvement cycle of Plan, Do, Check, Act. These steps are the Plan portion.

Once the community is accepted into the CLEAN Community Challenge, they will begin to implement their identified projects (DO), check in with the stakeholders at regular intervals as determined in the plan (CHECK), and follow up with any areas that need to be addressed due to the regular review of data and implementation (ACT).

City of Fishers, Indiana

Fishers is a city located in the southeast corner of Hamilton County, Indiana. As of the 2010 U.S. Census, the population was 76,794, and by 2016 the estimated population was 90,127. Fishers has seen rapid growth as a suburb of the City of Indianapolis. After a passage of a referendum on Fishers' status as a municipality in 2012, it transitioned from a town to a city on January 1, 2015. The first mayor, Scott Fadness, was sworn in on December 21, 2014. Prior to 2012, Fishers operated using a council-manager government with an elected seven-member town council and a clerk-treasurer.

According to the 2010 U.S. census, Fishers has a total area of 35.839 square miles of which 33.59 square miles is land and 2.249 square miles is water. Fishers has won numerous awards and earned recognition from many entities. One of their most recent achievements was being rated in 2017 by *Money* magazine as the number one city in the Top 100 Best Places to live in America.

Fishers as a Clean Community Member

Fishers became a CLEAN Community member in 2008. Through collaboration with IDEM, Fishers developed a Quality of Life Plan. As follows is a summary of the initial Environmental Improvement Initiatives that they selected to focus on for their first term 2008–2011 in the CLEAN program.

City of Fishers—Summary of Environmental Improvement Initiatives, 2008–2011

Objective 1: Reduce Resource and Energy Use

Objective: Reduce consumption of natural gas and electricity by town facilities

Target: Reduce energy consumption of town buildings by 10% by December 31, 2010

Measurement: Kilowatt hour usage per month, Therms usage per month

Action Plan: Conduct an energy audit of town facilities, pilot program of motion sensor lights, coordinate information technology updates to occur on specific day(s) of the week, seal windows/doors

Results: See Table 4.3

Table 4.3 Objective 1: Reduce Resource and Energy Use Results

Baseline	*Progress*
2007 Gas Usage Baseline: 49,929.204 Therms 2007 Electricity Baseline: 2,499,596 kWh 2008 Gas Usage Total: 66,017.155 Therms 2008 Electricity Total: 2,599,662 kWh 2010 Gas Usage Total: 65,673.00 Therms 2010 Electricity Total: 2,515,950 kWh	2008 Progress made as follows: CLEAN Resolution passed Town Council 7/7/2008. Although 2008 electricity increased, specific facilities achieved reductions. Fire departments 2008 data reported a reduction of 22,763 kWh Eller Garage 2008 data reported a reduction of 24,400 kWh 2009 Progress made as follows: Feasibility study, Energy Systems Group (ESG/Vectren) 6/24/09 Strategic Energy Master Plan. Upgrade of existing software and remote controls of 10 buildings to increase energy efficiency and retrofitting metal-halide bulbs in streetlights to LED through an Energy Efficiency and Conservation Block Grant (EECBG) application. Installed motion sensor lighting. EECBG Grant approved for $610,000 in upgrades. 2010 Progress made as follows: EECBG Grant secured for $55,700 for LED bulb retrofits to replace metal-halide bulbs at Fishers Town Hall. Building Superintendent began first steps of energy consumption database to track consumption at each town-owned facility and in total.

Objective 2: Reduce Solid Waste
Objective: Reduce solid waste through recycling
Target: Increase the amount of recyclables collected from Town departments by 25% by December 31, 2010
Measurement: Tons of recyclables collected per month, number of ink cartridges recycled per month
Action Plan: Enroll in Republic's pilot recycling program for aluminum, plastic, and paper products, implement a recycling collection and disposal program for all Town facilities, implement a paperless claims system for invoices on purchases, implement an ink cartridge recycling program, and educate town employees on new recycling programs
Results: See Table 4.4

Objective 3: Encourage Sustainable Land Use
Objective: Establish a high priority for the planting of native plants while promoting the importance of urban forestry

Table 4.4 Objective 2: Reduce Solid Waste Results

Baseline	*Progress*
Inventory of plastic bottle usage vs. five gallon jugs. In 2008, 5,985 bottles of water used and in 2009, 1,470 bottles. No recycling done at Town Center until September 2008 Republic initiated and suspended a recycling program for "credit", but it was cancelled. In 2009, all waste management services per facility were inventoried, in order to order recycle bins for locations. Fire Department initiated aluminum recycling and collection from municipal complex. Establish a way to monitor and maintain data. In 2010, recycling was instituted more widely with internal recycling options increasing to accept paper, plastics, and aluminum. However, poundage of recyclables was not collected to compare to the baseline.	Calendar year 2008: Progress made: Hauled approximately 2,213 lbs. to eight cubic yard bins that included metal, plastic, paper from Town Center. Republic started recycling at municipal complex for last six months of year. Calendar year 2009: Progress made: Eliminated bottled water usage in June 2009, to five-gallon tanks instead of 6,000 bottles/per year added solid waste. In 2009, 209 lbs. of paper and plastic were recycled through June. Hauled approximately 20 bins of metal, plastic, paper, cardboard. In September 2011, Public Works department leased a new Republic eight cubic yard recycling bin for Fire Station 92 and the Parks Department offices. No data has been collected for this new bin at this time.

Target: Increase the number of planting projects incorporating native plants and trees by 5% by December 31, 2010

Measurement: Number of trees planted annually, number of projects completed using native plants per year

Action Plan: Collect baseline data, join Tree City USA, develop a community forestry program and incorporate the program into the town budget, and incorporate native/low maintenance plants into the town's streetscape plans

Results: See Table 4.5

Table 4.5 Objective 3: Encourage Sustainable Land Use Results

Baseline	*Progress Made*
No quantifiable data on the amount of planting projects that incorporated native plants and trees was recorded before the CLEAN designation. Establish a way to monitor and maintain data.	Calendar year 2008: Progress made: Included membership to Tree City USA designation, Parks and Recreation introduced the CLEAN program with examples. Ordinance 012208B created to implement a Tree Board January 2008. Applied for TREE City USA and developed criteria for 2008. Passed Environmental Sustainability ordinance July 2008 listing commitments to CLEAN program. Heritage Park designated as a site of new green building roof. Calendar year 2009: Progress made: Included initiatives at Cyntheanne and Heritage Park at White River for water conservation. Landscaping, sports fields, new facilities will incorporate native plants and trees in their design. Created Urban Forestry initiative publicized on town website for approved trees, permits, planting guidelines, unapproved trees, tree care, and street tree ordinance. Constructed first "green" live roof technology at Heritage State Park to showcase a sustainable design technique using native plants, gardens, landscaping, walking paths, and bridges. Hurdles overcome include data for trees and parks started, but departmental changes have interfered in collection efforts since personnel has changed. Calendar year 2010: Initiated "Plant a Tree, Grant a Tree" matching grant program for community tree planting. The town will match investment by homeowner's associations or residents who plant trees adjacent to town right of way. This will help replace dying ash trees and enhance community roadways with more trees.

Objective 4: Encourage Environmental Design Standards

Objective: Implement environmentally conscientious design for construction and land-use improvements

Target: Increase the number of ordinances and incentives that encourage "green" design by 5% by December 31, 2010

Measurement: Number of ordinances eliminated or modified, number of new ordinances approved, number of incentives created

Action Plan: Eliminate or modify ordinances that prohibit green or any development that is environmentally friendly, write new or revise existing ordinances to accommodate green development, move ordinances through approval and certification process, and create incentives for pervious surface use

Results: See Table 4.6

Table 4.6 Objective 4: Encourage Environmental Design Standards

Baseline	*Progress Made*
None established at this time due to target approach of 5% not being measured to date. Modification needed to design baseline information.	Calendar year 2008: Progress made through citizen education on website regarding water pollutants, household hazardous waste, storm water, fertilizer, yard habits, and rain barrel usage. Calendar year 2009: Progress made included e-procurement purchasing for cost savings and efficiency, because each department had separate process. Develop a working definition of "Green" to evaluate unified development ordinance (UDO) standards. Drafts started on ordinances for conservation easement and preservation easement. New language for general development standards related to parking lots and number of spaces to promote low-impact development, products, and techniques used. Shared parking promoted to reduce construction. New language for architectural design, and landscape design is undergoing a complete rewrite. Hurdles included the time to research and to draft legal language for approval. Calendar year 2010: Progress made on resident education of environmental initiatives.

Objective 5: Eco-Purchasing of Chemicals and Fertilizers

Objective: Reduce the consumption of products and chemicals that are not environmentally friendly

Target: Reduce consumption of non-eco-friendly products by 10% by August 1, 2011

Measurement: Amount of chemical and nonchemical fertilizers used per month, amount of chemical and nonchemical cleaners used per month

Action Plan: Develop baseline of chemical and fertilizer use, evaluate organic or environmentally friendly alternatives, and convert to usage of environmentally friendly alternatives

Results: Table 4.7

Table 4.7 Objective 5: Eco-Purchasing of Chemicals and Fertilizers Results

Baseline	*Progress Made*
For newly reorganized Parks and Public Works departments, designing methods to establish a way to monitor and maintain data that is needed for baseline.	Calendar year 2008: Progress made was identification of chemical usage, by creating baseline of what is used where, and frequency. Broadleaf weed control program for municipal complex identifies product, purpose, acreage, and amount for 43,560 ft^2. Calendar year 2009: Progress made was reduced chemical usage in all medians by cutting out all services eliminating fertilizer and weed control products. No measurement of chemical usage was recorded previously due to being contracted out to vendor. Calendar year 2010: Began using slow release polymer-coated fertilizer and lower amounts of fertilizer overall to conserve and to protect from waste and runoff. In addition, Public Works employed cultural practices that avoided using chemicals for fertilizers and instead used air, sunlight, and/or mechanical means to stimulate plant and lawn growth. Calendar year 2012: Investigated organic fertilizers and technology to use half the current amounts. Same with cleaning supplies, investigating "green" or organic products.

Table 4.8 Environmental Goal 1: Increase Community Recycling Results

12-Month Baseline	*Reporting Year 2012*	*Reporting Year 2013*	*Reporting Year 2014*	*Total Progress over Membership Term*
One	16 tons	22 tons	15 tons	53 tons

Fishers decided that they would continue in the CLEAN Community Program from 2012 to 2015 and renewed their membership. They chose five new environmental goals to focus on for this next term.

Environmental Goal #1: Increase Community Recycling
Aspect: Waste and recycling—recyclable materials
Impact: Extend landfill life
Objective: Provide an opportunity for Fishers residents to recycle household materials by establishing availability of curbside recycling for all Fishers residents.
Target: Increase recycling totals, based on tonnage of materials recycled, by 25% by October 2013
Results: See Table 4.8

Fishers' Parks Department worked with their storm water division and Department of Public Works to organize and set up the event. Cones were needed to guide traffic into the parking lots; volunteers were needed to help efficiently off-load materials from people's vehicles; Dao Recycling placed all materials in their semitrucks and had staff to help load heavy items. Pro Shred provided confidential shredding services for no cost.

Environmental Goal #2: Reduce Municipal Carbon Footprint
Aspect: Energy and air—lighting
Impact: Deplete natural resources
Objective: Measure current carbon footprint and employ educational campaign to reduce energy usage and carbon emissions
Target: Decrease municipal carbon footprint by 10% by January 2013
Results: See Table 4.9

Table 4.9 Environmental Goal 2: Reduce Municipal Carbon Footprint Results

12-Month Baseline	*Reporting Year 2012*	*Reporting Year 2013*	*Reporting Year 2014*	*Total Progress over Membership Term*
None	Est. 5%–10%	Est. 5%–10%	Est. 5%–10%	Est. 5%–10%

The first year, Fishers had a difficult time employing the U.S. EPA Carbon Calculator. It is very sophisticated; however, they estimate that they reduced or mitigated 5%–10% emissions. The second year was smoother in terms of utilizing the calculator; however, their challenge was determining what metrics to input and truly how to measure the progress. In the Quality of Life Plan/Goals, they indicated that they would measure building energy usage at our buildings and also calculate tree plantings over the course of the year in association with our Tree City USA application to the Indiana Department of Natural Resources. With those measurements, they estimated approximately 5%–10% decrease in emissions. Building energy usage included gas and electric energy consumption. Note: This did not include their wastewater treatment plan usage, which is one of the largest energy consumers.

Environmental Goal #3: Reduce emissions from traffic congestion and idle times
Aspect: Land use and planning, energy and air
Impact: Degrade air quality
Objective: Improve traffic flow, minimize idle time, reduce emissions, and improve air quality
Target: Decrease traffic idle time by 10% by December 2013
Results: See Table 4.10

The "real-time traffic signal system" has not yet been installed as it was intended to be in 2012. It was intended to be installed and running by late 2014 but was not. This goal has not been reached as the system has not been in place.

Environmental Goal #4: Reduce Municipal Water Usage
Aspect: Water flow in toilets and sinks
Impact: Add load to wastewater treatment plant
Objective: Change attitudes and behaviors related to the environment
Target: Reduce municipal water consumption by 25% by December 2013
Results: See Table 4.11

Table 4.10 Environmental Goal 3: Reduce Emissions Results

12-Month Baseline	*Reporting Year 2012*	*Reporting Year 2013*	*Reporting Year 2014*	*Total Progress over Membership Term*
None	0	0	0	0

Table 4.11 Environmental Goal 4: Reduce Municipal Water Usage Results

12-Month Baseline	*Reporting Year 2012*	*Reporting Year 2013*	*Reporting Year 2014*	*Total Progress over Membership Term*
None	3%–5%	3%–5%	3%–5%	3%–5%

This goal also struggled to launch as "green" storm water capture and building fixtures had not yet been installed. Internally, Fishers believed that it achieved a 3%–5% water reduction as a result of internal education and using pond and well water to irrigate rather than potable water. One area of water usage reduction, although not measured, was based on their rain barrel giveaway program. Through this program, hundreds of rain barrels were given to residents to capture rainwater for usage in gardens and/or irrigation. Although this program had tremendous success, the results were not measured.

Environmental Goal #5: Reduce Municipal Paper Usage
Aspect: Solid waste (paper towels, cans, food, plastic, paper, and trash bags)
Impact: Decrease landfill life
Objective: Reduce waste as a result of meetings. This includes paper, bottles, cans, etc.
Target: Reduce Town paper usage by 25% by January 2013
Results: See Table 4.12

Table 4.12 Environmental Goal 5: Reduce Municipal Paper Usage Results

12-Month Baseline	*Reporting Year 2012*	*Reporting Year 2013*	*Reporting Year 2014*	*Total Progress over Membership Term*
None	0%	10%	20%	Nearly 20%

As people have become used to the technology implemented, paper usage decreased significantly. In conjunction with this goal, the Town also held an internal "cleanup day" for employees to get rid of old paper files (shredding and recycling) and load all important documents digitally into SharePoint (common, shared data hub). This effort drastically reduced the overall amount of paper in their offices and began a new era of opportunities to file and even sign some documents electronically rather than on paper. Finally, Fishers has promoted a health and environmentally conscious effort to use BPA-free water bottles in the organization rather than paper/Styrofoam cups.

Evaluating Progress toward Goals

As mentioned previously, the Quality of Life Plan includes a portion to identify how the CLEAN community will measure their progress toward their goals and make updates based on feedback from each person tasked with an action item. The Quality of Life Plan developed includes directions to the Task Force and municipal staff under the Monitoring and Progress Review portion. Typical elements of this portion of the plan include stating who is responsible for tracking and reporting on the progress of each initiative, how often the group will check in with each other, how the data will be compiled for review, and what type of reporting mechanism will be used.

Here is the language from the Quality of Life Plan for Fishers (Attachment B) under the Monitoring and Progress Review portion. It states,

> The taskforce will be responsible for tracking and reporting on the progress of each initiative set forth in the Quality of Life Plan. Quarterly meetings will be held to report on the progress of these initiatives. Minutes will be kept of each meeting to record decisions and progress. Data gathered and entered into the taskforce's data sheets will be reviewed to monitor the taskforce's progress. These quarterly meetings will also allow the taskforce to adjust the Quality of Life Plan and its respective action plans according to the organization's current circumstances. Progress on the initiatives will be reported internally in Quarterly Progress Report Cards to the Town Manager and Department Directors to ensure continual improvement.
>
> An internal audit will be conducted annually in September to track the progress and effectiveness of the current Quality of Life Plan. This audit will be done with the aid of IDEM's CLEAN programs check list and the advisement of IDEM's CLEAN representatives. The audit will include a comparison of all performance measurements to the baselines established for each active action plan. The audit will also look for evidence that the procedures identified in the Quality of Life Plan are being implemented and are effective for Fishers. Audit reports from previous years will be evaluated along with the current report to ensure continual improvement. The taskforce will assign a committee member to follow up on any deficiencies that are identified during the audit. The audit results will be reported to the Town Manager and disseminated to the Town Council. The results will also be reported to IDEM and included in IDEM's Annual Performance Report. Along with the Quality of Life Plan itself, all audit results

will be stored in the Town's document management system and will be available to all Town employees.

Fishers has used this systematic approach of monitoring and progress review to successfully implement these environmental goals for its community. They use the continuous improvement cycle to evaluate and improve their Quality of Life Plan. By establishing this continuous feedback loop to educate and inform the department managers and the mayor, they have established an effective way to manage their environmental impacts and provide open and honest dialogue about issues encountered during the implementation phase of each project.

Lessons Learned

1 Ensure that baseline data is established.
   a It is critical to determine what the metric is being measured and how the data will be collected on a routine basis.
   b Educate operators or participants on what changes are being adopted, what measurements are being tracked, and how often data are to be recorded and who is responsible for collecting the data.
   c Automation in collecting the data will help to ensure that the data is collected.
   d The projects that had clear baselines established were easier to measure the progress toward the reduction goal. It is worth the time spent on establishing a baseline.
2 Municipalities may have difficulties in implementing projects due to lack of staffing or turn over.
3 Once an Environmental Management System is developed, it is important to follow the continuous improvement cycle of Plan, Do, Check, Act. The projects that followed this process were able to push through hurdles or objectives were modified to allow for continued progress.
4 Municipalities may need assistance in using some of the available tools to calculate their reductions due to lack of experience with them.
5 As inviting as it may be to work on projects based on their popularity, it is crucial to look at the municipal operations and identify the significant aspects through a systematic ranking exercise in order to address those most pressing areas with the most significant environmental impacts. This will create significant pollution prevention reductions and save the municipality money.

Note

1 Vincent Ostrom was the first scholar to differentiate between the provision versus the production of municipal services. Service provision is based upon how a municipality chooses to administer a public good or provide a public service. Service production is the act of producing the public good or delivering the public service (Ostrom, Tiebout, & Warren, 1961).

References

Apotheker, S. (2010). Moving toward sustainability, Part 2. *Resource recycling* February 14–20.

Brown, B. J., Hanson, M. E., Liverman, D. M., & Merideth, R. W. (1987). Global sustainability: toward definition. *Environmental Management*, *11*(6), 713–719.

C40 Cities. (2017). *About C40*. Accessed at www.c40.org/about.

City of Austin. (2011). *Austin resource recovery master plan*.

Cohen, S., Eimicke, W., & Miller, A. (2015). *Sustainability policy: Hastening the transition to a cleaner economy*. Hoboken, NJ: Jossey-Bass.

Davis, M. W. (2014). *Examining the efficiency and equity of solid waste service production at the municipal level* (Doctoral dissertation). Retrieved from www.ucdenver.edu/academics/colleges/SPA/PhD/Documents/Davis,%20 Dissertation.pdf.

Dietz, T., Dolsak, N., Ostrom, E., & Stern, P. C. (2002). The drama of the commons. In E. Ostrom et al. (Eds.), *The drama of the commons*. Washington, DC: National Academy Press.

Environmental Protection Agency. (2017a). *Sustainable materials management: Non-hazardous materials and waste management hierarchy*. Accessed at https://www.epa.gov/smm/sustainable-materials-management-non-hazardous-materials-and-waste-management-hierarchy.

Environmental Protection Agency. (2017b). *Resource conservation and recovery act (RCRA) laws and regulations*. Accessed at www.epa.gov/rcra.

Environmental Protection Agency. (2017c). *Waste reduction model (WARM)*. Accessed at www.epa.gov/warm.

Fryrear, B. (2002). Pollution prevention. In J. E. Leonard & G. D. Robinson (Eds.), *Managing hazardous materials: A definitive text*. Rockville, MD: Institute of Hazardous Materials Management.

Hillman, T., & Ramaswami, A. (2009). Greenhouse gas emission footprints and energy use benchmarks for eight U.S. cities. *Energy Science & Technology*, *44*(6), 1902–1910.

ICLEI. (2017). *ICLEI—Local governments for sustainability*. Accessed at www.iclei.org/.

Kennedy, C., Steinberger, J., Gasson, B., Hansen, Y., Hillman, T., Havránek, M., ... Mendez, G. V. (2009a). Greenhouse gas emissions from global cities. *Energy Science & Technology*, *43*(19), 7297–7302.

Kennedy, C., Steinberger, J., Gasson, B., Hansen, Y., Hillman, T., Havránek, M., ... Mendez, G. V. (2009b). Methodology for inventorying greenhouse gas emissions for global cities. *Energy Policy*, *38*(9), 4828–4837. doi:10.1016/j.enpol.2009.08.050.

Kinsella, S., & Gertman, R. (2007). *Single stream recycling best practices implementation guide*. Conservatree and Environmental Planning Consultants. Available at: http://www.calrecycle.ca.gov/publications/Documents/BevContainer/2011028.pdf.

Layzer, J. (2014). *Municipal curbside compostables collection: What works and why?* Department of Urban Studies and Planning, Massachusetts Institute of Technology.

LBA Associates and Skumatz Economic Research Associates. (2008). *Best Management Practices for Glass Recycling in Northern Colorado*. Submitted to the City of Loveland, the City of Fort Collins, and Larimer County, CO.

Lund, H. F. (2001). *The McGraw-Hill recycling handbook—Second edition*. New York, NY: McGraw-Hill.

McGinnis, M. (2011). An introduction to IAD and the language of the Ostrom workshop: A simple guide to a complex framework. *Policy Studies Journal*, *39*(1): 169–183.

Morawski, C. (2010). Single-stream uncovered. *Resource Recycling*, February 21–28.

Oakerson, R. J. (1999). *Governing local public economies: Creating the civic metropolis*. San Francisco, CA: Institute for Contemporary Studies Press.

Opp, S. M. (2017). The forgotten pillar: A definition for the measurement of social sustainability in American cities. *Local Environment*, *22*(3), 286–305.

Ostrom, V., Tiebout, C. M., & Warren, R. (1961). The organization of government in metropolitan areas: A theoretical inquiry. In M. D. McGinnis (Ed.), *Polycentricity and local public economies (1999)*, pp. 31–51, Ann Arbor: University of Michigan Press.

Putnam, R. D. (2001). *Bowling alone: The collapse and revival of American community*. New York: Simon and Schuster.

Ramaswami, A., Hillman, T., Janson, B., Reiner, M., & Thomas, G. (2008). A demand-centered, hybrid life-cycle methodology for city-scale greenhouse gas inventories. *Energy Science & Technology* 42(17), 6455–6461.

Ringquist, E. (2006). Environmental Justice: Normative Concerns, Empirical Evidence, and Government Action. In Norman J. Vig & Michael E. Kraft (Eds.), *Environmental policy: New directions for the twenty-first century*. Washington, DC: CQ Press.

San Francisco. (2017). Zero Waste City. Accessed at https://sfenvironment.org/zero-waste-by-2020.

Skumatz, L. A. & Freeman, J. (2006). *Pay as You Throw (PAYT) in the US: 2006 update and analysis*. Skumatz Economic Research Associates Report for EPA Office of Solid Waste, Washington, DC.

Skumatz, L. A., Freeman, J., D'Souza, D., & BeMent, D. (2010). *Recycling incentive alternatives: Results of an analysis of performance pros, and cons of recycle bank, recycling credits, and pay as you throw (PAYT)*. Project co-funded by SERA and EPA via Econservation Institute. Available at: http://paytnow.org/PAYT_RecyBank.

The Natural Step. (2017). Accessed at www.thenaturalstep.org/.

U.S. Composting Council. (1996). Accessed at www.compostingcouncil.org.

Wagner, T. P. (2016). The rise of EPS ordinances. *Plastics recycling update*. Accessed at https://resource-recycling.com/plastics/2016/12/08/rise-eps-ordinances/.

5 Energy and Resource Conservation

Resource conservation is critically important for municipalities due to its interconnectedness to so many aspects of municipal life. It can have a real and meaningful impact on the environment, influence the quality of life for residents, affect localities' economic competitiveness, and can also have long-term positive impacts on municipalities' fiscal sustainability via ongoing cost savings. Because of this local level interconnection, municipalities offer the perfect ecosystem for the integration of sustainability principals and resource conservation for governmental entities, private sector ventures, and individual citizens and their households. This chapter focuses on two areas of resource conservation: water and energy. These two examples certainly represent two of the more critical resource concerns for municipalities. Conservation efforts are an *effective* means to save both physical resources and likewise preserve limited monetary reserves. For example, the Abington Free Library (AFL) Case Study profiled at the end of this chapter provides a sustainability and fiscal success story: measures enacted by the library reduced their electricity usage by 16%, reduced their natural gas usage by 25%, and reduced their operating costs by $8,200 annually. The addition of new conservation measures is likewise an *efficient* investment; money invested in new conservation infrastructure generally has a rapid payback period. For the AFL Case Study, the conservation improvements were found to have a payback period of less than five years. Likewise, many municipalities have found replacing traditional traffic light bulbs with LED bulbs to be a very efficient investment. The City of Chicago reduced their traffic light electricity usage by 85% with an initial investment that was paid for within two years from the electricity cost savings alone (www.c40.org, 2011).

Finally, resource conservation is *equitable* in that it lowers costs for all, but can have the greatest proportional positive benefit for those least financially secure. For water utilities, a tiered pricing system utilizing what is termed an *increasing block rate structure* (where the largest water users pay the highest per unit price and the lowest water users pay the lowest per unit price) is an example of a progressive pricing structure that helps protect those least able to afford their utility bill while imparting—via price signals—encouragement to all water users to conserve. For example, in 2004, the Water Utility for Colorado Springs, Colorado, moved from a flat block rate structure (per unit price of water is the same for all volumes of usage) to this increasing block rate structure. Colorado Springs Utility found the price signal indeed encouraged large volume customers to use less water, but they also found the new rate structure effectively awarded small volume users a smaller and more equitable total water bill that was more reflective of their actual usage (Colorado Springs Utility, 2017).

In addition to these clear, direct savings to municipalities, there are additional sustainability benefits "upstream" from where the water, energy, or electricity is physically utilized. Globally infrastructure is aging, but reports (American Society of Civil Engineers, 2017) indicate this problem of aging infrastructure is particularly critical in the United States today. By original design, most older infrastructure is significantly less efficient than new infrastructure constructed today utilizing newer technologies. Moreover, beyond this structural inefficiency, an aging infrastructure can have much higher maintenance costs than newer technologies.

With regard to water conservation, depending on the location of the city, there may be issues related to water shortages due to climate change and drought. Still other municipalities face water degradation concerns connected to impervious surfaces, runoff, pollution infiltration, and poor storm water management practices. Likewise, aging pipes tend to suffer from leakage. Anytime there are leaks within a water delivery system inefficiency is created. The utility must process more water at the treatment plant to deliver the lesser amount of water needed by the customers. This is not just a water resource inefficiency, this is a financial inefficiency; utilities are paid for water delivered and not water processed.

The electricity grid likewise suffers from similar inefficiencies. Electricity must travel via electric power lines to the point of use. Even the most efficient electric grid has what is termed *loss*—that is, electricity lost across transmission lines as the electricity travels from the point of power generation to the point of ultimate use. Depending on the distance electricity has to travel, this loss can reach as high as 50% of the electricity being lost from point of generation to point of ultimate use. Thus, when a consumer saves 1 kW of electricity from conservation, this can be as much as 2 kW of electricity saved at the point of generation. These savings have a multiplying effect in terms of physical resources saved, costs avoided, and environmental benefits reaped. Amory Lovins coined the term "Negawatt" to refer to the megawatt of electricity that never needs to be created in the first place. These Negawatt conservation savings are good for consumers, good for municipalities, good for utilities, and good for the environment (Lovins, 2017).

Returning to the tap water example again, producing ready-to-drink quality tap water can be an energy-intensive endeavor. Thus, for a gallon of water saved via conservation, there is both the water savings itself and the electricity savings from not creating that gallon of tap water in the first place. Once again, conservation generates multiplying sustainability benefits.

Municipal Operations: Leading the Way

Municipalities do much more than serve a regulatory or compliance function. They can also lead by example through the adoption of best practices related to the sustainability of their own operations. Cities responding to our survey demonstrate that a vast majority have adopted or implemented a significant number of the water, energy, and resource conservation policies or practices related to municipal operations (see Chapter 9 for a more complete discussion of municipal operation sustainability).

Among municipalities responding to our survey, less than 10% indicated having not adopted *any* energy and resource conservation polices or practices related to their own operations. On the opposite end of the spectrum, 83% of responding municipalities have installed upgraded energy efficient lighting, 66% upgraded to higher energy efficiency street lights, 62% have conducted energy audits of government buildings, 47% upgraded traffic signals to high-efficiency LED lights, 45% of cities have installed energy management systems (EMSs) in government buildings, and 42% of municipalities have increased the fuel efficiency of their fleet vehicles. The next two figures illustrate the "top ten" measures adopted across the municipalities surveyed. Figure 5.1 illustrates the top four water conservation measures adopted. Figure 5.2 illustrates these top six energy conservation measures adopted.

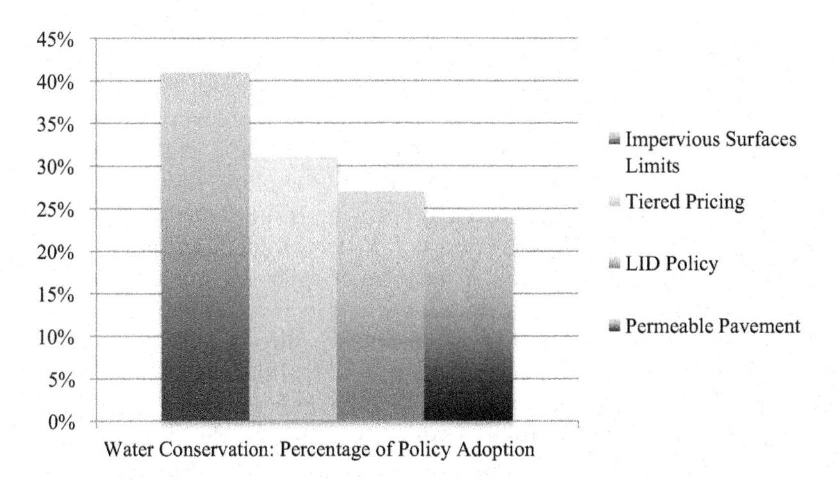

Figure 5.1 Top 4 Water Conservation Measures.

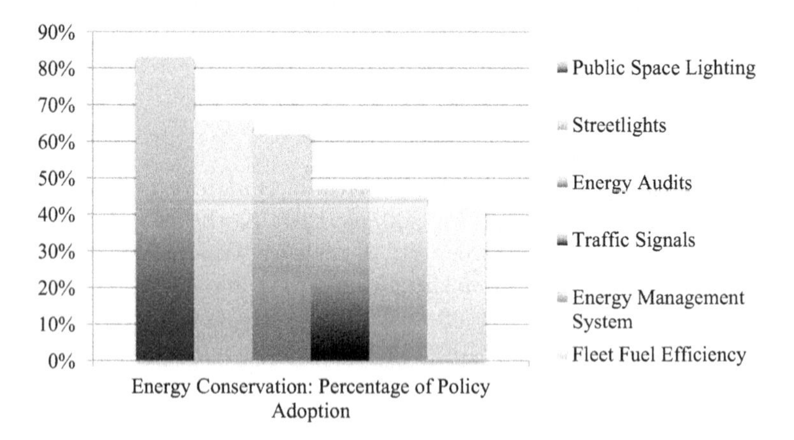

Figure 5.2 Top 6 Energy Conservation Measures.

Many localities are taking a comprehensive strategic approach to seeking a sustainable approach in their operations. Chula Vista, California, for example, crafted a *City Operations Sustainability Plan*, which "provides a powerful policy framework for the city...to pursue external funding and to leverage existing municipal program to effectively integrate sustainability throughout its operations" (City of Chula Vista, 2014). Chula Vista's plan addresses seven key sustainability areas, including energy and water use. Within each sustainability area, the document sets a quantifiable goal, outlines specific strategies designed to meet the stated target, and identifies specific performance metrics. Integrated into each area is a listing of existing policies and documents, as well as a set of potential funding opportunities. This plan serves as a best practice example.

The issues facing municipalities in the areas of sustainability and resource conservation are numerous. The good news is that municipalities today face these problems with an ever-increasing inventory of solutions, tactics, and approaches to address these critical issues. The remainder of this chapter will more fully explore various municipal resource conservation efforts. First, a more in-depth look at the various paths to water conservation will be explored—and specifically, treated tap water conservation. Next, the chapter will turn to energy conservation efforts. This discussion will be in three parts: electricity conservation, direct resource conservation for direct building heating (particularly from natural gas and other fossil fuel sources), and conservation via fleet vehicle fuel efficiency. The chapter then will close with a discussion of efforts by municipalities to monitor the performance of sustainability-focused city operations; discuss potential performance metrics, sample measures, and sample goals related to energy and water conservation; offer some final conclusions on the effectiveness, efficiency, and equity of resource conservation; and provide the reader the AFL Case Study.

Energy Efficiency and Energy Conservation: Policies and Performance

Energy efficiency and energy conservation are sustainability concepts that are related but are not identical. Energy efficiency is based on power usage to achieve a particular output. Take two identical outputs, for example, a pair of clean loads of laundry. If one clean load of laundry is completed in a washing machine that uses less electricity than another washing machine, the first is more energy efficient than the second. The Environmental Protection Agency's (EPA) Energy Star program, implemented in partnership with the Department of Energy, product manufacturers, local utilities, and retailers, is an excellent illustration of energy efficiency in action. Energy Star rates the efficiency of appliances and compares these appliances against other comparable products. The ranking for appliances is based on an average annualized cost of utilizing a particular appliance compared against equivalent appliances. Figure 5.3 is a sample Energy Star rating label. (In this case, the appliance is fictional and the label is purely an example.) The range provided is the range of annual operating costs for the particular class of appliance being considered and then the bar is the ranking for the particular appliance under consideration. This allows a consumer to bring the energy consumption (and the cost of this energy consumption) into their decision-making as they choose an appliance to purchase.

Beyond the aforementioned Energy Star Program, EPA has a number of programs aimed at energy efficiency. For example, EPA's Green Lights encourages the installation of upgraded lighting systems that utilize less electricity than the previous system and often improve lighting quality at the same time. Climate Wise is a voluntary program to help participants improve energy efficiency, reduce GHG emissions, and save money. To close, the Oak Ridge National Research Laboratory describes energy efficiency as "the least expensive and most rapidly deployable energy resource available today" (Friedman, 2008).

While energy conservation is the act of utilizing less energy, energy efficiency is but one of a number of paths toward this end. The next three subsections of this chapter will discuss these many paths to energy conservation from three perspectives: water conservation, energy conservation from an electricity standpoint and heating standpoint electricity conservation, energy conservation in direct building heating, and fuel efficiency in fleet vehicles. Table 5.1 outlines the policies adopted by cities and if performance measurements are utilized.

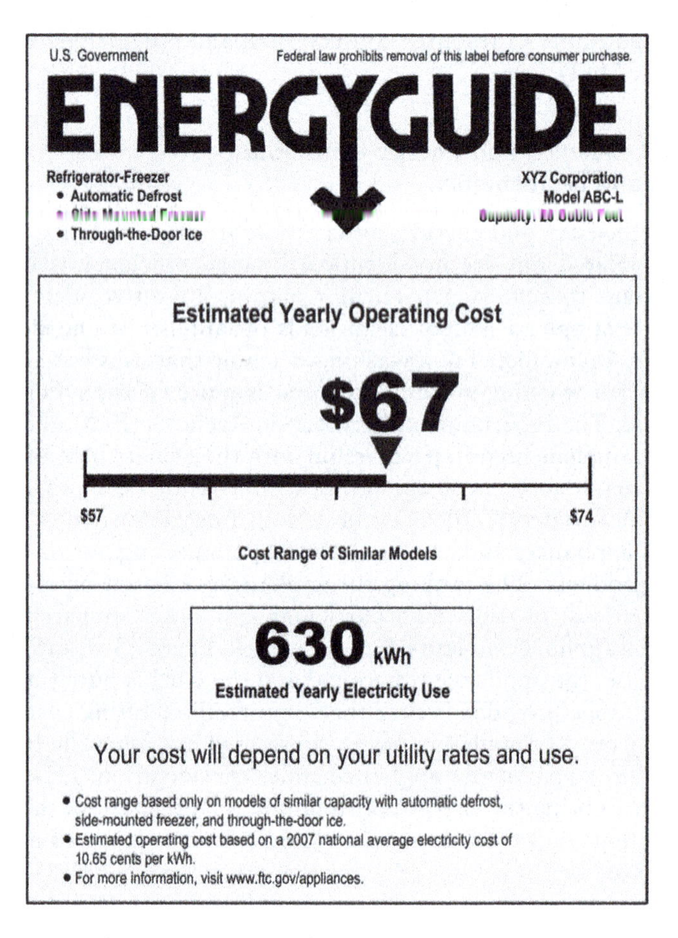

Figure 5.3 Sample Energy Star Label.

Water Conservation

Just like any household and any business, a municipality is a consumer of water. Many municipalities are also often the utility that provides drinking water to customers within a given locality. This section will discuss water conservation measures from both of these perspectives: as a customer/consumer utilizing water and as a utility providing the water. In the customer/consumer role, the link to a water conservation ethic is fairly straightforward: as a customer/consumer, water conservation simply makes logical sense. Even discounting the environmental and natural resource benefits of conservation, it is economically sensible to reduce costs by using the least amount required: water conservation saves money. Changes that are efficient, in that they do not in any way alter a consumer's usage experience but deliver a smaller amount of

Table 5.1 Linking Conservation Measures, Performance Measurement, and Municipal Budgets

	Conservation Program Measure	*Percentage of Municipalities Surveyed That Implemented This Conservation Effort (%)*	*Percentage of Municipalities That Linked Conservation Efforts to Performance Measurements (%)*	*Percentage of Municipalities That Linked Performance Measurements to Municipal Budget (%)*
Water resource conservation	Placed limits on impervious surfaces	41	4	1
	Tiered water utility pricing	22	11	3
	Have LID policies	21	3	0
	Using of permeable pavement	24	6	1
	Incentivizing private businesses to utilize permeable pavement	7	2	0
	Grey water reclamation systems	16	5	1
	Utilize other water conservation policies not listed	26	ND	ND
Energy resource conservation	Offer energy efficiency or renewable energy incentives for homeowners	21	6	1
	Offer energy efficiency or renewable energy incentives for local businesses	13	7	1
	Offered energy audits at low or no cost to homeowners	13	6	0
	Purchased compressed natural gas vehicles	14	7	1
	Offered energy audits at low or no cost to local businesses	13	6	0
	Tiered energy utility pricing structure to encourage conservation	5	2	0
	Conducted energy audits of public buildings	62	27	5
	Installed EMSs in public buildings	45	29	2

water per use include the following: low-flow water-conserving equipment including showerheads, faucets, and toilets (Fryrear, 2002). Today, there are both low-flow and now even no-flow versions of urinals available (Bristow, McClure & Fisher, 2006). Heat and/or motion detecting equipment further maximize efficiencies by automatically stopping water flow after the heat source leaves or the motion ceases. These devices tend to defeat individual carelessness toward water usage, particularly the forgotten-and-left-running faucet.

Turning to the perspective of the utility providing the water, this conservation ethic is not as straightforward yet still sound. At first glance, we might think a water utility would simply want to maximize profits by selling as much of their "product" as possible. In arid regions, this approach would come against the physical limitation of resource availability. Yet even in regions where fresh water is plentiful a conservation ethic is still more logical than a pure profit motive due to an "oddity" in the pricing of water. As a commodity, tap water is essentially free (Glennon, 2009). In the United States, a water bill is designed to cover two costs: the costs of constructing the physical infrastructure (pipes, pump stations, wells, etc.) to deliver the water to a customer and the cost of processing the fresh water from a "raw water" state to a treated "potable" drinking water state. Because of this pricing, it makes economic sense for a utility to want their customers to be conservative consumers. The construction of water treatment plants and water lines is an expensive proposition. Thus, encouraging customers to conserve enough water to avoid having to build large water lines or new and larger water treatment plants makes clear economic sense for a water utility. Furthermore, in arid regions, first obtaining and second affording water rights can be a costly scheme within a labyrinth of byzantine rules for the allocation of water (Glennon, 2009; Reisner, 1993). Finally, the multiplying effect of conservation is yet again in play. While this chapter does not cover the issue of wastewater and sewage, the physical infrastructure for wastewater is equally as expensive to its drinking water infrastructure counterparts. Any efforts to reduce water usage have a back-end benefit of reduced wastewater infrastructure and treatment costs. The next section of this chapter will look at a number of effective, efficient, and equitable water conservation measures, practices, and policies that can help ensure a sustainable conservation ethic.

So how best to approach water conservation? Effective measures including acknowledging the link between water and energy; better appreciating the role played by water in both the economy and the ecosystem; and finally, just simply abandoning a "business as usual" mentality. Effective practices include fostering creative conservation, creating incentives for both homeowners and businesses, and proper storm water management. Effective policies including using price signals such as tiered pricing and water metering of all customers, creating market-based incentives, incentivizing green development and discouraging unsustainable development, and developing dual pipe distribution system for drinking water and reclaimed water (often termed grey water).

From the municipalities that responded to our survey, we found: 41% place limits on impervious surfaces for new development or redevelopment, 22% utilize a tiered price (increasing block rate structure) for water utility pricing, 21% have low impact development (LID) policies, 24% of cities are making use of permeable pavement for new infrastructure, 16% use grey water or reclaimed water systems, 7% offer incentives for permeable pavement utilized by private businesses, and 26% utilize other water conservation policy (not included in this list).

Most of these measures noted above are focused on protecting water supplies and keeping water sources as clean as possible. Buildings, roads, and parking lots create impervious surfaces in the urban environment. Permeable pavements are a change in design that returns both roads and parking lots to a water-permeable rather than water-impermeable circumstance. Thus, the combination of measures that limited future developments' usage of impermeable pavements in concert with adoption of permeable pavement designs helps cities to better manage storm water and provide better water filtration of rainwaters that percolate into groundwater. These measures very directly influence and help to improve the quality of local drinking water sources by more closely mirroring natural hydrologic functions compared to their impermeable counterparts. Coupling these permeable designs with LID policies can further these sustainability efforts.

As has been noted earlier, generating drinking water is expensive. Because of this, it makes little sense to pay this substantial cost to simply utilize the treated drinking water to water lawns, parks, and golf courses. However, most cities only have one water delivery means and thus are forced into this inefficiency reality. Grey water and reclaimed water systems are increasingly being installed as a secondary and parallel water delivery system with untreated, minimally treated, or recycled water, termed "grey water" for use on lawns, parks, and golf courses—more simply stated, uses that do not require drinking water quality. A growing but promising movement to conceptualize how we view water is that of the "one water" initiative. Under a one water perspective, all water has value and a different way of delivering water must be pursued to accommodate the changes in population, climate, and other factors limiting water availability. Denver Water's "recycled" water program is a model of this type of plan. The Denver Water Utility estimates that when completed their currently in construction recycled water infrastructure "will free up enough drinking water to serve almost 43,000 households" in their service area (Denver Water, 2017).

Effective and Efficient Energy Conservation: Electricity

Respondents to our municipal survey indicated a number of electricity conservation measures, practices, and policies both within municipal buildings and outside in the greater urban environment. Table 5.1 outlines these findings from the survey. Chapter 9 revisits several of these topics in the broader discussion of greening the municipal operations.

Many sustainability efforts fall into the physical measure category, with lightening improvements of one kind or another ranking highly; 83% of the municipalities surveyed upgraded lightening for energy efficiency within public buildings and in public spaces. 66% of municipalities surveyed upgraded street lighting. Street lighting is commonly either a municipalities' first or secondary primary source of electricity usage. Nearly half (47%) likewise upgraded traffic signals for energy efficiency purposes. While these measures quite literally shine a light on sustainability efforts, less visible improvements likewise offer effective sustainability benefits. And there is a further benefit: Whether the replacement lighting is a compact fluorescent light (CFL) or a light-emitting diode (LED) unit—both have significantly longer usable lives compared to traditional incandescent lighting—generating maintenance cost savings over and above the energy cost savings already noted.

One example is that nearly half (45%) of the surveyed municipalities have installed is EMSs in public buildings. These computerized control systems actively monitor a building's mechanical, electrical, ventilation, heating and cooling, and lighting systems. They are fully programmable across various times of the day and different seasons throughout the year. EMSs allow a building to break from a 24/7 approach that keeps heating and lighting constant. Instead a building's managers can capitalize on the ebbs and flows of a building's usage by its occupants, actively monitor and focus on energy consumption needs, and maximize the efficiency of the building's electricity and direct heating usage. Constant data collection allows for deeper analysis for further improvements and provides an early "data defense" if a building maintenance issue develops such as a heating, ventilation, and air conditioning (HVAC) system leak or electricity issue that might otherwise go unnoticed and draw inefficient quantities of energy due to non-detection.

Energy audits are an inspection and analysis of a building that allow for a deep analysis of a building's efficiency with the goal of improving a building's electrical and energy efficiency and ultimately reducing a building's operational carbon footprint. Of the cities surveyed, 62% have completed an energy audit. Energy audits include a review of the efficiency of the buildings' exterior interface, inclusive of walls and ceilings/roofs, floors, doors, windows, and skylights. Leak detection, thermal efficiency, and thermal resistance (termed "*R*-value") are analyzed.

Deeper audits can even take into account the building's orientation in terms of sunlight and surrounding foliage to further enhance efficiencies.

Green building certifications have become a means to provide a further level of building analysis (followed by physical design improvements and operational efficiency maximization). Coupled with these efficiency improvements, green building certifications are both public/transparent and an external accreditation of a building's efficiency. One commonly utilized and generally accepted green building certification is Leadership in Energy and Environmental Design (LEED). It is a green building certification that was developed by the U.S. Green Building Council—a not-for-profit organization dedicated to improving the environmental efficiency and sustainability of buildings from design and construction to operation and maintenance. Today, LEED has four levels of certification: Certified, Silver, Gold, and Platinum. These levels of certification are based on point systems that evaluate a building's efficiencies from the perspectives of design, construction, operation, and maintenance.

While smaller in total numbers, many municipalities have taken "leading by example" to a deeper level for energy efficiency audit/reviews and physical sustainability improvements by offering these same sustainability activities to homeowners and business owners located within municipalities' jurisdictions. From our survey respondents, 14% offer energy audits at low or no cost to homeowners and 13% offer these audits to local businesses. Likewise, 21% offer energy efficiency or renewable energy incentives to homeowners and 13% offer these incentives to local businesses. Finally, 29% of survey respondents have adopted a formal resolution stating policy goals specifically pertaining to energy conservation.

A final sustainability measure public organizations, private sector businesses, and individuals are utilizing today is the option to purchase "green energy" or "renewable energy credit". Sometimes this purchase is particularly direct in nature: 29% of our survey respondents had physically installed solar panels on public buildings. Another path to green energy is purchasing and/or credit options that designate that the utility providing electricity to the purchaser will provide, at a minimum, an equivalent amount of power to the grid from a green energy source such as renewable energy from wind or solar. This is caused because of the physical interconnectedness of the grid in which electrons flow as needed, and, therefore, it is impossible to ensure a green purchaser actually receives the specific equivalent green electrons. Proponents of green energy purchasing options advocate that these purchases are a driver toward increased construction and increased production of renewable electricity and can be a further driver toward replacing fossil fuel-based electricity production—particularly replacing coal due to its intense carbon footprint.

To close, we find our survey and national trends suggest a three-prong approach emerging toward enhancing the sustainability of electricity production and usage: first, enacting conservation measures as needed; second, improving energy efficiency; and third, advocating for and purchasing green electricity. LEED estimates that for every one dollar spent on efficient electrical equipment two dollars are saved in terms of new investments required for electricity supply.

Effective and Efficient Energy Conservation: Direct Heating

The most recent data available from the Department of Energy indicate that 93% of the total energy consumed in commercial buildings (which is inclusive of municipal buildings) is from either electricity or natural gas (DOE, 2012). The electricity is primarily utilized toward lighting, computers, and other office equipment; the natural gas is primarily used to directly heat water and interior spaces within buildings (DOE, 2012). Today, heating oil is largely limited to the residential rather than the commercial market and furthermore that residential usage is largely limited to the Northeastern United States. The most recent data available from the Department of Energy indicate there are approximately 6 million households in the United States utilizing heating oil today and of these 84% of those households are in five states in the Northeast: Connecticut, Maine, Massachusetts, New York, and Pennsylvania (DOE, 2015).

A more environmentally sustainable form of interior space heating is the use of geothermal wells (also termed "heat pump systems"). These geothermal systems operate by exchanging heat between the ground and buildings. These geothermal systems take advantage of the near constant temperature found below ground. This consistency is used to pump heat from the ground in the winter, when the underground temperature is on average above surface air temperatures, and do the reverse in the summer, when the underground temperature is on average below surface air temperatures (Morgan et al., 2014). Figure 5.4 is an illustration of this kind of closed-loop geothermal system.

Today, geothermal systems of this kind are such a small percentage of the total energy market they are simply subsumed into the greater energy data from renewable sources (DOE, 2016). There are, however, some exceptional case study examples of public institutions that are leading the way in the adoption of geothermal wells and geothermal systems: Ball State University in Muncie, Indiana, and West Chester University in West Chester, Pennsylvania, are two such examples.

Ball State University began their conversion from aging coal boilers to geothermal wells in 2012. The system will ultimately comprise approximately 3,600 wells and Ball State estimates

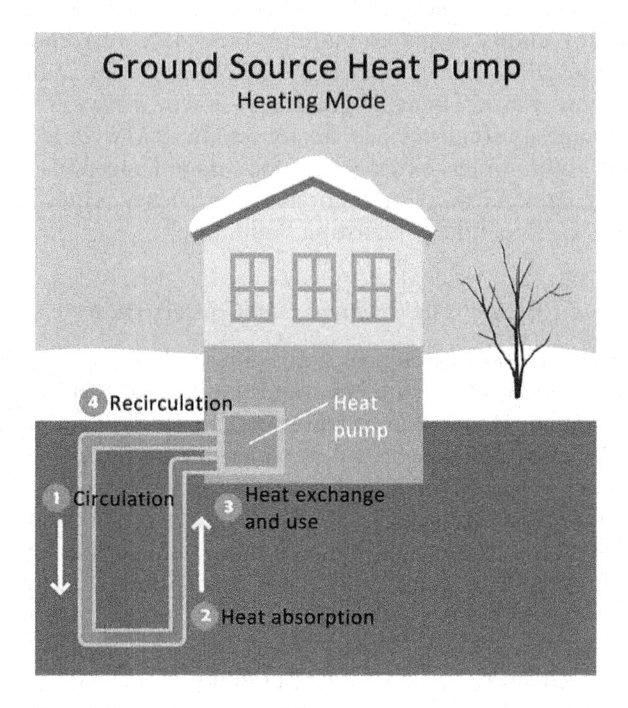

Figure 5.4 Closed-Loop Geothermal System.

> when the system is fully operational, the university will be able to shut down the [coal] boilers, thereby cutting the campus carbon footprint nearly in half. The system will heat and cool 47 buildings and result in $2 million in annual savings.
>
> (Ball State University, 2017)

The inception of the West Chester University geothermal initiative began in 2007. The completed system will include 1,400 closed-loop geothermal exchange wells. When completed, the system is projected to save $1 million annually and will be 49% more energy efficient than the coal-fired boiler it replaces. West Chester University's coal boiler was decommissioned in 2012, replaced by a combination of the geothermal wells installed to date and a new high-efficiency natural gas boiler. It is estimated this transition has reduced the University's annual carbon footprint by 7,500 tons of CO_2 annually (West Chester University, 2017).

While most conservation examples noted by respondents to the municipal survey indicated electricity conservation measures, there are several direct energy-conservation measures of note to come out of the survey. As noted in Table 5.1, 62% of responding municipalities conducted energy audits of public buildings and 45% of responding municipalities installed EMSs in their public buildings. In addition to the electricity conservation benefits previously noted, these efforts likewise bring direct energy efficiency benefits for buildings as well. Likewise, improvements to buildings' exterior interface via enhanced insulation and replacing aging windows with high-energy efficiency windows likewise improve the sustainability of existing buildings.

Effective and Efficient Fleet Vehicle Fuel Conservation

Conservation measures, practices, and policies should also be inclusive of the fleets of vehicles operated by municipalities (see Chapters 3 and 9 for more detailed information on transportation and municipal greening efforts). From the public works department to the police department, municipalities generally own and operate significant numbers of vehicles. Given that the replacement of these vehicles on a regular schedule is a constant within municipal budgeting and purchasing, fleet vehicles represent an excellent opportunity for municipalities to effectively improve their sustainability credentials. From our municipal survey, 42% of responding municipalities noted adding either fuel-efficient or hybrid vehicles to their fleets and 14% of responding municipalities indicated adding compressed natural gas vehicles to their fleet to replace gasoline- or diesel-powered vehicles.

The more fuel efficient a vehicle is the lower its annual operating costs and the smaller its carbon footprint. Clearly, municipalities must always balance the functional use of fleet vehicles against initial investment costs, operating costs over the life of the vehicles, and the environmental (and specifically the carbon) footprint of vehicles. As noted in our survey, many municipalities are increasingly seeing the sustainability component of this calculation as both critical and economical.

Hybrid vehicles likewise offer enhanced fuel efficiency but via a different technological path. Hybrid vehicles are partially powered by an electric motor and partially powered by a traditional gasoline engine. A battery within the car, that is charged utilizing regenerative breaking, powers the electric motor. There is an option for a diesel hybrid vehicle, but they are currently primarily sold in Europe and represent a very small percentage of the overall hybrid market. There is also a small but growing number of "plug in hybrids" that provide additional battery power by plugging these vehicles into an electric charging station when not in use to further maximize the battery utilization and electric motor operation. While these vehicles certainly greatly increase the fuel efficiency of vehicles, they are more expensive to purchase than simple internal combustion engine-powered vehicles, thus an analysis weighing monetary costs and environmental benefits must be completed.

Fleet vehicles today are also seeing forays into vehicles powered by natural gas rather than gasoline or diesel. Today, there is extremely limited infrastructure for fueling natural gas vehicles, particularly compared against the ubiquity of gasoline stations. However, fleet vehicles, often with centralized fueling, offer a good opportunity for natural gas vehicle utilization. Natural gas vehicles also offer sound environmental credentials compared against their gasoline-powered counterparts and lower annual fuel costs. Best estimates indicate that natural gas-powered vehicles emit 25% less greenhouse gas emissions than their gasoline counterparts, are less expensive to operate, and can give fleet vehicle managers resiliency against wild swings in the price of gasoline and/or diesel. By contrast, natural gas prices are significantly more stable over time and are today at historically low prices—with no indications of this changing anytime soon. Perhaps one of the most exciting developments on this front are new natural gas *and* hybrid-electric garbage trucks. With the stop-and-go nature of trash collection, these vehicles are ideally suited to take full advantage of regenerative breaking in combination with the environmental efficiency of natural gas.

Fully electric cars are exclusively powered by an electric motor rather than the combination seen in hybrid models that combine both an electric motor and a gasoline engine. While fully electric cars are gaining favor among some individual consumers, municipal fleet vehicles adoption has been slower and primarily in larger cities. Our city survey indicated minimal adoption among survey participants. However, many communities find that the installation of electric car charging stations provides good public opportunities to show their sustainability aspirations. Electric cars do offer one interesting sustainability advantage over the other vehicles discussed within this section. Electric vehicles (and to a significantly lesser extent plug-in hybrid vehicles) are the only vehicles that can operate greener over time and can actually achieve continuous environmental improvement. This is because as the electric power grid itself becomes greener over time—via further adoption of renewable energy sources and further retirement of the most inefficient fossil fuel power sources—the operation of an electric vehicle likewise becomes greener over time.

Monitoring Performance of Sustainability Focused City Operations

It is understandable that much of the focus at the local level has been to identify and to implement conservation efforts, rather than to quantify and evaluate the effectiveness and efficiency of their efforts. We must also acknowledge that the collection and reporting of performance measurements data in the area of sustainability are wholly voluntary in nature. Additionally, there has yet to emerge universal municipal-level

Table 5.2 Performance Metrics for Conservation Goals

	Performance Metrics	*Sample Measures/Goals*
Water conservation	• Limits on impervious surfaces and use of permeable pavement	**Indianapolis, Indiana Measures:** Has established a comprehensive design code for permeable pavements and clear guidelines for when appropriate to use. Tied these designs to storm water management practices.
	• Tiered water utility pricing (increasing block rates)	**Colorado Springs Utility, Colorado Goal:** Reduce total water usage and reduced per customer percentage usage.
	• LID policies	**Redmond, Washington Goal and Measures:** Protect groundwater particularly in light of city's high water table. Measures included creating code revision specific to LID in concert with updated storm water management plan.
	• Grey water/water reclamation systems	**Denver Water, Colorado Sample Measures and Goals:** Goal is reduced demand for treated drinking water and measure is average per household capacity of drinking water made available by customers converting to grey water system water usage.
	• Incentivizing private businesses to utilize permeable pavement	**Portland, Oregon Measures:** Grey to green initiative for Eco-roof adoption. Incentives included expedited permitting, decreased fees, zoning upgrades, and reduced storm water requirements and fees.
	• Offer energy efficiency or renewable energy incentives for homeowners and/or businesses/offered energy audits at low or no cost to homeowners and/or businesses	**Scottsdale, Arizona:** Comprehensive green building construction codes designed to address: summer heat island effect, mitigation of transportation impacts, resource-efficient building materials, energy efficiency for building envelope HVAC, and lighting.
	• Tiered energy utility pricing structure to encourage conservation	**San Diego Gas and Electric, California, Measure:** Electricity rates rise progressively as electricity usage rises across three pricing tiers. Prices differ from winter to summer as well.
Certification standards	• Energy Star energy efficiency	**Sample Measure:** Energy usage and energy cost ranking

sustainability performance measurements for cities. Put another way, unlike LEED for buildings or Energy Star for appliances, there are as yet no standard metrics of what is effective, efficient, and equitable on the sustainability front—this volume itself being an early effort on this front. As discussed earlier in this work, less than half (39%) of localities are measuring the performance of their policies or programs related to sustainability. While there is progress to be made in this area, municipalities should not be faulted for the lack of evaluation of their approaches to bringing sustainability to their operations. There are not many resources for localities with regard to understanding how other places have sought to understand the performance of their policies and practices designed to enhance their sustainability. Among surveyed municipalities, lack of resources was the top barrier to programmatic success. In part, this can explain low adoption of energy and resource conservation measures, which may be more costly compared to other sustainability initiatives, and face difficulties in adequately assessing these policies and linking performance to budget decisions.

There is an old public administration adage, "What gets measured gets managed". There is certainly still work to be done on the front of fully linking conservation and sustainability programs to performance measurements and municipal budgets. To further this dialog, Table 5.2 suggests some methods, metrics, and goals that have been successfully utilized by municipalities across the United States. These examples can serve as models for communities seeking to set sustainability goals or apply measures and metrics by which they can assess the performance of their sustainability efforts.

Conclusions and Concepts in Action

These issues are so critical that the United Nations includes, among its Sustainable Development Goals (SDGs), two goals that focus specifically on energy and water conservation. SDG 6: Ensure access to water and sanitation for all includes a number of goals and targets for the world to achieve by 2030. Included among the targets to achieve this outcome are the following water conservation-related goals: "improve water quality by reducing pollution" and "substantially increase water-use efficiency across all sectors". While this only represents a sampling of Goal 6's targets, they are consistent with the water resource and conservation goals omnipresent in a vast majority of municipalities in the United States. Similarly, SDG 7 seeks to "ensur[ing] access to affordable, reliable, sustainable, and modern energy for all". Energy efficiency is one of the associated targets, with an aim of doubling the rate of improvement globally (United Nations, 2017).

The case study that follows is an illustration of energy conservation and energy efficiency initiatives undertaken by the AFL in Abington

Township, Pennsylvania. What is perhaps the most impressive aspect of this case study is that by combining simple operational changes along with relatively low-cost equipment changes the library's two facilities achieved both significant electricity and natural gas usage savings. The two facilities reduced their electricity usage by 16% and natural gas usage by 25%. The initial investment in these conservation and efficiency measures was found to have a payback period of less than five years from the cost savings realized from the reduced usage.

ENERGY EFFICIENCY CASE STUDIES GREATER PHILADELPHIA REGION: ABINGTON FREE LIBRARY, ABINGTON, PA[1]

By: Delaware Valley Regional Planning Commission

Abington Township, located in Montgomery County, Pennsylvania, began numerous efforts in 2002 to improve energy efficiency in the AFL and a satellite library facility in Roslyn. The AFL is a 26,000 ft^2 building that was built in 1956 and has undergone several renovations during its lifetime. AFL's satellite branch in Roslyn is a 1,750 ft^2 building composed of two portable classrooms. Efforts to reduce energy use at both facilities began with an examination of current operations to identify no- or low-cost improvements. The library management team tested a variety of energy reduction strategies and monitored their impact on energy usage to reach their goals. In the preceding years, the library's energy consumption and expenditures had been steadily rising, and it became clear that energy reduction strategies would be a good way to reduce costs while increasing overall sustainability. The library facilities manager implemented a series of operational improvements that maximize energy efficiency without compromising occupant comfort.

Project Details and Operational Improvements to the Abington Free Library

HVAC Controls

Initially, after a 1999 renovation of the AFL, the building's HVAC system was programmed to start the boiler when the outdoor temperature was colder than 50°F and turn on the air conditioning when the outdoor temperature was warmer than 50°F. This setting worked well in the winter and summer months when temperatures rarely fluctuate; however, this was problematic in spring and autumn when the temperature would often be below 50°F at night and above 50°F during the day.

In 2001, AFL reprogrammed its HVAC so that the boiler started only when the outdoor temperature was under 40/45°F and turn on the air conditioner if it was warmer than 60°F. Additionally, the library started manually disabling the boiler between April and October, when it was not necessary.

HVAC Scheduling

The building management determined that during the winter it was unnecessary to run the boiler throughout the night. By disabling the boiler from 9:00 pm to 7:00 am, the library's temperature would drop from 72°F to 60°F. By restarting the boiler an hour before the library opened, the temperature is easily brought back up to a comfortable setting by 9:00 am when patrons arrived.

Energy Management System

In 2002, the library installed a pulse contact electric meter for $1,000 and the building's EMS (Johnson Controls) was upgraded at a cost of $1,500. Both features enable building managers to measure energy use on an ongoing basis. Using the new systems, the AFL reduced its mechanical system's operation schedule from 93 hours a week to 82 hours a week. By 2003, this change alone led to an 11% decrease in energy use and a $4,000 savings for the following year.

Air Flow Management

In 2009, the library initiated maximums on its Saftronics system to control airflow and increase efficiency. The library set the system to 75% of maximum airflow in the winter, 80%–85% in the spring and fall, and 90%–95% in the summer.

Lighting

Lighting Scheduling

AFL scaled back is light usage in 2008 by turning the indoor lights on at 8:55 am when the library staff arrives instead of at 7:30 am when the maintenance staff arrives. Parking lot light controls were set to turn on after dark and turn off at 9:30 pm, instead of 11 pm.

Energy Savings Investments	
Energy Efficient Windows (26 total)	$35,000
LED Exit Signs (14 total)	$476
Pulse Contact Meter	$1,000
Johnson Control System	$1,500
Summary of Savings	
Total Load Factor Improvement	14%
Electricity Usage Reduction (kWh)	16%
Natural Gas Usage Reduction (ccf)	25%
Savings from Natural Gas Reduction (annually)	$4,200
Savings from Johnson Control System Upgrade	$4,000
Greenhouse Gas Reduction (Tons COe)	28

Figure 5.5 Energy Savings Investments.

However, some of the potential energy savings was offset by the installation of extra spotlights in the parking lot and an increase in the parking light wattage from 175 to 250 W to address safety concerns. Upgrade Lighting Technology 14 of the building's exit signs were upgraded from incandescent lamps to LED lamps. The lights came as part of a retrofit kit purchased from Graingers, at a cost of $34 each. Due to the low cost, the library was able to purchase these lamps out of its operating budget.

Reducing Peak Demand

The building was originally equipped with three compressor units that were designed to meet a projected maximum cooling load. In practice, it was only during rare heat waves that the third compressor was actually used, turning on briefly to augment the other units. On those days, the spike in electricity use caused by the use of the compressor significantly increased their peak load profile and resulted in a substantially higher kilowatt hour price for that month. To avoid high electric costs, AFL decided to utilize two air conditioners to cool the library. The right sizing of their mechanical equipment greatly lowered their peak energy demands and helped the library develop a better load profile, saving them money. They have received very few complaints from library patrons regarding the indoor air temperature.

Other Capital Projects–Windows and Panels

In 2004, double-paned windows with insulated glass were installed at a cost of $35,000. Also, the library recently installed a 1.25 kW solar panel on its roof. The Redevelopment Fund provided the solar panel after the township agreed to purchase 20% of the electricity used for its municipal operations from renewable sources. Between November 2009 and June 2010, the solar panel has generated 885 kWh of electricity.

Performance

The AFL's energy improvement programs were successful in reducing both energy consumption and expenditure. A baseline comparison reveals that the library used 16% less electricity and 25% less gas in 2009 than in 2004. The load factor for the facility also increased by 14%, indicating more level energy usage with lower peak and therefore a lower kilowatt hour price. Additionally, the improvements have led to significant cost savings with expenditures on gas decreasing by 13% over the span of the improvements. Table 5.3 outlines the energy savings achieved through the various improvements to the facility.

Project Details and Operational Improvements to the Roslyn Library

Building Control Systems

The Roslyn Branch consists of two portable classrooms that were originally climate controlled using two coil electric heaters and two electric air conditioners. In 2005, the library invested in a Trane heat pump to supply the building's heating and cooling load. The system led to a 37% energy reduction and will recoup its $9,200 cost in about five years.

Table 5.3 Energy Savings—AFL

Energy Savings Investments: AFL	
Energy-efficient windows (26 total)	$35,000
LED exit signs (14 total)	$476
Pulse contact meter	$1,000
Johnson control system	$1,500
Summary of savings	
Total load factor improvement	14%
Electricity usage reduction (kWh)	16%
Natural gas usage reduction (ccf)	25%
Savings from natural gas reduction (annually)	$4,200
Savings from Johnson control system upgrade	$4,000
Greenhouse gas reduction (tons COe)	28

Windows, Lighting, and Carpet

In 2003, the Roslyn Branch installed new carpet that insulated the rooms and resulted in lower energy use. The following year, the library spent $1,775 to replace the windows with new double-paned units. At the same time, the library removed 40 light bulbs and replaced them with reflectors. Together, the new carpet, windows, and reflectors led to an almost 15% reduction in energy use.

Performance

The Roslyn branch has cut its electricity use by almost 50% saving almost $3,500 during the last five years on their total bills of just over $20,000: a 17% savings. Many of the library's improvements were operational and free to implement, leading to a significant savings. Table 5.4 outlines the total savings associated with upgrades to the facility.

Lessons Learned

The AFL and the Roslyn branch have put in tremendous effort over the past nine years to improve energy efficiency. The main lesson learned was to examine current usage and operations first to identify simple, inexpensive opportunities to save energy. After their operational changes started to show decreases in energy use and expenditures, the staff had proven accomplishments that they could leverage to encourage the Township to make further energy-saving improvements. Many of the township's efforts were borrowed from best practices of other successful building retrofits by their peers. In the end, the AFL reduced its energy consumption and financial cost through strategic capital improvements and operational changes.

Table 5.4 Energy Savings—Roslyn Library

Energy Savings Investments: Roslyn Library	
Energy-efficient windows (five total)	$1,775
Heat pump thermostat	$9,200
Summary of savings	
Total load factor improvement	10%
Electricity usage reduction (kWh)	50%
Energy cost savings in 2009	$1,400
Energy cost savings—last five years	17%
Greenhouse gas reduction (tons COe)	5

Note

1 This is one of a series of Energy Efficiency Case Studies developed by DVRPC in collaboration with the City of Philadelphia and U.S. EPA to profile replicable and cost-effective energy-efficiency projects in the Greater Philadelphia region. For more information, see www.dvrpc.org/EnergyClimate. DVRPC, 2010.

This publication was developed under Grant Assistance Agreement No. XA-97365801-DVRPC awarded by the U.S. EPA. It has not been formally reviewed by the EPA. The views expressed in this document are solely those of the Delaware Valley Regional Planning Commission, and the EPA does not endorse any product or commercial services mentioned in this publication.

References

American Society of Civil Engineers. (2017). *2017 infrastructure report card.* Accessed at www.asce.org.

Ball State University. (2017). *Geothermal energy system.* Accessed at http://cms.bsu.edu/About/Geothermal.

Bristow, G., McClure, J. D., Fisher D. (2006). Waterless urinals: Features, benefits, and applications. *Journal of Green Building 1*(1), 55–62.

City of Chula Vista. (2014). *City operations sustainability plan.* Accessed at www.chulavistaca.gov/home/showdocument?id=9725.

Colorado Springs Utility. (2017). *Tiered water rates.* Accessed at www.csu.org.

C40Cities.org. (2011). *Case study: LED traffic lights reduce energy use in Chicago by 85%.* Accessed at www.c40.org/case_studies/led-traffic-lights-reduce-energy-use-in-chicago-by-85.

Denver Water. (2017). *Recycled water.* Accessed at www.denverwater.org/your-water/recycled-water.

Department of Energy. (2012). Energy use in commercial buildings. Accessed at www.eia.gov/energyexplained/index.cfm?page=us_energy_commercial#tab2.

Department of Energy. (2015). Who uses heating oil? Accessed at www.eia.gov/energyexplained/index.cfm?page=heating_oil_use.

Department of Energy. (2016). Renewable energy explained. Accessed at www.eia.gov/energyexplained/index.cfm?page=renewable_home#tab2.

Friedman, T. (2008). *Hot, flat, and crowded: Why we need a green revolution—and how it can renew America.* New York: Farrar, Straus, and Giroux.

Fryrear, B. (2002). Pollution prevention. In Jack E. Leonard and Gary D. Robinson (Eds.) *Managing hazardous materials: A definitive text.* Rockville, MD: Institute of Hazardous Materials Management.

Glennon, R. (2009). *Unquenchable: America's water crisis and what to do about it.* Washington, DC: Island Press.

Lovins, A. B. (2017). *The Negawatt Revolution—Rocky Mountain Institute.* Accessed at www.rmi.org.

Morgan, P., Helmke, M., Fritschle, J., Cuprak, G., Clark, T., & Lattanze, J. (2013). Geothermal Initiative at West Chester University: Sustainability for institutional success. Accessed at www.pagreencolleges.org/Resources/Documents/2014%20Posters/PERC%20Geothermal%20Poster%202014.pdf.

Reisner, M. (1993). *Cadillac desert.* New York: Penguin Books.

United Nations. (2017). *Sustainable development goals: 17 goals to transform our world*. Accessed at www.un.org/sustainabledevelopment/sustainable-development-goals/.

West Chester University. (2017). *Office of sustainability: initiatives*. Accessed at www.wcupa.edu/sustainability/initiatives.aspx.

6 Sustainable Economic Development

Sustainable economic development policies are some of the most common examples of local sustainability initiatives across the United States (Opp & Osgood, 2013; Opp & Saunders, 2013). The lingering impacts of the Great Recession prompted many cities to search for new and creative ways to meet the economic needs of their communities. As discussed previously in this book, past research has demonstrated that the policies with the most potential for revenue generation and/or cost savings are significantly more likely to be adopted than sustainability policies without these types of economic benefits (see, for example, Opp, Osgood & Rugeley, 2014; Osgood, Opp & Demasters, 2017). In each policy area in this book, we see some evidence of economic co-benefits playing a role in what policies are more likely to be adopted. Given the overall prevalence of sustainable economic development policies across the United States, it is very important to understand this particular area of sustainability. Furthermore, as concerns continue to mount about the potential for serious unintended consequences resulting from sustainable economic development efforts, it is also necessary to consider the overall performance and outcomes of the adopted sustainable economic development policies.

This chapter focuses on local economic development and the relationship that it holds with sustainability. In addition to detailing the level of local engagement in this policy area, this chapter also introduces the performance measurement activities occurring in this policy area in American cities. Given the sheer scope of activities that can be considered economic development, this chapter focuses somewhat narrowly on a more traditional economic development focus—as opposed to a broader look at the intersection of the environment and economic development. However, the next chapter examines a number of policies that can also be considered part of a city's sustainable economic development tool kit. This chapter and the following chapter can be treated as complementary and contributing to a more comprehensive and complete understanding of local sustainable development policy. Although the next chapter approaches sustainability from a land-use planning perspective, significant synergies exist between land-use planning and economic development. As a result, the two areas should be taken together in order to better understand the complexity of sustainable development. This chapter starts with an overview of the practice and the goals of local economic development and then narrows to a focus on how sustainable economic development fits into this policy area. This chapter then moves into a study of the performance measurement activities in sustainable economic development and completes with a case study to provide the reader with a demonstration of the concepts in action as told by a practicing administrator.

Local Economic Development: An Introduction

Economic development is defined by the U.S. Economic Development Administration (EDA) as being the efforts that "...create the conditions for economic growth and improved quality of life..." (EDA, 2017). Economic development is considered to be one of the most important tasks for local governments in the United States by many observers: "... increased levels of economic activity fill tax coffers. Higher levels of economic activity lead to a 'virtuous cycle' of increases in property values, greater retail sales, higher personal incomes, larger corporate profits, and increases in other sources of government revenue" (Koven & Lyons, 2010, p. 7). Local governments often find themselves in a position to adopt policies to try to improve the economic condition of their city because cities are frequently faced with significant and ever-increasing service demands coupled with declining intergovernmental support and legally limited revenue raising capacity.

Traditional economic development is usually approached through a "needs-based" perspective. This needs-based approach will generally result in a community assessing the current local problems and related economic needs and then developing policies to try and satisfy those needs. This approach is generally a top-down effort in that it begins at the macrolevel and usually does not include a great deal of community participation or even neighborhood-level analysis. Needs-based economic development has been criticized by many onlookers for the seemingly heavy reliance on attracting investment or businesses to fill various identified needs and for ultimately contributing to cycles of boom-and-bust in a community (Read, nd).

The most common economic development goals found across cities in the United States include increasing local revenues, creating or expanding jobs in the community, and/or increasing overall local wealth. According to 2014 International City/County Management Association (ICMA) economic development data, more than 85% of cities prioritize job creation and increasing the tax base in their economic development programs. Only 45% prioritize sustainability and a mere 26% prioritize social equity. Our 2016 survey provides additional evidence that shows

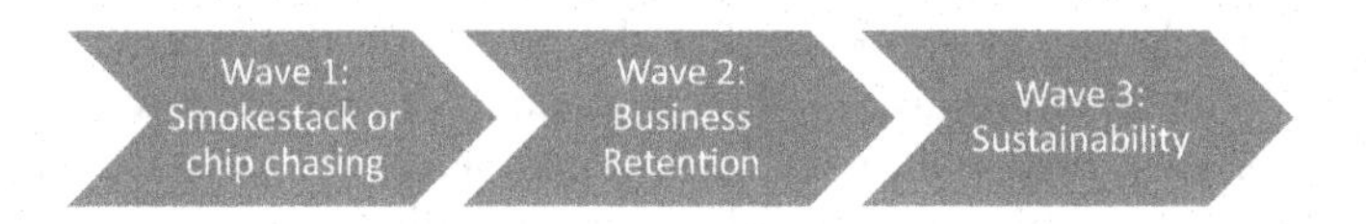

Figure 6.1 Waves of Economic Development.

a general prioritization of jobs and taxes over other types of economic development goals.

To understand the nature and history of local economic development, it is possible to view these local efforts through the lens of a series of three evolutionary and progressive waves (Koven & Lyons, 2010; Osgood, Opp, & Bernotsky, 2012). Although cities tend to move through these three waves sequentially, research has shown that most communities will still draw strategies from more than one wave at any given point in time (Koven & Lyons, 2010; Osgood, Opp, & Bernotsky, 2012). Furthermore, recent research has shown that a changing economic condition can prompt a community to *regress* along the waves and return to earlier wave strategies in their quest to achieve local economic development goals. Overall, latter stage waves are thought to be qualitatively *better* than earlier wave strategies because of the correlation those strategies have with fewer negative consequences for the city. Furthermore, wave three economic development is believed to most closely align with what we would term sustainable development and tends to depart from the needs-based approach to economic development. Figure 6.1 provides a visual depiction of the three waves' framework for economic development. The following section will discuss each of the three waves in greater detail.

Three Waves of Economic Development: A Path to Sustainable Development?

Wave one economic development is usually defined as a reliance on policies and tools focusing on business attraction through incentive provision. These incentives most often consist of some combination of grants, loans, tax credits, or other types of financial inducements meant to attract businesses to a city. Policies that are associated with wave one usually have poor outcomes for the community and are sometimes pejoratively referred to as "smokestack or chip chasing" due to the focus on attracting and capturing businesses for the community (Koven & Lyons, 2010). These types of policies are known to create an environment whereby cities compete with other cities to *win* a business by offering various and oftentimes increasing incentives to lure them to their community and away from a competing community. In some cases, this interjurisdictional competition prompts cities to offer increasingly large incentive packages to the point that the return on the investment does not even match the outlays of the investment let alone create any additional economic benefits for the community (Peters & Fisher, 2004).

Wave two strategies are considered marginally better than wave one strategies by virtue of their internal focus on existing businesses as opposed to businesses located elsewhere. Incentives may still be a policy choice under a wave two economic development effort; however, any incentives offered will be focused on current and existing businesses as opposed to new businesses located elsewhere. By focusing local development efforts on existing businesses, a city is thought to minimize the risk of entering into a bidding war with other communities over finite levels of economic investment. Furthermore, communities focusing their economic development efforts in this wave will likely have started to move away from the top-down nature associated with wave one and instead will begin to focus more of their attention internally on the community and specific lower level needs that may exist.

Lastly, cities engaging in wave three economic development policymaking are generally considered to be pursuing policies that can be labeled as sustainable economic development. Wave three policies focus economic development efforts on creating an environment that is conducive for economic development as opposed to directly targeting specific businesses or industries. These policies seek to find ways to create and to maintain a high quality of life so that both residents and businesses will *want* to be part of the community. It is thought that focusing on the quality of *place* will work as an attractant in and of itself, therefore reducing the need to provide direct incentives to private businesses to encourage them to invest in the community. Furthermore, this wave departs from the needs-based approach to economic development by focusing attention, resources, and efforts toward making the community a better place instead of identifying gaps in the economy or problems that need to be fixed. Under wave three, business attraction and retention is not a central focus. However, in some communities, wave three economic development may include a small-business or microenterprise component. Any focus on small business development is thought to be another form of an investment into the community and the area residents and not on equal footing with the smokestack chasing found in wave one strategies.

Much is known about how and when communities engage across the different waves of economic development. For example, recent research has demonstrated that the changing economic condition of a community influences the set of economic development strategies that the city utilizes (Opp, Osgood, & Rugeley, 2014). Recent survey data from ICMA also show that cities will provide financial incentives—wave one efforts—more often during recessionary times than they will during times of economic plenty (Osgood, Opp, & Bernotsky, 2012). Furthermore, previous research has also shown that when cities perceive higher levels of competition for economic development, they tend to adopt more incentive-based policies (Opp, Osgood, & Rugeley, 2014). Although economic development policy has a long history of research outlining the pros and cons of specific policies and tools, comparatively little is known about the nuances of sustainable economic development in American cities. Even less is known about the performance of these policies.

Sustainable Economic Development

Urban planners have searched for solutions to balance the tension between development demands and environmental degradation for at least a century (Wheeler & Beatley, 2009). As introduced in Chapter 1, the most common definition of sustainable economic development originates from the 1987 report *Our Common Future,* which defined sustainable development as, "development that meets the needs of the present without compromising the ability of future generations to meet their needs" (Bruntland et al., 1987). In the years following this report's publication, the concept has been embraced by many cities in their local economic development efforts. Surveying the literature as well as all available data sources on local economic development provides evidence of two major categories of sustainable economic development: redevelopment and revitalization efforts and unique place-based development strategies. More will be said on both of these categories in the text that follows.

Redevelopment and Revitalization as Sustainable Economic Development

Land available for development purposes can be categorized into three groups: greenfields, grayfields, and brownfields (Opp & Osgood, 2013). Greenfields are defined as the undeveloped parcels of land in a community. Local greenfields are usually made up of some combination of open space, natural areas, and/or farmland. These types of properties are most often found on the periphery of a city and may not have extensive existing infrastructure or public service availability associated with them. Grayfields, unlike greenfields, are properties that have been previously developed within a community. These properties are most often abandoned or underutilized commercial space such as an old shopping mall or big box store. Grayfields get their name from the large areas of gray surface parking lots found on many of these properties, which give them a gray appearance. Brownfields, similar to grayfields, have been previously developed. However, unlike grayfields, brownfield properties' reuse and redevelopment is complicated by the actual or the potential presence of environmental contamination. Contamination on brownfield properties can include toxins in the building envelope or in the ground or groundwater. Brownfield properties generally require some level of remediation of the contamination in order for them to be reused and/or redeveloped. Historically, the concern over the presence of contamination has worked as a significant deterrent to the redevelopment of these properties. As a result, many communities face a significant problem with the presence of brownfields in their jurisdiction (Opp, 2009).

Sustainable economic development efforts that focus on revitalization and/or redevelopment generally utilize various policies to try and pursue development in a way that minimizes or outright avoids developing a community's greenfield properties. Policies in this category will usually focus development inward toward the areas in the city that are already well developed. Revitalization and redevelopment policies will also often seek to decrease sprawl and to preserve open space in a community while still pursuing economic development goals related to jobs, tax revenue, or wealth increases (Opp & Osgood, 2013). In addition to the environmental benefits associated with reducing or limiting sprawl; evidence demonstrates that focusing development on existing properties within a community will create an additional economic benefit by decreasing infrastructure costs for both the developer and the city (Opp & Hollis, 2005).

Smart Growth, a topic covered extensively in Chapter 7, is largely focused on sustainable economic development through policies like infill, main street programs, brownfields revitalization, and other common forms of local redevelopment and revitalization efforts. Although these policies are certainly an important part of pursuing sustainable economic development, the details of these policies are focused on in Chapter 7 and will not be covered in depth in this chapter. Instead, this chapter will focus on the second major category of sustainable economic development: unique place-based economic development strategies. Additionally, this chapter will highlight some additional economic development tools that are sometimes used in sustainable economic development efforts across the country.

Unique Place-Based Economic Development: Amenities, Assets, and Innovation

This category of economic development can be best described as unique place-based economic development. This approach to economic development is sometimes referred to as "placemaking"; however, placemaking can also refer to an approach to public spaces (Project for Public Spaces, 2009). Unique place-based economic development is a catchall phrase for efforts that focus on unique attributes, assets, and/or opportunities related to a specific place (i.e. city or neighborhood) to achieve economic development goals (Hildreth & Bailey, 2014; Williamson,

Imbroscio, & Alperovitz, 2003). Specific policies or strategies that often fall under this phrase include amenity-based economic development, asset-based economic development, and innovation-focused development.

Amenity and Asset-Based Development

Both amenity- and asset-based development strategies are uniquely place based and more bottom-up than traditional economic development strategies. These strategies emphasize protecting and promoting attributes of the community such as natural resources, culture, climate, and other unique features of the local area to accomplish local economic development goals. As previously mentioned, traditional economic development practice usually begins with an investigation into the economic needs or problems of a community and follows with policy development to try to satisfy that identified need or problem. As an example of the prevalence of this needs-based approach to local economic development, Chapter 6 of the popular local economic development planning book *Planning Local Economic Development: Theory and Practice* discusses the analytical tools used by local economic development planners to identify gaps in the local economy so that policies can be created to address those needs (Leigh & Blakely, 2017). Unlike traditional economic development, both amenity- and asset-based development practices are more bottom-up in nature and deviate from the traditional strategy of identifying *needs* or *problems* and then developing a policy to address the identified issue.

Both of these strategies are relatively new to the local economic development discussions; however, both show promise in assisting with local sustainability goals. "Such a strategy would differ from traditional economic development strategies in its focus on quality of life as a key determinant of firm location" (Gottlieb, 1994, p. 270). Although some foundational differences exist between amenity- and asset-based economic development, the similarities are far more numerous and obvious. The most significant difference often found between these two categories is related to the level of emphasis on social goals and community engagement. Amenity-based economic development tends to focus on developing, preserving, and marketing local amenities to achieve development goals. Although asset-based economic development also focuses on these local assets or amenities, it will usually do so with an expectation or encouragement of the active engagement of local residents in the economic development process. More specifically, under asset-based economic development, the local residents are deliberately included in the process and in the determination of what exactly constitutes a local amenity (Kretzmann & McKnight, 1996). One other common difference sometimes found between these two forms of economic development is that asset-based development is more often associated with rural development than is amenity-based development (Nzaku & Bukenya,

2005). Both of these two economic development strategies are closely associated with quality of life in a community and in the creation of a quality *place*. As Koven and Lyons (2010) say, "[q]uality of life is an amorphous term used to connote a bundle of amenities generally recognized as positive assets in any given community" (p. 125).

Research has repeatedly demonstrated a positive empirical relationship between economic growth, resident wealth levels, and the presence of amenities within a community (Brueckner, Thisse, & Zenou, 1997). Many types of amenities exist that can serve an important economic development role; however, the most common amenity focused on in this type of economic development is that of natural amenities.

The United States Department of Agriculture (USDA) has studied natural amenities and the various economic impacts these amenities have on communities and on individuals. According to the USDA, "... people are drawn to areas with varied topography; lakes, ponds or oceanfront; warm, sunny winters; and temperate, low-humidity summers" (USDA Overview, 2016). Additionally, the USDA states that "...scenery with a mix of forest and open country is attractive to people, much more so than scenery that is either largely treeless or extensively forested..." (USDA Measures of Natural Amenities and Their Research Use, 2017). By most definitions, natural amenities consist of geographic features like bodies of water (ponds, oceans, rivers), natural spaces (greenfields), forests, mountains, or other such environmental amenities associated with a location. Recognizing that the presence or absence of natural amenities within a community works as an attractant to people and to businesses suggests that there is an important role for environmental protection, preservation, and management in economic development efforts. "Empirical analysis of exurban growth in the western United States has found that not only is population growth linked to natural amenities, but so is economic restructuring and economic well-being" (Marcouiller & Clendenning, 2005, p. 7). A community that chooses to pursue economic development in a way that reduces the availability or the attractiveness of these types of natural amenities will not reap the economic benefits known to be associated with the presence of these amenities. While these natural amenities are the most commonly identified target for these types of sustainable development efforts, other categories of amenities exist that can facilitate economic development. This is an important realization for the many communities that face a deficit of natural amenities by virtue of their specific geographic realities.

Historical or cultural amenities are an increasingly popular focus of local amenity-based development efforts. Historical amenities are generally defined as "...monuments, buildings, parks, and other urban infrastructure from past eras that are aesthetically pleasing to current residents of the city" (Brueckner et al., 1999, p. 94). Amenity-based economic development policies that focus on preserving or utilizing historical amenities in their economic development efforts tend to span multiple other policy areas within a city. One of the most common policies that a community pursues related to historical amenities is that of historic preservation. Historic preservation laws exist at all levels of government in the United States and include definitions, processes, and mechanisms meant to preserve historical properties in a community. Past research has offered evidence that historic preservation efforts produce more jobs, more local revenue, and higher property values as compared to other forms of economic investment (Gilderbloom, Hanka, & Ambrosius, 2009). Other common types of historical amenity development efforts in cities include the revitalization of historic trolleys (Nittler & Boyd, 2012), industrial heritage sites (Kerstetter, Confer, & Bricker, 2008), and battlefield sites (Ryan, 2007) among others. The specific type of historical amenity being focused on in this form of economic development isn't the most important factor for pursuing sustainable economic development. Rather the important part is that this strategy helps achieve sustainability goals by focusing economic development efforts on parts of a community that are already developed as opposed to greenfield sites on the periphery of the community. Furthermore, this inward-looking development effort helps minimize the negative outcomes associated with smokestack chasing and helps reduce the possibility of interjurisdictional competition for development while also conserving local resources for future generations. Finally, this type of economic development effort will lead to a higher quality of life for residents in the community as opposed to dedicating resources to pursuing businesses through incentive provision.

As noted in an earlier section, asset-based community development (ABCD) is similar to amenity-based economic development in that it focuses on using positive and unique attributes of a community to pursue economic development goals. While the assets of a community often include the amenities discussed before, in ABCD, the focus of economic development will often include an additional explicit social consideration (Mathie & Cunningham, 2003). "…ABCD rests on the principle that recognition of strengths and assets is more likely to inspire positive action for change in a community than is an exclusive focus on needs and problems" (Mathie & Cunningham, 2003, p. 477). More specifically, ABCD calls for the deliberate inclusion of residents in the community to shape the local development efforts and to also assist in defining the positive assets that exist in that community. Additionally, it is relatively common to see ABCD efforts focus explicitly on poorer and/or rural communities, whereas the asset-based development efforts do not necessarily share this same geographic focus.

At their core, both amenity- and asset-based development align closely with the third wave strategy discussed at the beginning of this chapter (Koven & Lyons, 2010). Third wave strategies, by definition, include policies that seek to improve the attractiveness of a community and focus on what makes that place unique. Both amenity- and asset-based development have quality of life and *place* as their central goal. Ultimately, both of these development categories seek to maintain, expand, and develop unique local amenities including natural resources and cultural/historical sites to create a place ripe for economic investment instead of providing incentives to businesses to entice them to relocate to the community.

Both of these economic development strategies align well with sustainability goals. Sustainability, as discussed extensively in Chapter 1, is concerned with creating and sustaining a high quality of life. The incentive-heavy economic development strategies of the past have been shown to be both ineffective and to blame for significant negative externalities that reduce the quality of life in a community. However, amenity- and asset-based economic development strategies hold some promise for the viability of the pursuit of sustainability. These efforts naturally work to preserve open space, focus on protecting important assets, and provide for unique and attractive entertainment options for residents—all of which contribute to long-term sustainability goals. At the same time, these two strategies have the secondary benefit of reducing the interjurisdictional competition and all the problems that are known to come with high levels of competition.

Innovation Efforts

Innovation and the relationship it has to economic development has been a focus of study for decades (Koven & Lyons, 2010). Innovation can be defined as "A mindset, a pervasive attitude, or a way of thinking focused beyond the present into the future vision" (Kuczmarski, 2003, p. 536). When it comes to local economic development, scholars have dissected various aspects of innovation. In some studies, universities are highlighted as centers for innovation that can create important economic development spillovers for a city (Youtie & Shapira, 2008). In other studies, innovation is viewed more broadly as knowledge creation and the externalities that accompany that new knowledge (Trullen & Boix, 2008). In still other sources, innovation is discussed through a narrower lens whereby research and development and new technology is the focus of innovation (Koven & Lyons, 2010; Leigh & Blakely, 2017). Regardless of which lens innovation is viewed through, this concept can be important for approaching sustainable development in cities across the United States.

Pursuing economic development through an innovation focus can include a variety of tools and strategies. One such strategy can be that of universities and tech-transfer. Previous researchers have highlighted the fact that universities and technology-transfer schemes have become a common phenomenon across the country. Universities use tech-transfer as a viable source of funding for research and the cities can use it as a policy tool for business creation (Geuna & Muscio, 2009). Although the evidence is mixed concerning whether tech-transfer programs achieve local economic development goals (see, for example, Feldman & Desrochers, 2003), a partnership with a local university can contribute positively to local economic development and place-based initiatives.

Returning to the overall place-based economic development idea can provide important insights into other ways to use innovation for sustainable economic development. An emerging focus in some communities is on "Maker's Places" or "Makerspaces". A Maker's Place can be defined as spaces where individual entrepreneurs can access equipment to manufacture an item with the goal to eventually bring it to market. Many cities have provided free or reduced public property (such as a library or vacant building) for the purpose of offering a space for shared equipment and small-scale manufacturing activities to spur innovation and small business creation. Furthermore, shared kitchens (sometimes called kitchen or food incubators) are a popular and growing extension of maker's places. Shared kitchens are usually low-cost commercial grade kitchens that can be utilized by individual entrepreneurs to create food products to bring to market. These maker's spaces can provide for economic development through a focus on innovation in individuals within a community. Although relatively new to the economic development realm, maker's places are growing in popularity and have seen some important successes in achieving economic development goals (ACT, 2016).

As a final statement on innovation and economic development, it is important to recognize that approaching economic development through an innovation framework can provide the necessary encouragement and space for creative policymaking—something that is very important in sustainability efforts. This creative policymaking can lead to successes with economic goals, conserving public resources, and achieving overall sustainability goals. For example, the case study presented at the end of this chapter highlights one such innovation-focused strategy—Camp Small—in Baltimore, Maryland. Baltimore, Maryland, created the Innovation Fund in 2012 with the goal to provide seed money to projects that are expected to, among other things, provide economic benefits to the community. Camp Small provides a very unique program that was successful in balancing economic, environment, and social needs through creativity and innovation.

Other Tools and Strategies for Sustainable Economic Development

In addition to the sustainable economic development efforts that focus on place-based economic development, there are other tools and strategies that may help support local sustainability efforts. Specific tools such as tax increment financing (TIF), cluster-based strategies, and alternative development policies such as childcare incentives can all contribute to a local sustainability effort and are important to highlight in this chapter.

Tax Increment Financing (TIF)

TIF is a common economic development tool that, when used appropriately, focuses public resources on the redevelopment of distressed areas in a city. These distressed areas almost certainly involve brownfields or grayfields as opposed to greenfield properties. TIF can serve as a valuable financial tool for communities seeking to redevelop distressed and underutilized portions of their community. TIF has a long history of being an important source of financing for projects in cities across the United States. The use of this tool generally involves some slight variation on the following steps (Opp & Osgood, 2013):

1. Determine if a need for development exists
2. Determine if the area meets state and local rules for the use of TIF
3. Draw boundaries and set the base year for the TIF district
4. Assess the base year property value
    a. In some states, a sales tax backed TIF can be used and property value will be less relevant
5. Issue bonds to finance the redevelopment expenses
6. Complete the project
7. Use the incremental tax receipts gained from the project to pay off the municipal (or authority) issued bonds
    a. The "base" tax remains with the taxing jurisdictions in the district and the "incremental" tax receipts are used to pay off the bonds

Although each state has slightly different rules guiding the use of TIF, most rely on a "but-for" principle to justify the use of public bonds for this type of project (Opp & Osgood, 2013). The "but-for" principle typically requires that a city or a local authority demonstrate that the proposed development would not have occurred "but for" the improvements gained through the TIF-funded expenditures. At its core, TIF is expected to be used to finance development in distressed parts of a community. This implies a natural orientation toward brownfields or grayfields. By focusing attention away from greenfield development, TIF can be closely aligned with sustainable economic development. Unfortunately, TIF has been misused by many cities across the United States, prompting several states to develop more stringent rules on the use of this financing tool for development (Guimond, Duffany, Krcmarik, & Pingenot, 2016; Luce, 2003).

Cluster-Based Economic Development

Industry clusters are defined as concentrations of interrelated and interconnected industries/businesses within a specified geographic region (Koven & Lyons, 2010). For example, New York City (NYC) is well known as a hub for financial services. In other words, NYC has an industry cluster consisting of various financial service businesses. An economic development strategy that focuses to some degree on industry clusters enjoys some of the same benefits that might be derived from the other place-based economic development efforts discussed in this chapter. Cluster-based economic development relies on the relative competitive advantage of a specific place to attract economic investment as opposed to simply incentivizing any business to (re)locate within a given community (Koven & Lyons, 2010; Leigh & Blakely, 2017). This concept is so well accepted in economic development practice that the EDA has sponsored an online resource meant to assist with mapping industry clusters across the United States (Cluster Mapping, 2014). Presumably, the EDA hopes that communities will use the mapping resource to better target their economic development efforts on businesses that are already clustered in their region as opposed to engaging in traditional wave one type efforts to attract *any* development.

Overall, industry clusters are thought to contribute to sustainability efforts in a couple of important ways. First, these clusters are expected to result in a competitive advantage for both the businesses and the geographic area. This competitive advantage is believed to provide important and valuable benefits to the specific businesses located within that community through their ability to engage in information sharing, networking, and collaboration with other similar businesses. This competitive advantage may translate into a business that is more successful and resilient than one that is located in a community without an industry cluster. Second, having industry clusters is believed to require fewer resource investments by the local government. This reduction in resource use is thought to come, at least in part, from an expectation that less public infrastructure will be demanded by businesses due to similar industry needs and from the ability of the industry to create their own linkages in the supply chain (Read, nd). "Clusters benefit from technical and specialized information with the area. This allows firms to be more productive and permits sophisticated buyers to gain information that meets their company's needs" (Koven & Lyons, 2010, p. 203). In short, industry clusters are thought to provide some level of economic stability for the community, potentially provide industry with a competitive advantage, perhaps provide a path for reduced public infrastructure demands, and ultimately contribute to sustainability efforts.

Business Incentives/Support for Childcare

Alternative and unique economic development programs exist across American cities that can be identified as being part of a community's sustainable economic development efforts. One such alternative program is one that focuses on encouraging childcare in the community. This specific economic development program has significant relevance to social sustainability (see Chapter 8) through the added focus on providing for a community's social needs in addition to the economic benefits to be had. This type of program will typically involve the use of public resources to support the provision of childcare for local employees. Although this type of effort relies on providing incentives, it does so without engaging in the traditional competitive race to attract a business. The foundational economic development rationale for this type of program centers on an understanding that childcare is an important part of a city's economic development infrastructure (Warner, 2017). Recent research has provided evidence of the economic benefits that can result from a local investment into childcare. Some of the identified economic benefits have included higher worker productivity, increases in consumer spending, and the creation of new jobs—all which are typical economic development goals for cities (America's Edge, 2011). Similar to the other tools and strategies outlined in this chapter, this particular tool maintains a focus on existing businesses and the long-term well-being of the community, therefore making a potential contribution to sustainability efforts. Given the uniqueness of this type of economic development tool, it is instructive to briefly examine a city that has adopted this type of program to glean some insights in how this might work in practice.

Concept in Action: Williston, North Dakota

Williston, North Dakota, has a population of approximately 26,426. The community has experienced rapid population growth—tripling in size in a 10-year span. As the population of the community grows, the city has identified a need for expanded childcare services to support the increase in workforce. In the 2010 comprehensive plan, the city identified childcare shortage as a key workforce threat and made an explicit effort to address this problem through a city-funded economic development program. This program is currently funded through a 1% local sales tax and has as its primary goal to increase Williston's childcare capacity (Krause, 2016). This program provides up to $1,000 in annual assistance for licensed childcare providers to offset state licensing costs, replacement of equipment, and to provide a general incentive award for existing providers (Williston Economic Development, 2017). Given the relatively small size of Williston, it is commendable to have this type of incentive program in the local economic development toolbox. In addition to the positive impact this program is expected to have on the workforce, this type of program may also have spillover employment effects as additional childcare providers set up businesses in the community. Furthermore, of consequence, this is one of the few cities across the country that has created a dedicated local funding stream specifically for childcare development incentives. Many, and perhaps most, other local efforts to incentivize childcare businesses across the country rely on state or regional funding mechanisms as opposed to using their own revenue stream to support this form of an alternative development program. By having an incentive specifically focused on childcare, Williston is improving the quality of life for residents and also potentially creating additional jobs and businesses in the city. This type of incentive works without engaging in the types of incentive provision that have been shown to create or to exacerbate interjurisdictional competition.

Concerns with Sustainable Economic Development Efforts

Even with promise that these sustainable economic development efforts and tools hold for sustainability, many of these economic development strategies raise concerns about social equity, gentrification, and socioeconomic segregation. Perhaps of immediate concern is the emerging evidence that indicates that the cities labeled as highly sustainable are the same ones that have a very high cost of living (Opp, 2016). Many of the sustainable economic development strategies discussed in this chapter and those covered in the next chapter have been connected to some very serious social equity concerns. In fact, "[t]he theory shows that the relative location of different income groups depends on the spatial pattern of amenities in a city" (Brueckner et al., 1999, p. 91). In simple terms, people want to live in a high-quality *place* and the more amenities that exist within a community the higher the likelihood of a wealthier resident population.

In the absence of robust public efforts to ensure that a community is accessible to all income levels, successful quality of life policies developed under the banner of sustainable economic development might lead to an imbalance in housing and in jobs. This imbalance may be to blame for an increased cost of living in some of the most desirable locations as defined by the presence of amenities, high quality of life, and robust sustainability engagement. This emerging concern begs the question of how do we ensure that these types of sustainability efforts do not simply exacerbate the trends of the past concerning concentrated and segregated wealth and poverty. To be sure, Tiebout's (1956) "vote with your feet" theory has been criticized for assuming that people can relocate easily and without cost (Bewley, 1981). However, at the same time, evidence has supported the basic premise of Tiebout's theory by showing that individuals do often relocate to locations that more closely match their desired service and tax level (John, Dowding, & Biggs, 1995). Does this mean that these types of sustainable economic development programs and policies contribute to the creation of exclusionary communities? One solution offered to try to avoid this outcome is the encouragement of the planning paradigm known as Smart Growth (discussed further in Chapter 7). Furthermore, social sustainability has been trumpeted as a way to address these types of social challenges (discussed further in Chapter 8). To be sure, a community with a spatial mismatch in jobs and housing will likely suffer unintended negative externalities associated with a need for lower income individuals to commute in to work. For the remainder of this chapter, another potential avenue to combat unintended consequences related to sustainable economic development efforts is studied. A robust and ongoing performance measurement effort can provide a city with the necessary mechanism to identify negative and unintended consequences and can hopefully provide an opportunity to correct any problems before they get out of hand and difficult to correct.

Performance Measurement and Sustainable Economic Development

As previously explained, Chapter 7 will focus on a number of policies and programs that can be considered sustainable economic development efforts. For the remaining portions of this chapter, we focus on a narrow set of economic development policies that have less overlap with other areas of sustainability and can be measured through a survey. Table 6.1 provides the summary of the percentage of cities that report having each of the 11 economic development policies asked about in the 2016 survey distributed for this project. The policies in bold text are the ones that most closely align with sustainable economic development principles. This table also provides an overview of the level of engagement in performance measurement activities and also the stated goals of the cities' local economic development programs.

Based upon the responses to the 2016 survey, cities remain focused on the traditional economic development strategies such as tax credits (36%) and grants for job creation (36%). The reported level of performance measurement across these policies is concurringly low in the sample. Only 11% of the responding communities that use tax credits for job creation or retention report measuring the performance of these efforts and less than 6% report measuring the performance of their local grant programs. Furthermore, as can be seen in Table 6.1, TIF remains one of the more popular economic development tools with almost half

Table 6.1 Economic Development Policies

Policy (Percentage of Cities Reporting, 2016 Survey)	*Performance Measurement: Percentage of Cities Reporting (Performance Linked to the Budget) (%)*	*Primary Goals for Economic Development (Percentage of Cities Reporting)*
1 Job training programs (18.8%)	4.2 (0.5)	1 Jobs (73.2%)
2 **Business assistance, loans, or grants to support childcare (8%)**	2.2 (1.9)	2 Wealth creation (17.8%)
		3 New businesses (60.9%)
3 **Industry Cluster Program/ Strategy (16.3%)**	2.8 (0.5)	4 Higher tax revenue (52.9%)
4 **Innovation Strategy (10.1%)**	1.4 (0)	5 Property value increase (52.2%)
5 **Asset-based strategy (6.5%)**	0.5 (0)	6 Other (4.3%)
6 Tax credits for job creation or retention (35.9%)	11 (5.6)	
7 Grants for job creation or retention (35.9%)	5.5 (2.3)	
8 Loans for job creation or retention (23.9%)	6 (1.9)	
9 Infrastructure provision for job creation or retention (25%)	6 (2.4)	
10 **Tax Increment Financing (47.1%)**	11.1 (6)	
11 **Historic Preservation Policy/ Program (47.8%)**	10 (1.4)	

Note: Bolded policies are more closely aligned with sustainability.

of the cities reporting that they utilize TIF for economic development purposes. Although, TIF enjoys the highest level of engagement in performance measurement of any of these policies at 11.1% of cities, this is still a concerning level of performance measurement. Given the mounting evidence of TIF misuse, this low level of engagement in performance measurement does not provide assurances that TIF is achieving the goal of revitalization and redevelopment. Furthermore, many states require that communities collect and provide extensive justification and forecasting of the revenues expected from the projects financed with TIF funds. This level of justification and planning implies that measuring the performance of TIF efforts could be a bit easier than some other economic development tools where a similar level of documentation is not required. The fact that only 1 in 10 cities routinely measure the performance, efficiency, or effectiveness of their TIF efforts is certainly concerning from an accountability perspective.

Unsurprisingly, the alternative economic development program related to business incentives for childcare is not widely adopted by these cities. Only 8% of the cities in this sample report having an economic development program focused on childcare. In the communities that do report having this type of economic development program, most do not assess the performance. In fact, according to the survey data, only 2.2% of the cities engage in performance measurement for this program and only 1.9% links the program/policy to the budgeting process to ensure accountability. Much work remains to be done in this area from both an adoption standpoint and from an accountability perspective.

Industry cluster economic development strategies are present in 16.3% of the cities in the survey with 2.8% measuring the performance of these cluster efforts. Even worse, less than 1% of the cities in this sample tie the performance of their cluster development program to the budgeting process for that program. Given the popularity of cluster-based economic development and the availability of federal tools to assist in this effort, it is unfortunate that so few cities assess how these efforts are faring at achieving economic development goals. Furthermore, it is unclear whether cities have a mechanism in place to help prevent some of the poor social equity consequences that might come from economic development efforts.

Innovation strategies are reported to be present in just over 10% of the cities with slightly more than 1% measuring the performance of these efforts. Somewhat unsurprisingly, most of the cities in this survey that indicated having an innovation focus to their economic development programs are ones that also house a major research university. For example, State University Pennsylvania indicates that they use an innovation strategy for economic development. This community is home to Pennsylvania State University where an extensive innovation and tech-transfer effort exists through the "innovation park".[1] Innovation as a place-based economic development strategy has a long way to go in American cities.

Asset-based strategies for economic development were reported in only 6.5% of the cities in the sample, and less than 1% of the cities indicate that they measure the performance of these efforts. Unfortunately, not one city in this sample affirmed that they tie the performance of their asset-based economic development programs to the budget for that program or policy. To be sure, asset-based economic development is relatively new to the local economic development discussions and toolbox; so hopefully, with time, we will see an increase in both the engagement in this type of economic development effort and in the assessment of performance and accountability.

The final remaining policy area in this part of the survey that has relevance to sustainable economic development is that of a historic preservation policy. This policy was the most widely adopted of all the economic development policies at almost half of the cities affirming the presence of historic preservation policy/program within their community. Additionally, 10% of the cities report measuring the performance of their historic preservation policy, and approximately 1% tie the performance of the policy to the budget for that program.

Moving away from a summary of what policies exist in these communities, it is instructive to see what cities cite as reasons for having difficulty achieving success in economic development. In this survey, the most common reason cited for having difficulty in achieving economic development success is simply a lack of resources. Human capital constraints and a lack of infrastructure are reported as secondary barriers to achieving success among these cities. Based upon this reality, it appears that many communities struggle with a problem akin to the chicken and the egg. Economic development has as one of its central goals to increase resources and revenues for the city, but it seems that cities report the most significant barrier to achieving this goal is the very lack of resources they are trying to grow! If a community needs economic development in order to increase local resources, but, at the same time cannot achieve economic development goals without resources—which comes first? To be sure, this is a difficult and challenging dilemma for cities. It is not hard to see why many cities are attracted to the wave one policies—attracting a large business to your community can surely have an immediate economic and political payoff.

Given the reality that a lack of resources creates challenges to achieving economic development goals, performance measurement activities are more important than ever. If a community is facing resource scarcity and is using some of those scarce resources on economic development efforts, it is of utmost importance that these programs perform well. Policy failure in this area can further strain limited resources and contribute to a vicious cycle. Table 6.2 provides a list of the performance metrics reported to be used by the cities that measure the performance of their economic development programs. This table also provides readers with some potential benchmarks and comparison metrics so that

Table 6.2 Metrics for Measuring Economic Development Policy Performance

Performance Metrics	*Sample Benchmarks*
• Value of commercial property	**Fort Collins, Colorado:** Target is $90 per capital for new commercial construction.
• Commercial permits issued:	**Tampa, Florida:** 2017—494 permits issued
• Office vacancy rates	**Bellevue, Washington:** 12% downtown office vacancy rate 2014
• Unemployment rate	**Pittsburgh, Pennsylvania Goal:** 3.7% or less
• Number of businesses (new or retained)	**Phoenix, Arizona:** Goal to retain 500 jobs
• Number of patents	**San Diego, California:** 16,908 patent cooperation treaty (PCT) filings in 2017

(*Continued*)

Performance Metrics	*Sample Benchmarks*
• Other creative class measure (i.e. number of artists)	**Pittsburgh, Pennsylvania Goal:** 167.6 jobs in arts and cultural establishments per 100,000 residents (based on average of comparison regions)
• Job counts (created or retained)	**Baltimore, Maryland:** 6.9% change in numbers of jobs created through development programs (2013–2017)
• Building permits issued	**Centennial, Colorado:** 8,264 historical three-year average
• Return on investment metric	**Lewisville, Texas:** 2.2 dollars per $1 spent. Goal is less than $1 per $1 spent.
• Size of financial assistance packages	**Seattle, Washington:** 2016—$5.85 million lent to Seattle businesses
• Tax receipts	**San Jose, California:** Estimated taxes from new businesses FY 2011–2012 was $1,036,865
• Percent of community with access to high-speed internet	**Grand Rapids, Michigan:** 100%
• Tourism counts/ tourists	**Chattanooga, Tennessee:** Goal to increase hotel tax revenue monthly. April 2017—$633,151.29 in hotel tax revenue.
• Festivals in the community or other creative class measure	**Austin, Texas:** Goal to have 500 contracts with arts professionals or arts organizations

communities seeking to develop their own performance measurement program for economic development can have some comparison examples. Similar to the other chapters in this book, these provided sample benchmarks can serve as a starting point for discussing ways to approach the performance assessment for these types of programs.

Concept in Action—Sustainable Economic Development in Baltimore, Maryland: The Story of Camp Small

While this chapter has provided readers with an overview of the primary avenues for sustainable economic development policy and program building, it is instructive to learn about a specific case as detailed by someone working with the program. Kirsten Silveira, a dedicated local public servant, tells the story of a creative project known as "Camp Small". Through patience and creativity, the city of Baltimore was able to turn an environmental and economic liability into a real opportunity for the city and the residents. By encouraging innovation and focusing on performance, Baltimore has planted a seed of economic potential that also spills over into the environment and social sphere.

By: Kirsten C. Silveira

Shaun Preston was hired to do the seemingly impossible: turn liability into opportunity. Baltimore's Department of Recreation and Parks (BCRP) Forestry Division maintains the city's 100,000+ tree canopy; for decades, every branch, leaf, stump, and log piled up on a piece of five-acre property a few miles north of City Hall. When the accumulation became unmanageable—like in 2011 when it nearly caught fire—the city paid as much as $350,000 for contractors to clear the space, known as Camp Small, so that they could continue to use the property for the storage of this debris.

This lot, found at the end of a tree-lined dirt road, is Preston's office. On his first day as Camp Small Yard Master, he was tasked with figuring out how to process a football field's worth of urban debris and then sell it. Stepping out of the traditional government role in more ways than one, Camp Small is a municipal enterprise that transforms urban waste into high-quality, marketable compost, mulch, and logs.

Urban Sustainability

Baltimore adopted its first sustainability plan in 2009, outlining measurable steps to achieve social, economic, and environmental sustainability. The plan focuses on seven areas in which the city would incorporate the tenants of sustainability into policymaking and service provision: cleanliness, pollution prevention, resource conservation, greening, transportation, education and awareness, and the green economy.

The plan aims to connect previously fragmented sustainability efforts, ensuring that all city programs and initiatives are working with the aforementioned tenants in mind. Camp Small—while not directly involved in building standards, zoning codes, or the city's comprehensive master plan—is a display of commitment to a broad, inclusive, and community-centric definition of urban sustainability. The initiative is part of a continuum of programming that positively impact Baltimore's long-term viability. For example, as the city seeks to grow its urban canopy to temper climate, provide habitat for wildlife, conserve energy, and much more, the volume of tree waste will increase. Camp Small turns that waste into an economically viable, "green" product—generating revenue for the city, eliminating the previously prohibitive cost of disposal.

Preston describes his first impression of the Camp Small lot as "a disaster"—he would spend the next six months cleaning up

25-foot-high piles of organic materials to make room for the plan to come to fruition. Solo, Preston used a Terex Powerscreen Warrior 600—a heavy piece of machinery used to screen and separate materials—to process more than 16,000 cubic yards of Legacy Mulch. The piles, he said, began forming 20 years ago and some of the material had already decomposed into compost. The screening process divided the material into three piles, each serving its own purpose:

1 Logs and other debris that were too large to fall through the two-inch square screen;
2 Materials that passed through the two-inch screen but are too large to fall through a 5/8th-inch screen—mulch for planting trees along city streets and green spaces; and
3 Material that had decomposed enough to pass through both screens—rich, wood compost.

These materials were utilized by local government and nonprofit partners—city agencies, Tree Baltimore, Growing Green Initiative, Homegrown Baltimore Land Lease Initiative, and the Parks and People Foundation. These entities spend significant resources on purchasing woodchips and compost, and this material was able to be used in place of the normal purchases they would make each year.

With the majority of the mulch gone, Preston had room to accommodate the daily influx of logs from city streetscaping projects. Of the roughly 100,000 board feet dropped off annually, Preston sorts and grades the wood into piles labeled prime, seconds, and thirds. Table 6.3 demonstrates the difference in the labeled piles.

BCRP's long-term vision is to use less-desirable logs and other urban debris to kick-start an Organics Composting Facility. Rather than paying for a contractor to chip the wood and begin another mulch pile on the site, BCRP will explore entering a Service Agreement to rent three acres of the site to a private business to operate

Table 6.3 Wood Pile Sorting Piles by Grade

Grade	*Description*
Prime	Logs over 8′6″ in length and with little to no defects (e.g. knots, branches, holes, scars)
Seconds	Logs with several or more defects. Can be any length
Thirds	Logs with more significant damage and defects

a composting facility. A major theme throughout the plan is the transformation of waste to wealth; "it wasn't just greening. Of course we wanted to reduce waste, but we also want to create economic opportunity", said Andy Cook, Environmental Planner for Baltimore's Office of Sustainability (BOS).

The 2009 sustainability strategy outlined ways to reuse waste created by the city, growing the urban canopy to curb the heat island effect and establishing a "green collar" workforce. Camp Small is the fruition of many of these goals; the program facilitates conservation, greening, and economic prosperity by repurposing tree waste into organic compost, woodchips for city projects, and unique, funky logs coveted by artisan woodworkers.

Because the city mostly removes only trees that must come down because of rot or storm damage, Log Thirds make up roughly 75% of Camp Small's annual intake. Prime Logs account for the smallest percentage of wood Preston processes each year; Preston estimates only 5% of the annual intake are top quality. Most Camp Small logs have been sold for local mulch production. Other possible uses are compost, biofuel, biochar, and playground fiber.

Innovation Fund Process

Anne Draddy, BOS Sustainability Coordinator, said there have been "a lot of starts" on the path to a Zero Waste initiative over the last nine years. In Fiscal 2016, BCRP and BOS teamed up to submit a $98,000 proposal to the city's Innovation Fund. Managed by the Bureau of the Budget and Management Research (BBMR), the Innovation Fund provides seed money for one-time investments that will lead to improved results, increased revenue, and/or reduced ongoing operating costs for city services. The proposal included confirmation from local sawmills, businesses, and nonprofits that the city's sale of logs, compost, and mulch would be of interest to their enterprise. The analysis estimated revenue at $95,000 in the first year and roughly $30,000 annually in subsequent years. In addition to identifying a market for the recycled materials, the project would eliminate the need to pay a third-party vendor to remove wood waste from the site—an estimated $103,000 annually. Table 6.4 outlines the estimate revenue base for recycled materials.

Baltimore's Innovation Fund is meant to be self-sustaining; savings from the investments are returned to the fund so that other projects may be supported. Designed to rigorously evaluate proposals for risk versus reward, the review process includes a written application explaining the venture, a cost-benefit analysis, metrics

Table 6.4 Revenue Generated by Recycled Materials

Material		*Price/Unit*
Compost	Small Bulk Sales *(11–50 yards)*	$18.00
	Bulk Sales *(50+ cubic yards)*	$12.00
	Resident Sales *(1–10 cubic yards)*	$25.00
Mulch	Small Bulk Sales *(11–50 yards)*	$1.00
	Bulk Sales *(50+ cubic yards)*	$0.25
	Resident Sales *(1–10 cubic yards)*	$10.00
Logs	Prime	*board-foot unit based on quarterly timber market reports*
	Seconds	$0.30 per board food
	Thirds	$1 per 10 tons

to use as a baseline for measuring program success, and finally an in-person pitch presentation. The programs' operational success would be measured by the tonnage of log sales, revenue generated, and cost savings from waste disposal.

Applicants are also asked to exhibit the proposal's connection to the Baltimore's population-level outcomes—this ensures that Innovation Fund monies are spent on initiatives that further the city's long-term goals. The Camp Small Zero Waste Initiative honed in on Growing Economy, Innovative Government, and a Cleaner City. The site's log sorting operation would save approximately 5,000 tons of wood annually from being chipped and mulched—redirecting the wood to construction and artisan projects and the longer term goal of establishing an Organics Composting Facility, which has the opportunity to accept and process 17,000 tons of organic waste annually from city operations—offsetting the cost of waste disposal and generating revenue from the sale of compost products.

A partnership with Baltimore Gas and Electric (BGE) allows the company to establish a new energy transfer substation on a portion of Camp Small in exchange for the construction of necessary concrete pads, roads, and storm water infrastructure. The agreement also included a land-swap and mitigation of the historic Melvale Rye Whiskey distillery site, located in Baltimore's Jones Falls area. This public-private partnership represents a major savings to the city and enhances BCRP's ability to conduct business on site.

Challenges

Baltimore's Innovation Fund took Camp Small from a well-laid plan to a true possibility. Getting from money in a budget account number to a well-oiled urban wood enterprise required months of trial-and-error. At more than one point, Preston found himself thinking: "how do I get rid of all this material...who's going to buy it?"

Risk Aversion

Programs like Camp Small require public servants to shift the perspective of their organization; facing financial constraints, cities are often hesitant to "commit scant resources to something nobody is sure will work", said Draddy.

Prior to submitting an application for Innovation Fund support, BCRP and BOS conducted their own field study to determine whether the market would support the city selling its urban wood. A number of regional sawmills and artisans showed interest in the material and subsequently provided letters of support to supplement a thorough cost-benefit analysis and loan application. Although Camp Small showed promise of return on investment and aligned with Baltimore's Sustainability Plan, the addition of industry commitment to support the initiative provided the Innovation Fund Committee with the assurance that the project was a sound investment.

From "Buyers" to "Sellers"

Traditionally, cities sit on the purchasing side of commercial transactions; while it's standard to collect revenue for permits, user fees, or taxes, the idea of regularly selling a product to a consumer was new to Baltimore. Designing the sales process required collaboration with BBMR, the Bureau of Purchasing, the Bureau of Revenue Collections, the Bureau of Accounting, and the Law Department.

The first approach to selling wood at Camp Small was through the city's Surplus Property Program, where prequalified buyers could bid on lots of "choice logs" curated by Preston. Unfortunately, nobody bid. The city then relisted the lot with no minimum bid requirement and, despite a vocalized interest in Camp Small logs, there were still no bids. Preston reached out to the prequalified bidders and found that the bundling of logs into lots made the material unattractive to local businesses—"it was the wrong species, the wrong amount and people didn't like the process".

Through this experience, Preston realized that Camp Small would only work if the city worked to "meet people where they are". He pulled together contacts from the Department of Finance and the Law Department to figure out how the city could make the material more accessible for the businesses interested in buying logs—everything from the "super funky street trees" to the straight trees perfect for logging. It's important to note that Camp Small doesn't present as a typical storefront—it's a dusty, four-wheel-recommended spot piled with urban wood of all shapes and sizes. Although the long-term plan is to have a small facility on-site, it wouldn't make sense for the city to have a traditional point-of-sale operation.

For Camp Small to be successful as a business enterprise, it was critical that the city listen to the voice of its customer and adapt its practices to fit their needs. An innovation will die on the spot if leaders are unwilling to take risks and try new things. After workshopping a few ideas—hours of operation where Preston could collect payment, a different approach to online purchasing (think Amazon for wood)—the group landed on purchasing Preston a tablet and a Square Magstrip Reader so he could collect payment anywhere and from anyone without being subject to any fees. This also circumvented the need to manually create invoices for every log-sale. The concept was met with some hesitancy from the city's Information Technology operation, but was eventually approved. The city's Treasury Office facilitated the setup of a regular ACH Wire Transfer and the Revenue team set up a specific account for the funds to be deposited into and tracked. Preston is now able to sell Camp Small materials to any interested buyer, from anywhere.

How to Show Savings to City Government

The Camp Small Zero Waste Initiative has the potential to save the city some money each year by using materials like mulch and compost for municipal projects. Contracts for landscaping or Capital Improvement Plan initiatives often require third-party partners to procure materials at market value for use on projects; however, if the materials are owned by the city and available for use already, Request for Proposals (RFPs) and contracts can be written to require the use of these materials first. Baltimore's Bureau of Purchasing is trying this out with a new RFP for tree-pit digging, which would not only lower financial burden to the City, but would create a demonstrable savings as a result of the Innovation Fund's investment in Camp Small.

Urban wood is also being used in the renovation of the city's Cahill Performing Arts Center; 17,000 board feet is being used for walling in the 40-year-old West Baltimore facility. This application of Camp Small materials has an estimated $80,000 market value. The log value, transportation, sawing, drying, finishing, and delivery of the Cahill project wood only cost them $36,000, demonstrating how the city can repurpose its own waste for creative results at a fraction of the market cost. In this case, using Camp Small materials frees up significant resources for enhancements to other recreation facilities included in the $185,000 plan. Showing how Camp Small materials help mitigate other everyday costs is a little more tricky—for example, if the Department of Transportation uses mulch to landscape a median rather than purchasing it wholesale, Preston would need to work with the agency to identify the hard dollars saved down to the specific budget account number for that fiscal year. At this point, the savings resulting from the use of Camp Small materials is in "soft dollars"—anecdotal, instead of using savings from one project to repay the Innovation Fund loan. Preston led the charge on sending citywide communications about material availability and keeping track of the market value of the amount other municipal agencies were using for projects. While finance folks might baulk at the idea of "soft savings", it's important to remember that projects—especially environmentally focused ones—often rank larger goals such as environmental sustainability and economic opportunity as higher priorities than financial return on investment.

Sustaining the Success

Growing pains—every program has them. Day-to-day, Preston is responsible for basic housekeeping of Camp Small, ensuring that the age-old practices of collecting and dumping urban forestry waste are modified to fit new policies. Every so often, he will find things like old tires in his wood piles or receive more/less wood than he was expecting in a week. Preston doesn't mind, though, because his visceral love for woodworking and nature drives his commitment to Camp Small's success. He patiently reexplains procedures, advocates for needed equipment, and enjoys when random logs show up and he "gets to do some science" to figure out the species. Now that Camp Small has a well-oiled sales process, Preston is focusing on what needs to happen for the initiative to thrive and achieve longer term goals like broadening its market and expanding into formal organic composting operation.

Maximizing the Tree Inventory

The city's recent investment in a Tree Inventory enables Preston to predict the trees that will arrive at Camp Small. Of the 125,000+ street trees and large park network, the variety of logs can range from an invasive species like the Japanese Angelica Tree to a street-friendly Oak variety that was damaged by a storm. When a log arrives on site, it begins to decompose quickly, so the sooner Preston can begin marketing the wood to local sawmills, craftsman, and other interested buyers, the better. The idea that "an invasive species that is obnoxious to the city can be used for something" is the premise of Camp Small's contribution to the Waste to Wealth Initiative.

Material Processing and Transportation

Currently, Camp Small does not offer processing or delivery of materials. Once a log is sold, Preston writes the company name on the log and places it in the "purchased" pile. The lack of delivery options can be an obstacle for smaller businesses or, even, the artisan resident that may participate in the program. To grow the market beyond larger buyers, Preston explains, the city would need to invest in costly milling, grinding and screening equipment, and, potentially, additional personnel. Preston has begun to explore whether some of the equipment needed exists within other parts of the organization and what the true cost of offering processing and delivery would be to drive the conversation around potential next steps.

Impact on the Community

The return on investment is what sold Camp Small as a viable Innovation Fund project, but the impact on the community is the heart of the initiative. Baltimore's urban wood has an opportunity for a second life; Preston dedicates much of his time to communicating the availability to local businesses, woodworking clubs, universities, and community associations. Local woodworker Mark Supik has been visiting Camp Small since his Maryland Institute College of Art (MICA) days in the 1970s, when sculpture and environmental woodworking professors would source materials from the site. Supik has operated his made-to-order woodworking shop (Mark Supik & Company) since 1981, and each month he teaches a bowl turning course using almost exclusively Camp Small logs. This process, Supik explained, needs fresh cut wood and produces something completely unique you can't get in a store. Invasive trees like the Ailanthus, or Tree of Heaven, is a "crappy tree that grows out of sidewalk cracks—but it makes a nice bowl", he said. In addition to Supik's classes, he noted several regional woodworking clubs that Camp Small serves a need for—many artisans look for specific types of wood to work with, often those that are "bad street trees" but beautiful for other projects.

In addition to being used for woodworking, Preston has found other avenues to give urban logs another life. Prior to the Zero Waste initiative, there was an "unspoken club" where residents would come to get wood at the front entrance; Preston created the Woodhawks Club where anyone can pay an annual membership fee for 12 loads of unsplit firewood. This club ensures that Log Thirds, which make up roughly 75% of annual intake, are used and continues to engage long-time supporters.

In Camp Small's first year, the city used more than 30,000 board feet of Prime Logs and Seconds Logs. Projects included a recreation center wall cladding, nature pavilion construction, nature playgrounds, garden paths and trail borders, furniture, and festival seating. These accomplishments provide an inside peek into Preston's big ideas for what Camp Small may grow to be in years to come; he wants to see the site come alive, to be a fun place for local nature-lovers, recyclers, and artisans to gather.

Officially built into the city's Fiscal 2018 Operating Budget, the initiative is recognized as its own city program. Once BGE completes the substation work and installation of its energy transfer substation and infrastructure, Preston plans to host on-site demos with artists using Camp Small materials, partner with schools to provide learning experiences, and use leaf decomposition to inoculate mushrooms in natural logs. Nancy Supik, Mark's wife and the co-owner of the local woodworking business, said Camp Small brings purpose back to urban trees; "they were planted with a purpose and, when it's time to come down, they can still have a life".[2]

Notes

1 More information about innovation park can be found at www.innovationpark.psu.edu/.
2 To learn more about Camp Small, visit www.TreeBaltimore.org.

References

ACT. (2016). U.S. Kitchen Incubators: an industry update. Available at: www.actimpact.org/wp-content/uploads/2016/03/U.S.-Kitchen-Incubators-An-Industry-Update_Final.pdf.

America's Edge. (2011). Montana: strengthening Montana businesses through investments in early care and education, America's edge. Available at: http://s3.amazonaws.com/mildredwarner.org/attachments/000/000/169/original/report-5755193a.pdf.

Bewley, T. F. (1981). A critique of Tiebout's theory of local public expenditures. *Econometrica: Journal of the Econometric Society*, *49*(3), 713–740.
Brueckner, J. K., Thisse, J. F., & Zenou, Y. (1999). Why is central Paris rich and downtown Detroit poor?: An amenity-based theory. *European Economic Review*, *43*(1), 91–107.
Brundtland, G. H. (1987). *Report of the World Commission on environment and development: "our common future"*. United Nations.
Cluster Mapping. (2014). Mapping a nation of regional clusters. www.clustermapping.us/.
EDA. (2017). What is economic development? Available at www.eda.gov/.
Feldman, M., & Desrochers, P. (2003). Research universities and local economic development: Lessons from the history of the Johns Hopkins University. *Industry and Innovation*, *10*(1), 5–24.
Gilderbloom, J. I., Hanka, M. J., & Ambrosius, J. D. (2009). Historic preservation's impact on job creation, property values, and environmental sustainability. *Journal of Urbanism*, *2*(2), 83–101.
Gottlieb, P. D. (1994). Amenities as an economic development tool: Is there enough evidence? Economic development quarterly, *8*(3), 270–285.
Geuna, A., & Muscio, A. (2009). The governance of university knowledge transfer: A critical review of the literature. *Minerva*, *47*(1), 93–114.
Guimond, D., Duffany, B., Krcmarik, A., & Pingenot, G. (2016). Colorado tax increment financing changes. Available at: http://www.apacolorado.org/sites/default/files/sites/all/themes/apa_colorado/images/editor/Economic%20%26%20Planning%20Systems%20APA%20TIF.pdf.
Hildreth, P., & Bailey, D. (2014). Place-based economic development strategy in England: Filling the missing space. *Local Economy*, *29*(4–5), 363–377.
John, P., Dowding, K., & Biggs, S. (1995). Residential mobility in London: A micro-level test of the behavioural assumptions of the Tiebout model. *British Journal of Political Science*, *25*(3), 379–397.
Kerstetter, D., Confer, J., & Bricker, K. (1998). Industrial heritage attractions: Types and tourists. *Journal of Travel & Tourism Marketing*, *7*(2), 91–104.
Koven, S., Lyons, T. (2010). *Economic development: Strategies for state and local practice*. Washington, DC: International City/County Management Association.
Krause, M. (2016). Williston creates incentive program for child care providers. *Williston Herald*. Available at: www.willistonherald.com/news/williston-creates-incentive-program-for-child-care-providers/article_03b2e798-c1ac-11e6-8783-b70c35a65c30.html.
Kretzmann, J., & McKnight, J. P. (1996). Assets-based community development. *National Civic Review*, *85*(4), 23–29.
Kuczmarski, T. D. (2003). What is innovation? And why aren't companies doing more of it?. *Journal of consumer marketing*, *20*(6), 536–541.
Leigh, N. G., & Blakely, E. J. (2017). *Planning local economic development: Theory and practice*. Los Angeles, CA: Sage Publications.
Luce, T. F. (2003). *Reclaiming the intent: Tax increment finance in the Kansas City and St. Louis metropolitan areas*. Center on Urban and Metropolitan Policy, The Brookings Institution.

Marcouiller, D., & G. Clendenning. "The supply of natural amenities: Moving from empirical anecdotes to a theoretical basis." In Green, G. & Deller, S. & Marcouiller, D. (eds) (2005). *Amenities and rural development: theory, methods and public policy*. Northampton, MA: Edward Elgar Publishing.

Mathie, A., & Cunningham, G. (2003). From clients to citizens: Asset-based community development as a strategy for community-driven development. *Development in Practice*, *13*(5), 474–486.

Nittler, T., & Boyd, C. (2012). Ding! Ding! Ding!. *Roads & Bridges*, *50*(8), 18–20.

Nzaku, K., & Bukenya, J. O. (2005). Examining the relationship between quality of life amenities and economic development in the southeast USA. *Review of Urban & Regional Development Studies*, *17*(2), 89–103.

Opp, S. M., & Osgood Jr, J. L. (2013). *Local economic development and the environment: Finding common ground*. Boca Raton, FL: CRC Press.

Opp, S. M., Osgood Jr, J. L., & Rugeley, C. R. (2014). City limits in a postrecessionary world: Explaining the pursuit of developmental policies after the great recession. *State and Local Government Review*, *46*(4), 236–248.

Opp, S. M., & Saunders, K. L. (2013). Pillar talk: local sustainability initiatives and policies in the United States—finding evidence of the "three E's": economic development, environmental protection, and social equity. *Urban Affairs Review*, *49*(5), 678–717.

Osgood, J. L., Opp, S. M., & DeMasters, M. (2017). Exploring the intersection of local economic development and environmental policy. *Journal of Urban Affairs*, *39*(2), 260–276.

Peters, A., & Fisher, P. (2004). The failures of economic development incentives. *Journal of the American Planning Association*, *70*(1), 27–37.

Project for Public Spaces. (2009). Placemaking. https://www.pps.org/.

Read, A. (nd). Asset-based economic development and building sustainable rural communities. ICMA Center for Sustainable Communities. Available at: www.nado.org/wp-content/uploads/2012/11/Asset-Based-Economic-Development-Part-1.pdf.

Ryan, C. (Ed.). (2007). *Battlefield tourism: History, place and interpretation*. Routledge.

Tiebout, C. M. (1956). A pure theory of local expenditures. *Journal of political economy*, *64*(5), 416–424.

Trullen, J., & Boix, R. (2008). Knowledge externalities and networks of cities in the creative metropolis. In P. N. Cooke, & L. Lazzeretti (Eds.), *Creative cities, cultural clusters and local economic development*. Edward Elgar Publishing.

USDA Overview. (2016). Natural Amenities. Available at: www.ers.usda.gov/topics/rural-economy-population/natural-amenities/; www.ers.usda.gov/topics/rural-economy-population/natural-amenities/measures-of-natural-amenities-and-their-research-use/.

Warner, M. (2017). *Restructuring local government*. Available at: www.mildredwarner.org/econdev/child-care.

Williamson, T., Imbroscio, D., & Alperovitz, G. (2003). *Making a place for community: Local democracy in a global era*. New York: Routledge.

Williston Economic Development. (2017). Child Care Assistance Program. Available at: www.willistondevelopment.com/Opportunities/Williston-STAR-Fund/Child-Care-Assistance-Program.

Youtie, J., & Shapira, P. (2008). Building an innovation hub: A case study of the transformation of university roles in regional technological and economic development. *Research Policy*, 37(8), 1188–1204.

7 Smart Growth and Land-Use Planning

Local land-use planning activities naturally overlap with sustainability efforts in American cities. Land-use planners have a long history of searching for ways to balance the tensions between economic development, environmental protection, and social equity (Campbell, 1996; Opp & Saunders, 2013). This tension, sometimes termed "The Planner's Triangle" (see Figure 7.1), is usually illustrated as a triangle with each corner representing a competing dimension (Campbell, 1996).

The Planner's Triangle has been adapted by scholars studying sustainability to represent the similar tensions that exist in the pursuit of broader sustainability goals (Mazmanian & Kraft, 2009). To be sure, land-use planning choices and sustainability efforts are inextricably linked and are important to understand in the context of local sustainability policymaking and performance measurement. As Owens and Cowell (2002) say,

> In practice, land-use planning proved to be one of the most important arenas in which conceptions of sustainable development are contested. Here, more than anywhere else, it has become clear that trying to turn the broad consensual principles into policies, procedures, and decisions tends not to resolve conflicts, but to expose tensions inherent in the idea of sustainable development.
>
> (p. 28)

One of the newer land-use planning paradigms attempting to provide a prescription for how to balance these three dimensions is that of the smart growth movement. Most of this chapter focuses on this planning paradigm as it relates to the sustainability efforts of American cities. However, before focusing more narrowly on smart growth, it is necessary to provide a historical context of land-use planning in American cities so that the connection to sustainability is clear for all readers.

Land-Use Planning: Introduction and Overview

Land-use planning emerged as an important local responsibility over the last century in the United States. New York City had one of the very first

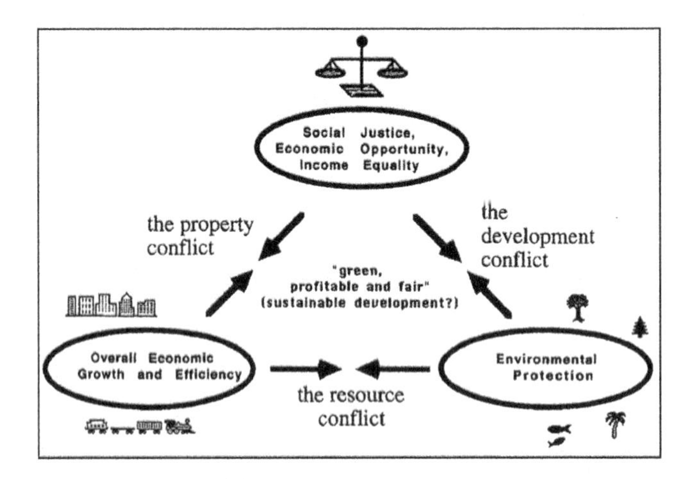

Figure 7.1 Planner's Triangle.

visible local land-use planning efforts when the city explored using land-use controls to combat congestion in the early 1900s (Akimoto, 2009). Over the course of the twentieth century, land-use planning efforts expanded and now most American cities engage in some form of planning and land-use control. Local planning efforts range from simple controls meant to ensure public safety to extensive and elaborate planning efforts meant to guide and to control all aspects of growth and development within the community (Levy, 2009). To understand land-use planning, it is instructive to break it into two broad categories: (1) land-use controls and (2) comprehensive planning processes. More will be said on each of these categories in the text that follows.

Land-Use Controls

Land-use planners have a number of tools available to them to accomplish development and planning goals. The most common land-use control tools include subdivision regulations, zoning, and review processes meant to control, to guide, or to limit development within a city. In the simplest terms, land-use controls limit the use of private property and, as a result, can sometimes be controversial and politically challenging for communities (Feiock, 2004; Levy, 2009).

Subdivision regulations are among the oldest forms of land-use control in America. These subdivision regulations have an impact on large areas of land across the country each year (Levy, 2009). "Every year thousands of acres of vacant land at the fringe of American cities are subdivided into building sites" (Reps, 1955, p. 258). Subdivision rules control how, and under what conditions, parcels of land within a community can be divided and used (Levy, 2009). Subdividing larger plots of land into smaller buildable lots directly impacts public service demands, population levels in the city, and the overall character of the community. Ultimately, adopting subdivision regulations provides local governments with a mechanism to control the impacts and the nature of development that occurs within the city. One of the most common subdivision rules found across the country is a requirement that the landowner provide or contribute to some of the necessary infrastructure (such as roads, public areas, and utility facilities) resulting from the increased demands generated from the newly subdivided land. Furthermore, some cities require that a landowner contribute financially, usually in the form of impact fees or a similar payment to the local government, to compensate for the added population that newly subdivided land brings to the community (Levy, 2009; Reps, 1955). The specific requirements and provisions found within local subdivision regulations can have a significant influence over how, and where, neighborhoods develop within a broader community. Furthermore, subdivision regulations can also have an impact on housing costs, open space acreage, commuting patterns, and overall social equity within a city. The more expensive or difficult it is to subdivide land, the less development that will likely occur. This is a double-edged sword. On one hand, less development may mean less sprawl and a higher likelihood for green space preservation—both are important to sustainability goals. On the other hand, less development may also mean higher housing costs and a resultant social equity concern (see Chapter 8).

Similar to subdivision regulations, local zoning ordinances also have a substantial impact on how a community develops and grows. Zoning ordinances are probably the most well known of all of the land-use controls and are sometimes blamed for serious environmental, economic, and social problems (Ketcham, 2009; Levy, 2009; Opp, 2016). The first comprehensive local zoning ordinance was adopted by New York in 1916 (McDonald & McMillen, 1998). Following the 1926 Supreme Court ruling declaring zoning ordinances to be constitutional, the Department of Commerce published the Standard Zoning Enabling Act (SZEA), which was subsequently adopted by many states and cities across America (Ketcham, 2009; Stever, 1986). SZEA, after the Supreme Court decision affirming the constitutionality of Euclid, Ohio's zoning codes, is commonly known as Euclidean zoning. Euclidean zoning generally calls for a separation of land uses into specific and like districts, which is something that has been pointed to as being problematic for social equity and environmental considerations. Modern zoning ordinances will usually include two major parts: (1) a zoning map and (2) details on what is allowable, or not, within a particular zone (Levy, 2009).

The specific definitions and rules contained within a zoning ordinance will have a significant influence over the nature of land development and which, if any, negative externalities will emerge from local development decisions. Under traditional Euclidean zoning, local zoning ordinances tend to be narrow and include instructions on specific layout and use requirements for a specified zone. These layout and use requirements will ultimately impact the density, land value, and permissible development types within a designated zone. Common requirements include minimum or maximum residential lot sizes, structural restrictions on property, and specific use restrictions (Levy, 2009). For example, Fort Collins, Colorado, has a very detailed land use code divided by various types of districts across the city. One such district is called the *Urban Estate District (U-E)*. The U-E district is "...intended to be a setting for a predominance of low-density and large-lot housing" (Division 4.2, Fort Collins Land Use Code). The land use code provides very specific rules, restrictions, and allowances for this zone such as including an allowance for accessory dwellings for farm animals and also dictating that the average density of this zone not exceed two dwellings per acre. These requirements will directly impact the density as well as the land value within this zone. Furthermore, these rules will also indirectly affect the environment through the resultant impacts on automobile traffic, congestion, and commuting patterns across the city.

Although Euclidean zoning remains one of the most popular forms of zoning in the United States, other variations on zoning have emerged as alternatives. For example, inclusive zoning, performance zoning, and form-based codes have all emerged as potential changes or replacements for Euclidean zoning (Elliott, 2008). Although each of these variations in zoning is important and useful to a city's land-use planning activities, this chapter will not focus on these alternatives and will instead focus on smart growth, one of the most promising approaches to balance sustainability concerns.

In addition to subdivision regulations and zoning ordinances, cities also have a variety of other land-use controls at their disposal that are worthy of mention. Other common land-use controls include review processes for development, historical preservation rules/requirements, and other unique provisions concerning the process and approval rules for development (Levy, 2009). These controls are quite diverse and are sometimes part of a city's comprehensive plan and other times are separate from any larger process that may be required in a city's planning process. Furthermore, these policies and land-use controls may have overlap and relevance to economic development efforts for a city (see Chapter 6).

Ultimately, the land-use controls that a city chooses to utilize will shape how that community grows and develops over time. As mentioned, traditional regulations on subdivisions and zoning often create homogenous groups of buildings and people. This end results achieved through land-use planning will directly influence all three E's of sustainability.

For example, areas zoned as low-density residential tend to result in areas prone to economic and racial segregation due to the resultant lack of diversity in housing choices and prices (Ketcham, 2009). Furthermore, traditional Euclidian zoning has been shown to increase the reliance on automobiles for commuting, increase obesity rates as walking is deterred, increase stress levels from long commutes, and ultimately contribute to sprawl (Ketcham, 2009; Pendall, Martin, & Puentes, 2006).

Comprehensive Planning

While land-use controls are the tools that a city uses to accomplish planning goals, comprehensive planning is a broader activity with just as significant of an influence on how, where, and when development occurs. In the early twentieth century, many cities adopted zoning ordinances but not comprehensive plans (Kaiser & Godschalk, 1995). By the mid-1950s, more and more cities were adopting comprehensive plans to help them deal with the postwar growth (Kaiser & Godschalk, 1995). While not all communities develop or adopt what is termed a comprehensive or master plan, by the 1980s many states passed laws requiring that every city within their state develop a comprehensive plan (Chapin, 2012). As a result of these state-level rules, comprehensive plans are far more common than they were in past decades. Although the level of detail and the scope of local comprehensive plans vary significantly across the United States, these plans do share some basic characteristics that can be summarized in the following paragraphs.

Most comprehensive plans are approached with a long-range view in mind, typically covering around 20 years. These plans also tend to share a focus on planning for the protection of health, safety, and public welfare (Levy, 2009). Comprehensive plans will also often establish a vision for the growth of the community tied to specific goals and objectives (Chapin, 2012). In some cases, the state government will heavily influence the nature of local comprehensive plans (such as is the case in Florida with the passage of the Growth Management Act of 1985), and in other cases, local governments have far more discretion over the nature and the content of their comprehensive plans. In simplest terms and as a summary, comprehensive planning seeks to manage growth in a way that protects public health, public safety, transportation infrastructure, public service adequacy, and local fiscal health (Chapin, 2012; Levy, 2009). A good comprehensive plan will enable a city to control and plan for future growth so that the local infrastructure is sufficient to serve that new population.

Although sustainability goals have not always shown up in a city's comprehensive plan, they have grown increasingly more common in recent years. Similar to everything else related to local governments, exactly how environmental and sustainability considerations show up in the comprehensive plan varies significantly. In some communities, sustainability planning is completed through a separate and distinct process from the traditional comprehensive planning efforts. For example, Los Angeles, California, developed a comprehensive sustainability plan titled the "pLAn" in 2015. This sustainability plan outlines an environmental vision for Los Angeles that includes all three E's of sustainability and identifies target dates for making progress (pLAn, 2015). In short, the pLAn works as the city's comprehensive plan for sustainability. In other communities, sustainability is more narrowly embedded within their traditional comprehensive plan and planning process. Finally, in some cities, sustainability is not a distinct consideration in any part of the community's planning process and is simply absent as a major consideration.

In addition to the sustainability considerations related to general land-use controls and comprehensive planning processes, sustainability shows up as a central part of a newer planning paradigm known as "Smart Growth". *Smart growth* proponents have more than a three-decade long history of experimentation, program development, and public resource provision at all levels of government in the United States. Since at least the 1990s, the United States Environmental Protection Agency (EPA) housed an office and a set of programs focused on promoting smart growth across cities in the United States (Laporte & Opp, 2016). Additionally, many states have adopted statewide smart growth programs to facilitate or to encourage the adoption of smart growth principles within the cities in their state (Ingram, Carbonell, Hong, & Flint, 2009). Perhaps most important to this book, as of 2017, thousands of cities embrace the general concept of smart growth in their comprehensive plans and land-use policy choices. Smart growth does not appear to be losing popularity and is the focus of the remaining parts of this chapter as part of this book's exploration of sustainability in America.

Smart Growth 101

According to the organization Smart Growth America, "Smart growth is an approach to development that encourages a mix of building types and uses, diverse housing and transportation options, development within existing neighborhoods, and community engagement" (Smart Growth America, 2017a, 2017b). Unlike traditional Euclidean zoning, smart growth seeks to diversify areas within the community. In general, 10 principles are thought to represent the foundation of a "Smart Growth" approach to local development (see Table 7.1). Each of these principles relates in varying ways to the sustainability goals discussed throughout this book.

The very name of this planning perspective implies that there is something that can be categorized as "not smart" or perhaps even "dumb" growth. So what exactly is thought to be "dumb" growth and why is

Table 7.1 Smart Growth Principles

	Connection to Sustainability
1 Mix land uses	By having a diversity of land uses in a block, it is possible to avoid socioeconomic segregation (see Chapter 8) and improve social capital. Additionally, mixed-use development is thought to increase the probability of residents being able to walk to work, shopping, and home, thereby reducing greenhouse gas (GHG) emissions from vehicles.
2 Compact design	Compact design practices encourage a more efficient land use that is thought to decrease greenfield development and farmland conversion for development. Also, compact design is thought to reduce the public expenditure demands associated with sprawling infrastructure.
3 Provide diverse housing options through mixed use and other efforts	Diversity in housing choices with respect to price and size. Housing affordability is an important aspect of social sustainability (see Chapter 8).
4 Create and encourage walkable neighborhoods	Neighborhoods that encourage walking by residents are thought to help combat obesity, reduce GHG emissions from transportation, and provide for increases in social capital.
5 Create unique, interesting, and quality communities with a strong "sense of place"	Developing neighborhoods that are attractive, unique, and diverse will attract residents and create a nice place to live. A community that is unique and attractive can help build social capital and encourage a sense of community among residents (which are thought to have important co-benefits like reduced crime). Parks, recreation, and other quality of life amenities are important considerations in this principle of smart growth.
6 Preserve open space, farmland, and greenfields	By making a dedicated effort to direct development to existing locations and protecting open space and farmland, environment benefits are expected to accrue from lower commuting patterns, less infrastructure requirements, and protecting the natural environment.
7 Prioritize infill development	Infill represents the goal of directing new development to areas that are already well developed. This will reduce sprawl, traffic congestion, and demands on public infrastructure.

(*Continued*)

		Connection to Sustainability
8	Provide a variety of transportation options	Providing public transit options, including biking and walking infrastructure, is expected to reduce automobile commuting and the environmental externalities that accompany it.
9	Ensure and enhance equal access to resources for all community residents	This principle is a fundamental social sustainability principle (see Chapter 8) where fairness and equality is important for development choices.
10	Encourage and facilitate collaboration in development decisions	Collaboration is important for social sustainability and also for economic and environmental protection goals.

Source: Adapted from Smartgrowthamerica.org and Ingram et al. (2009).

it so concerning? As discussed throughout many of the previous chapters, local governments have historically approached development within their community in ways that have encouraged sprawl, reduced or eliminated open space and farmland, increased demands on public infrastructure and resources, and ultimately negatively impacted the natural environment while also reducing social equity across their jurisdiction (Opp & Osgood, 2013). Through traditional Euclidean zoning practices, land regulation policies, and the basic human tendency to self-sort into homogenous groups, most American cities developed into fragmented and segregated communities where automobiles are a necessity and social ills are common (Opp & Osgood, 2013). The suburbanization trend and development patterns that occurred over most of the twentieth century is thought by many scholars to be to blame for several of America's wicked social problems. For example, as wealthier, and most often white, residents left central cities to pursue single-family homeownership in newly emerging suburbs, economic and racial segregation expanded. Zoning processes in many cities aided in this social sorting by race and income through the traditional separate-use scheme of Euclidean zoning. Additionally, as more people separated their place of residence from their place of employment, reliance on automobile commuting exploded. By 1970, more people lived in the suburbs than in the central cities in the United States and residential segregation by race and income became the norm (Morgan, England, & Pelissero, 2007; Opp & Osgood, 2013).

As suburbanization intensified in the mid-to-late 1900s, central cities across the United States suffered substantial reductions in population and in tax revenues. At the same time, wealthier and more exclusive suburban governments grew in areas that were previously farmland or open space. In addition to the environmental and social concerns associated with this type of growth, this fragmented structure also set the stage for the interjurisdictional competition for economic development highlighted in Chapter 6. Research has routinely demonstrated the negative aspects of interjurisdictional competition for certain types of people (e.g. those that can pay taxes) and for businesses that can provide jobs and sales tax revenues to support local interests (Opp, Osgood, & Rugeley, 2014; Peterson, 1981). The sprawl and competition that comes, at least partially, from traditional land-use planning is believed to reduce the quality of life for all residents in a community and is, therefore, what many might term *dumb* growth.

Over the past hundred years or so, land-use planning evolved from a fragmented set of local zoning policies to a wide-reaching and comprehensive effort to control land uses, direct growth, and regulate the future of communities across America (Feiock, 2004; Levy, 2009). Smart growth is one of the latest, and perhaps most common, perspectives on what is required of communities in order to create *better* places where all residents can enjoy a high quality of life (Levy, 2009). The level of engagement across the 10 smart growth principles identified in Table 7.1 varies significantly from city to city. Even with all of the perceived benefits stemming from smart growth, the paradigm is not without potential problems that must be considered. Some research has shown that a city's selective engagement in only some of the smart growth principles, while ignoring or refusing others, can lead to perverse outcomes (Godschalk, 2004; Opp, 2016; Quigley & Raphael, 2005). For example, a city that adopts policies to create walkable neighborhoods but doesn't adopt policies to ensure diverse housing options may result in the creation of an exclusionary community where only wealthier individuals can afford to live. In addition to the significant social ills that result from this consequence, environmental consequences can be expected to follow. A healthy economy will have needs for workers across all income groups. If lower wage or working-class individuals cannot live in the community, one of two potential outcomes is likely. (1) A shortage in available employees will exist and the community will not have sufficient access to demanded services and goods, or (2) commuting into the city will increase, as will the congestion and emissions related to that commuting. Neither of these outcomes is ideal or sustainable.

The 10 smart growth principles all share the common goal of creating livable, interesting, and great places for all people while, at the same time, avoiding the negative externalities associated with development and growth. As the Smart Growth Network (2006) says,

> When cities choose smart growth strategies, they can create new neighborhoods and maintain existing ones that are attractive, convenient, safe and healthy. They can foster design that encourages social, civic, and physical activity. They can protect the environment while stimulating economic growth.
>
> (p. 1)

In essence, smart growth provides a land-use and development perspective on the three E's of sustainability: environmental protection, economic development, and social equity. Smart growth can be viewed as one potential prescription for local sustainability.

In some communities, smart growth efforts are limited to just a few or perhaps just one specific principle. Alternatively, other communities more fully embrace smart growth across all 10 principles. It remains to be seen whether this paradigm and approach to development will achieve the goals it purports to be pursuing or whether significant and widespread unintended negative consequences will result. Nonetheless, with caution in mind, the general concept of smart growth provides a useful framework to explore sustainability in the United States with respect to land-use planning and development.

What Smart Growth Efforts Are Cities Adopting?

The first major data source providing an inventory of smart growth policy engagement across American local governments emerged from the 2010 municipal survey distributed by the International City/County Management Association (ICMA). In this survey, 17 policies were catalogued that can be at least partially considered smart growth efforts (see Table 7.2). In our 2016 survey, we catalogued 11 policies that are explicitly related to the 10 smart growth principles listed in Table 7.1. Of note, we also catalogued several other policies that can easily be considered smart growth oriented (such as walking and biking infrastructure) but have elected to discuss those policies in other chapters where the central focus is on that specific aspect of sustainability. Table 7.2 provides both the 2010 and the 2016 inventory of the smart growth policies across the United States.

Both surveys provide evidence that smart growth principles have been translated into local policies across the United States. For our 2016 survey, we focused on policies that either reflect a specific land-use planning tool, such as density zoning, or clearly represent a key principle of smart growth, such as infill development, without falling squarely into another area of sustainability, such as transportation efforts. More will be said on these policies in the text that follows.

Brownfields Program

The EPA defines a brownfield as a "...property, the expansion, redevelopment, or reuse of which may be complicated by the presence or potential presence of a hazardous substance, pollutant, or contaminant" (EPA, 2017). By definition, a community with active brownfields will struggle to redevelop or reuse those properties. A community facing difficulty in their redevelopment efforts will also likely struggle to be successful with

Table 7.2 Inventory of Smart Growth Policies

Smart Growth/Land-Use Planning Policies (Governments Reporting (%))	
ICMA 2010 Survey	*Opp, Mosier, and Osgood (2016) Survey*
1 Active Brownfields Program (22.5%)	1 Active Brownfields Program (25.4%)
2 Land conservation program (18.7%)	2 Downtown revitalization efforts (62%)
3 Program for the purchase or transfer of development rights to preserve open space (14.2%)	3 Mainstreet programs (37%)
4 Program for the purchase or transfer of development rights to create more efficient development (5.4%)	4 Policies or programs encouraging infill (34.8%)
5 Program for the purchase or transfer of development rights to preserve historic property (7.5%)	5 Incentives or programs to encourage mixed-use development (51.4%)
6 Permit higher density development near public transit modes (20.4%)	6 Density zoning variances for sustainable development (29.3%)
7 Permit higher density development where infrastructure is already in place (22.3%)	7 Parking zoning variances for sustainable development (27.9%)
8 Incentives other than increased density for new commercial development that are LEED certified (5.2%)	8 Open space preservation policies/programs (43.1%)
9 Incentives other than increased density for new single-family residential to be LEED certified or the equivalent (2.6%)	9 Farmland preservation programs/policies (12.7%)
10 Apply LEED neighborhood design standards (3.7%)	10 Park and recreation facility development (64.9%)
11 Provide density incentives for "sustainable development" (9.7%)	
12 Provide tax incentives for "sustainable" development (2.8%)	
13 Reduce fees for environmentally friendly development (3.5%)	
14 Fast track plan reviews and/or inspections for environmentally friendly development (8.7%)	
15 Residential zoning codes to permit solar installations, wind power, or other renewable energy production (20.8%)	
16 Residential zoning codes to permit higher densities through ancillary dwelling units or apartments (13.9%)	
17 Zoning codes encourage more mixed-use development (36.6%)	

an infill effort (Principle 7) particularly if a brownfield is located near an area where infill opportunities are present. The stigma associated with brownfields can deter investment in the entire surrounding area and can exacerbate problems with sprawl and prompt developers to pursue development on open spaces or farmland. While research indicates that more than half a million brownfield sites exist across the United States (Opp & Hollis, 2005), only 25.4% of the cities responding to our survey indicate they have an active brownfields program and, similarly, 22.5% reported this program in the 2010 data. To be sure, not all communities will face problems with brownfields, making the need for this program contingent upon the specific conditions of the community. It is to be expected that not all communities in America will have brownfields to contend with. It is possible that, particularly given our skew toward smaller communities, the low adoption level for this program is related to the difference in communities that have these properties versus those that do not. Alternatively, all 50 states have developed robust brownfields programs to support redevelopment and remediation (Opp, 2009). These state programs may work to decrease the need to create a local program to focus on this issue area because the state-level program might be expected to provide sufficient necessary public resources to remediate and redevelop these properties.

Downtown Revitalization Efforts/Mainstreet Programs

Downtown revitalization efforts and mainstreet programs can both be labeled as a sustainable economic development program (see Chapter 6). Although both of these programs focus on revitalizing a downtown area, mainstreet programs tend to be more often associated with rural communities than the broader downtown revitalization efforts. It is not absolutely necessary to differentiate between a mainstreet program and a downtown revitalization program; however, for the purposes of the survey conducted for this book, we elected to ask about them separately so that communities can self-select into the title they more closely associate their programs with. Downtown revitalization and mainstreet programs reflect the goals found in smart growth Principles 2, 5, 6, and 7. These programs traditionally focus and direct development efforts toward the older and potentially historic segments of the community. Furthermore, focusing development on downtown or mainstreet will likely make use of well-developed infrastructure and perhaps reduce the need for additional public investment for roads, transportation, or utilities. These programs also tend to have a shared emphasis on compact design, walkability, density, and attractive urban design of a community's downtown or mainstreet. Downtown revitalization efforts represent one of the most commonly adopted of all of the smart growth policies catalogued in these surveys, with 62% of the cities indicating they have a downtown revitalization program. Mainstreet programs were selected by 37% of the communities responding to the 2016 survey. This high level of adoption is not surprising given the connection these programs likely have with economic development needs in a city. As discussed in Chapter 1 as well as demonstrated in previous research, economic co-benefits are important factors driving the adoption of sustainability policies in many cities (Opp & Mosier, 2017; Opp, Osgood, & Rugeley, 2014). Understanding the relationship between economic co-benefits and sustainability is important for understanding why certain policies get adopted while others do not. As an example of this synergy between smart growth concepts and economic co-benefits, the case study for this chapter provides an example of this concept in action. Kansas City, Missouri, has been successful in developing a unique approach to downtown revitalization and economic development, and the community has seen important successes in increasing foot traffic, sales, and citizen satisfaction within the downtown—all while focusing on additional transportation options and making downtown unique.

Infill

Infill can be defined as the encouragement of new development within locations where existing development is already in place (Sustainable Cities Institute, 2013). More simply stated, infill is the act of developing open land that is enclosed by other development as opposed to developing farmland or open space on the low-density periphery of the community. Infill is one of the 10 principles of smart growth (number 7) and shares similar benefits of other policies discussed in this chapter. For example, many of the same benefits perceived to come from downtown revitalization and mainstreet programs are also likely possible outcomes from infill programs. It is believed that by encouraging infill in already well-developed areas of a community, sprawl, traffic congestion, and demands on public infrastructure will be reduced—all of which are important sustainability considerations. Infill policies or programs were reported as adopted by almost 35% of the cities in the 2016 survey. While a city does not necessarily need a formal program or policy on infill to actually encourage infill, it is a fair assumption that communities with formalized programs will be more successful in directing growth and development toward those well-developed areas of their city by virtue of a formal policy encouraging it.

Mixed-Use Development

Principle 3 of smart growth calls for mixed-use development to provide for diversity in housing choices, income of residents, and land uses across the city (see Table 7.1). In simple terms, mixed-use development is a zone within a city that allows for multiple uses (Tombari, 2005). Unlike Euclidean zoning, mixed-use zones would encourage various uses in the same zone including residential, commercial, and sometimes light industrial. By mixing allowable uses within a zone, it is believed that it will provide encouragement for residents to walk; it will diversify residents living in a specified area; and it will ultimately contribute to environmental, economic, and social sustainability (Opp, 2016; Tombari, 2005). Important to note is that mixed-use development or zoning does not necessarily mean that mixed income is the goal or the result. It is possible, and perhaps even likely, that many communities that engage in mixed-use development will not see mixed-income results from these efforts. If a city is truly approaching land-use planning and development through a smart growth lens, they must be concerned with equal access and income/racial diversity (Principle 9). Chapter 8 focuses in depth on this aspect of smart growth through the lens of social sustainability.

Over half of the cities in the 2016 survey indicate they have policies or programs in place to encourage mixed-use developments. A slightly smaller portion (36.6%) of the cities in 2010 indicated having a formal mixed-use effort embedded in their zoning codes. Of significance is that mixed-use development can exist as part of a zoning code or it can exist as part of a city's comprehensive plan where it is encouraged but not necessarily required. In some cases, cities can combine elements of infill with mixed-use and downtown revitalization to achieve smart growth goals. For example, in 2016, the City of Fort Collins approved an infill mixed-use development known as the "320 Maple" project (Duggan, 2016). This project combines an apartment building with commercial space in the historic downtown area of Fort Collins. The development is also considered infill due to the underutilized land being located within an otherwise well-developed area of the city.

Zoning Variances for Sustainable Development

Both the 2010 and the 2016 surveys asked about some of the most common zoning variances for sustainable development. Both surveys show a similar level of engagement in these types of zoning variances. In 2016, density variances were available in 29.3% of the cities and parking variances were available in 27.9% of the communities. In 2010, 22.3% reported having density variances and 20.8% of the cities reported having zoning codes that allowed solar, wind, or other renewable energy production mechanisms on residential developments. These types of zoning variances depart from traditional zoning practices to provide a mechanism to encourage various forms of sustainable development within existing zones. By allowing a developer to build at a higher density and/or with fewer parking requirements, it is thought to be possible to direct growth away from open space and greenfields and instead provide an incentive to direct growth where it will be more sustainable. Furthermore, by using land use codes to encourage sustainable development, a city might be able to approach growth in a *smarter* way than they otherwise would.

Open Space or Farmland Preservation

Open space and/or farmland preservation programs are both central aspects of smart growth representing Principle 6 in the list. A key consideration of a smart growth approach to development is that open space and working land is preserved as much as possible. While this is certainly present as a consideration in the previous policies discussed, a city might also have a standalone policy or program meant to ensure that open space or farmland is protected and preserved. It is thought by most researchers that land preservation will provide for environmental protection considerations and potentially contribute to economic considerations as well. For example, it is well known that "...open space increases the property values of nearby homes and attracts tourism and recreation. Working lands like farms and ranches support local economies, strengthen the tax base, and provide food" (Smart Growth Network, 2006, p. 14). In the 2010 survey, 18.7% of cities indicated they have a land conservation program and 14.2% report having a program to purchase or transfer development rights in order to preserve open space. In the 2016 survey, we see a higher level of engagement in open space preservation efforts with 43% of the cities surveyed indicating they have an explicit open space preservation program and another 12.7% affirming the adoption of a farmland preservation policy or program. Explicit open space preservation policies are some of the most criticized of all smart growth-related efforts, with concerns over the potential these programs have to increase social exclusion in cities. For example, growth restrictions and preservation policies in California are frequently cited as reasons for the high cost of housing (Frieden, 1983).

Park and Recreation Development

Park and recreation development programs are a bit less clearly related to smart growth than the other policies discussed in this chapter. However, a key outcome that smart growth seeks to achieve is that of a high-quality and livable place for all Americans. Parks and recreation development efforts are certainly related to the pursuit of Principle 5 of smart growth, creating a unique, interesting quality of life for residents. By explicitly focusing on the public provision of parks and recreation opportunities, it is believed that cities will create a place that improves the well-being of residents, provides for social capital, and ultimately improves the community's health. Parks and recreation development policies were the highest reported policy in smart growth with almost 65% of the cities affirming the presence of a public effort to provide parks and recreation opportunities. To be sure, this does not give us quite enough information to assess the fairness, distribution, or quality differences that might exist across a community in the provision of these parks and recreation. However, it does give us a glimpse into the tendency for cities to use public resources to develop parks and/or recreation opportunities for the residents of their communities. This is likely not a surprise to many local governments given this is such a common policy for local governments to have. However, if a community can make the connection between park provision and smart growth, sustainability might be a bit easier to reach. Providing parks throughout a community can increase physical activity (and therefore reduce public health expenses), lower stress levels, encourage social cohesion, and provide for a quality place where people want to live.

Overall Smart Growth

Although the 2010 and 2016 surveys provide us with evidence that smart growth policies are not rare across American cities, comparatively little is known about how well these policies are achieving their goals and how, if at all, communities are measuring the performance of these efforts. As previously mentioned, some significant concerns have been raised over the negative consequences of a city engaging in just a few of these smart growth principles while not fully engaging in others (Downs, 2003). As Downs (2003) points out, "The smart growth elements least likely to be adopted are those needing large public subsidies". Furthermore, Downs (2003) goes on to affirm that "...the other main smart growth policies restrict the supply of land usable for development. That normally places upward pressure on prices of both new and existing units, making housing less affordable than it would otherwise be". It does not take long to find examples of cities that are viewed as high quality, unique, and "smart-growthy" but that also suffer from significant affordable or low-income housing shortages. Given this very real concern over social sustainability problems associated with smart growth, it is important to understand and assess the performance of these efforts.

Performance Measurement in Smart Growth

The level of performance measurement reported in the 2016 sample is detailed in Table 7.3. Similar to most of the policies profiled across all of the chapters in this book, most cities do not measure the performance of their smart growth efforts. Even fewer report linking the performance of these policies to the budget for those efforts. If we are to use performance measurement as one mechanism to recognize and to try and avoid

Table 7.3 Performance Measurement in Smart Growth

Performance Measurement: Percentage of Cities Reporting (Performance Linked to the Budget)
1 Active Brownfields Program: 5.6% (2.4%)
2 Downtown revitalization efforts: 15.9% (6.5%)
3 Main Street programs: 10.2% (1.8%)
4 Policies or programs encouraging infill: 4.2% (0.5%)
5 Incentives or programs to encourage mixed-use development: 8.3% (1.4%)
6 Density zoning variances for sustainable development: 6.1% (0.9%)
7 Parking zoning variances for sustainable development: 6% (0.5%)
8 Open space preservation policies/programs: 9.3% (0.9%)
9 Farmland preservation programs/policies: 2.3% (0.9%)
10 Park and recreation facility development: 14.3% (7%)
11 Local historic preservation policies/programs: 10% (1.4%)

or mitigate negative outcomes from smart growth efforts, this low level of assessment is concerning.

The measurement of performance across these 11 policies ranges from a low of 1.8% for mainstreet programs to a high of 15.9% for the downtown revitalization efforts. This represents some of the lowest level of performance measurement seen across the various subsets of sustainability examined in this book. However, unlike other policy areas profiled in this book, every policy in the smart growth category had at least one city reporting that they linked the performance of that policy to the budget for that effort. When a city links performance of an effort to the budget, it is likely that the outcomes will be of greater importance for the continuation of that effort. Even though the overall engagement in performance measurement for smart growth efforts is low, much can be learned from the cities that do make an effort to measure how well the programs are doing so that other interested cities might find inspiration to develop metrics and processes of their own.

Performance Measurement: Common Metrics in Smart Growth

Table 7.4 outlines the performance metrics used by cities in the 2016 survey to gauge the effectiveness or efficiency of their smart growth efforts. This table also lists some sample goals and performance outcomes found in cities across the country. These sample goals and current performance levels can serve as a starting point for identifying potential benchmarks or targets for cities interested in expanding their performance measurement activities.

Table 7.4 Reported Metrics Used to Assess Smart Growth Efforts

Performance Metrics	*Sample Benchmarks*
• Acres of open space (per capita or otherwise)	**Oxford, Connecticut:** 40% of a subdivision site should be preserved as open space
• Jobs/housing ratios	**Fairfax, Virginia:** 1..5 jobs per household recommended target
• Acres/number of brownfields sites	**Minneapolis, Minnesota Measure:** Clean up 170 sites over 10 years
• Population density	**San Francisco, California:** 18,176 people per square mile and is compared against peer average of 8,863.
• Gentrification vulnerability measures	**Los Angeles, California:** Since 2000, the city hosts a geographic information system (GIS)-based tool for visualizing demographic changes by zip code. The "Los Angeles Index of Neighborhood Change". See www.arcgis.com/home/item.html?id=57e9231c3bd34d44ae49b309b0cb440e#overview
• Number of historical buildings preserved	**Alexandria, Virginia:** 100% of properties adhere to local regulations protecting historic sites
• Walkability measures	**New Rochelle, New York Goal:** Increase by 5% the number of streets served by sidewalks
• Developed land (per capita or otherwise)	**Baton Rouge, Louisiana:** At least 10% of all new development should consist of infill and redevelopment
• Percentage of housing near mass transit	**New Rochelle, New York Goal:** 65% of all new development within 1/2 mile of train station
• Expenditure on recreation and parks	**San Francisco, California:** $213 per resident spent on recreation and parks
• Other	**EPA:** The EPA houses information on a smart growth INDEX meant to assist in assessing local smart growth efforts. **www.epa.gov/smartgrowth/smart-growth-index**

The metrics shown in Table 7.4 can be largely categorized as output or outcome measures of local smart growth efforts. In this survey, no city reported a process or workload measure for their smart growth efforts. However, land-use planning processes—including smart growth specific efforts—can easily lend themselves to process performance measures. For example, most development approval processes require a formal review from some group in the city (commission or council is most common). The time that a development proposal spends in the review process could be an important indicator concerning the performance of the actual planning and development system of the local government. Long wait times for approval can deter development and would be cause for concern in many cities. Additionally, expedited review processes can be sought for development that is more sustainable in nature. Without a baseline measure for how long an average review takes to complete, it is difficult to assess the success or appropriateness of an expedited process for sustainable development. This type of performance measurement activity can provide important information to citizens, to prospective or current developers, and to the local government seeking to improve their processes.

Given the very low level of engagement in performance measurement coupled with the serious concerns over negative social outcomes from smart growth efforts, it is imperative that cities consider other possible metrics and mechanisms to assess and monitor the outcomes—intended and unintended—of their smart growth efforts. For example, many of the metrics presented in Table 8.2 in the next chapter can help a city avoid the common problems identified with smart growth. Furthermore, engaging in social sustainability (see Chapter 8) policies and programs can potentially provide an additional avenue to achieve sustainability goals related to development and growth without missing important social considerations or exacerbating challenging social conditions.

In order to better understand and to provide an example of this concept in action, the following case study on Kansas City, Missouri, provides a valuable inside look at one city's downtown revitalization efforts. Kansas City's case study shows a unique and historical streetcar development project that was able to overcome challenges, increase foot traffic, and provide economic benefits while also serving the residents of the city. As Eric Roche and Kolbe Krzyzanowski describe in the case that follows, Kansas City was able to successfully finance and develop a streetcar in their downtown to encourage alternative transit and to increase visitors to their downtown. This streetcar project, although not without problems, has provided a potentially transformative development to spur the continued revitalization of downtown Kansas City. This streetcar project represents several of the smart growth principles discussed in this chapter. First, this project represents a downtown revitalization project that focuses development attention on older, well-developed portions of the community. Second, this streetcar provides a mechanism to encourage walkable neighborhoods and to create a unique and interesting place (Principles 4 and 5). Finally, of consequence and as a point of praise for doing the work to collect this information, the authors detail the process of data gathering to assess this project through surveys. The authors readily admit that although this streetcar has many successes, it is also important to know the ongoing data collection has shown that the riders tend to be wealthier. This brings up the concerns about social sustainability discussed throughout this chapter. However, as an additional point of praise, Kansas City does an excellent job of assessing this project and being aware of these types of concerns and realities. Understanding and identifying these issues is perhaps half the battle.

CONCEPT IN ACTION: A STREETCAR FOR ECONOMIC DEVELOPMENT—THE STORY OF KANSAS CITY, MISSOURI

By: Eric Roche and Kolbe Krzyzanowski

Within a short period, Kansas City (KC) has experienced a cavalcade of proactive urban development. The KC Streetcar follows nearly 30 years of cultural and economic development projects in the downtown area of the city. In May 2016, KC's first modern streetcar began operation. It had been 59 years since the City's last streetcars stopped running in the community after this mode of transportation fell out of favor nationwide due, in part, to increased car ownership and the belief that buses would offer cheaper and more flexible public transportation options (Market Street Railway, 2017). At one point in history, KC had one of the most extensive streetcar systems in the United States (Horsley, 2013). However, in the 59 years since the KC streetcars stopped operation, the city became known as a "car town". Today, the city has more freeway lanes per capita than any other city in the United States (City Planning and Development, 2017). This translates to the fifth quickest average commute time among the 50 largest metro areas in the United States (Cronkleton, 2016). About 83% of metro workers drive alone to their places of employment in KC.

History

As Dodd (2002) recounts, the first franchise of the Metropolitan Street Railway Company was opened in Kansas City in 1870 by Thomas Corrigan and William Rockhill Nelson, and was converted from horse-drawn cars to electric cars in 1908. The electric streetcar system closed in 1957. The newly developed streetcar line marks the first operational streetcar line in KC in 59 years. The history of KC's modern streetcar development effort has its roots in the opening of the Leedy-Voulkos Gallery in 1985 and the establishment of the First Friday's art and culture events in 1995. Additional major downtown development included the construction of the Kansas City Power & Light districts between 2005 and 2008. The Power & Light district (see www.powerandlightdistrict.com) is a downtown development project that has garnered its share of criticisms from both voters and patrons, but nevertheless this particular development appears to be one of the primary catalytic projects in Kansas City. The streetcar project punctuates a major stage in this cycle of downtown development and in the development of Kansas City as a Midwestern metropolis ready to compete on a national and international scale.

Approval process in Kansas City, Missouri (KCMO)

A previous mayor, now a congressional representative, had once called the idea of building new streetcars in Kansas City "touristy frou-frou" (Diuguid, 2014). This image stuck with many KC residents and the new streetcar faced a steep challenge to find public approval. However, in 2012, residents within 1/3 of a mile of the proposed starter line approved both a 1% sales tax and a real property mill tax increase to fund the construction and the operation of the streetcar system.

Construction Financing and Financial Performance

With a budget of $102 million, the KC Streetcar is a project with middling cost that comes in lower than many other similar projects in other cities. For example, the cost per mile of track in KC is $25.35 million. This cost is only slightly higher than the costs realized by the city of Portland, Oregon ($22.43 million per mile). However, the KC Streetcar costs were less than several other national cohorts like Tucson, AZ ($28.26 million per mile), and Cincinnati, OH ($36.76 million per mile) (Horsley, 2015a). Still, the KC Streetcar has its own unique financial story that helps demonstrate the realities of this type of project.

The 2.2 mile route for the KC downtown streetcar project costs $102 million (Horsley, 2015a). The KC Streetcar uses *Transportation Development District* (TDD) financing, which levies a 1% sales tax (one cent on the dollar), and a special assessment on all properties within the designated TDD to help fund the streetcar project. The revenues from the TDD go toward paying debt service on $63,955,000 in special obligation bonds issued by the city to finance the initial streetcar development (Horsley, 2015a). Other funding for this project comes from two federal grants. The City of Kansas City received federal grants for roughly $17 million toward the streetcar project, followed by another $20 million in federal TIGER grants. Initial estimates put the KC Streetcar construction $250,000 under budget and initial operational costs under budget as well. The Kansas City Treasury Department reported that the sales tax collections in the TDD outperformed projections by almost a million dollars, citing a collection of $4.8 million versus a $3.9 million projection (Horsley, 2015a). These projections come on the heels of final construction, even before the opening of the streetcar.

The RideKC Streetcar authority reports a marked growth in property value relative to the streetcar line, with sales tax receipts growing by 58% since 2014 (see Figure 7.2). This growth was

ANNUAL SALES TAX RECEIPTS						
	2014	2015		2016		2014-2016
	Actual	Actual	Growth	Actual	Growth	Growth
Downtown TDD	$3,451,822	$4,772,466	38.3%	$5,458,896	14.4%	58%
City-wide Total	$198,085,065	$224,522,627	13.3%	$229,816,923	2.4%	16%

Figure 7.2 Tax Receipt Growth.

faster than the overall sales tax growth reported by the citywide sales tax receipts (16%).

Construction Process

Construction on the project began on May 22, 2014. Construction and testing would take nearly two years due to the considerable amount of time required to relocate utilities buried underneath the streets and the actual process of laying the track for the streetcar. During this time, the City' Water Services Department used the construction as an opportunity to replace water mains and sewer lines along the streetcar corridor, reducing the need to close the streetcar system down in the future due to water and sewer line breaks from old infrastructure. This is one instance in which the streetcar was used as a catalyst for necessary economic development goals, such as the construction of new infrastructure and updating of old systems.

One of the criticisms levied against the streetcar was that it would eliminate street parking in front of businesses. The logic from many in the business community is that this street parking was vital to the health of their businesses. Unfortunately, due to the realities of construction, many businesses did end up having their parking impacted during construction. However, public sentiment among shop owners along the route was that most seemed frustrated with the construction, but they were also understanding of the long-term benefits the streetcar would bring.

Construction was completed on the streetcar line in November 2015, marked by the arrival of car 801 in Kansas City (Horsley, 2015b). A period of testing followed with an official opening of the streetcar line for service on May 6, 2015. Much of the early testing of the streetcar involved towing by tow truck along the tracks to test the recently constructed routes, ballasting with sandbags to test weight tolerances, test-drivers, and test-passengers. Testing continued for seven months until the streetcar opened to the public on May 6, 2016 to great fanfare. City and streetcar employees worried about the public perception the testing process would generate. After all, the first vision people would have of the expensive, brand-new system would be a tow truck pulling it along the line. Ultimately, many residents seemed to understand the testing despite the long period of intensive testing that occurred.

Ridership

Ridership was originally estimated to average 2,700 passengers per day. However, in the first year of operation, the streetcar averaged 6,798 passengers per day. Ridership tends to peak around lunchtime and then peaks again around 7:00 pm (Figure 7.3).

The streetcar's performance has been very strong so far in Kansas City, MO, compared to other streetcar systems across the country. Average daily ridership is higher than several other systems. Passenger counts are still below that of the Portland, Oregon, Streetcar. However, Portland, Oregon, enjoys a much more built out and complete streetcar system than what KC currently has developed. When compared on a ridership-per-mile basis, the KC Streetcar ranks ahead of several of its peers. At least part of this can be explained by the streetcar line being located within the city's densest, most urban development. It will be interesting and telling to see how ridership per mile changes over time if the streetcar expands to less dense areas outside of the downtown (Figures 7.4 and 7.5).

These ridership figures have continued to grow since the initial launch of the streetcar, with average daily passengers increasing throughout the week. Saturdays remain the busiest day for streetcar travel.

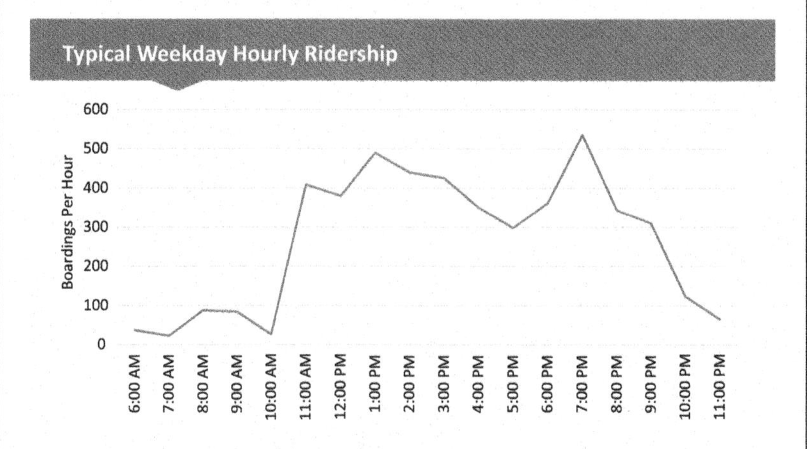

Figure 7.3 Typical Weekday Hourly Ridership.

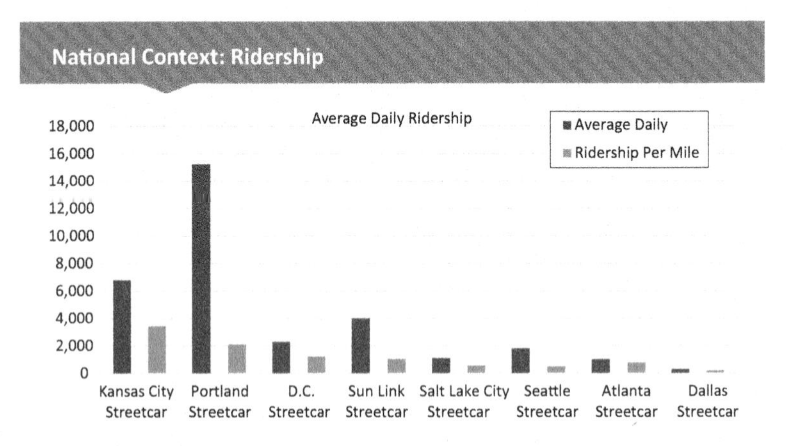

Figure 7.4 Ridership Comparison.
Source: http://us3.campaign-archive2.com/?u=c08008bb7ee39d4bfcccf757f&id=24b6842df5.

	Total	Total Average	Average Weekday	Average Saturday	Average Sunday
June 2016	182,248	6,075	5,270	9,421	5,625
June 2017	217,129	7,238	6,639	11,589	6,180

Figure 7.5 Year-to-Year Ridership.
Source: KC Streetcar.

Streetcar Business Survey

In the summer of 2016, the Streetcar Authority asked Kansas City's Office of Performance Management to perform a survey of businesses[1] to collect feedback on the impact of streetcar operations. The Office of Performance Management was selected to do this work because it functions as somewhat of an independent authority that does not report to the Streetcar Authority. The Office of Performance Management also had a great deal of experience in design of the user and resident surveys, and also agreed to perform the survey for free.

Employees ended up calling, emailing, or visiting over 80 small businesses in the process of gathering these data. The survey covered every known business within the streetcar financing district. Ultimately, 41 small businesses responded to the survey requests. The respondent's business type included a diversity of businesses including restaurants, retail, bars, coffee shops, and more.

One question on the survey asked respondents to detail the level of impact that the KC Streetcar has had on their business since it began operating; 97% of respondents said it has had an impact, whereas 22% said that it had had some impact (Figure 7.6).

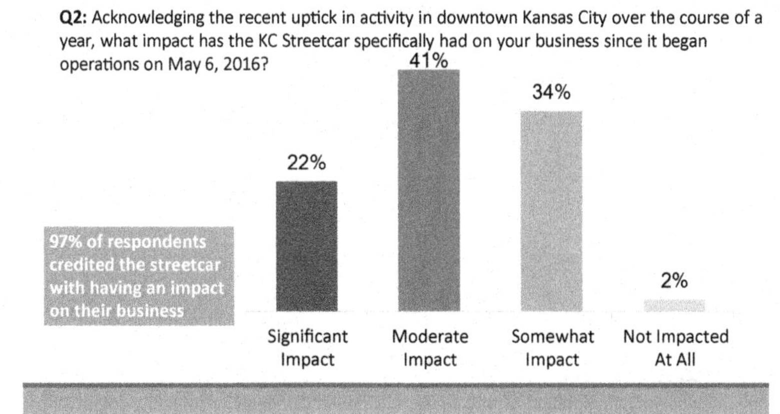

Figure 7.6 What Impact Has the KC Streetcar Specifically Had on Your Business since It Began?

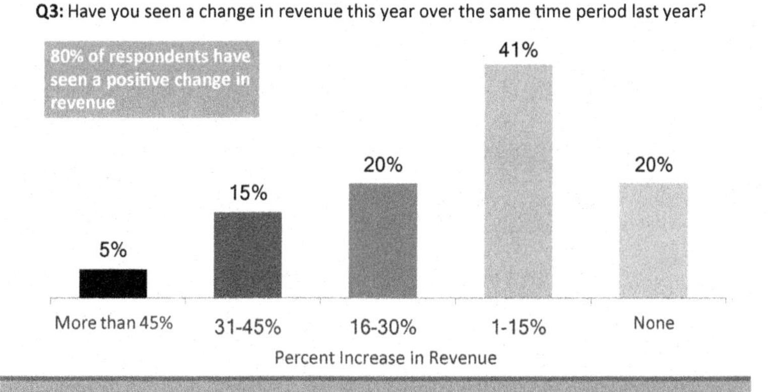

Figure 7.7 Have You Seen a Change in Revenue This Year over the Same Time Period Last Year?

Another question asked was whether the businesses had seen a change in revenue in the past year; 80% of businesses had seen a positive change in revenue since the launching of the streetcar (Figure 7.7).

Not surprisingly, and of importance, 83% of businesses reported seeing a positive change in foot traffic. Most of this comes during lunch hours (Figures 7.8 and 7.9).

The survey also asked "What adjustments have you made in your business due to the addition of the KC Streetcar to downtown?"

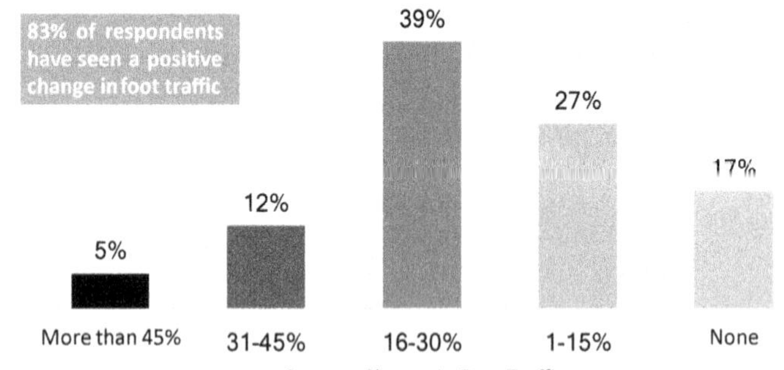

Figure 7.8 Have you Seen a Change in Foot Traffic This Year over the Same Time Period Last Year?

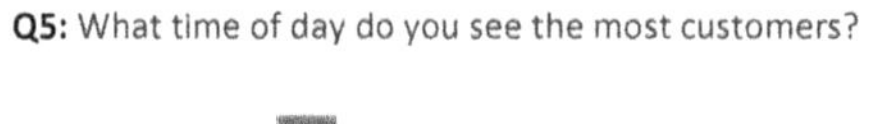

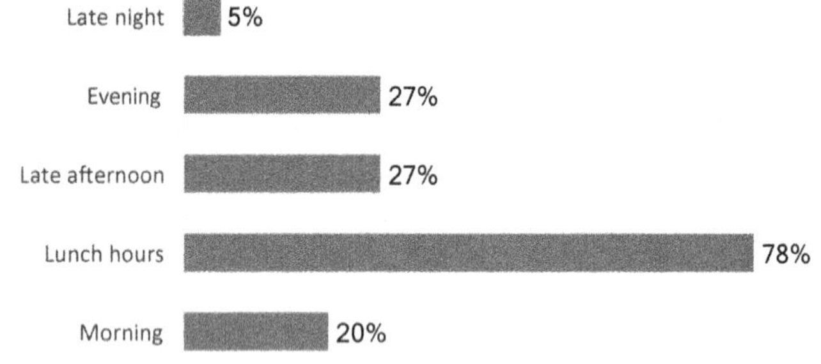

Figure 7.9 What Time of Day Do You See the Most Customers?

17% had changed their hours of operation, 39% had hired additional staff, and 13% had changed their service or menu. Respondents were also asked what further improvements to the KC Streetcar system would be beneficial to their business. The most common response was to "expand the streetcar line", but many of the other results had to do with a larger transportation ecosystem or with further strengthening the tie between the streetcar system and local businesses (Figure 7.10).

26 responses

Q8: What KC Streetcar related improvements would be beneficial to your business?

- Expand the streetcar line (9 responses)
- Satisfied with the results (4 responses)
- Plan for additional parking (4 responses)
- Develop a Park & Ride (2 responses)
- Advertising opportunities for those businesses with a Main Street address (4 responses)
- Develop a map pinpointing area restaurants (2 responses)
- Make improvements to traffic at certain intersections (1 response)

Figure 7.10 What KC Streetcar Related Improvements Would Be Beneficial to Your Business?

21 responses

Q9: Additional Comments

- Expand the streetcar line
- It has been a fantastic addition to the city
- We love the streetcar
- The streetcar is greatly impacting most local businesses in a positive manner.
- Glad the construction is done
- Without the streetcar as an option, customers would not have visited my store at the City Market
- We need more parking
- Investment of time, energy and construction detours have paid off
- We are happy to have the streetcar as a benefit to our employees and customers
- I see the streetcar bringing more people downtown.
- Bring more retail on the line
- Nothing but positive results to our business
- Construction impacted my business and revenue fell during construction
- With the streetcar people now have the option of exploring more of our city
- The streetcar and streetcar staff are some of the nicest and greatest additions to our city

Figure 7.11 Additional Comments.

About half of respondents also left an additional comment on the survey. Most were positive, although a few alluded to the cost (to the business) of streetcar system construction as a negative aspect of the project (Figure 7.11).

Citizen Survey Results

The City of Kansas City, Missouri, conducts a stratified random sample survey of residents to measure their satisfaction with a variety of city services. The survey is delivered by mail to approximately 9,000 households per year and has an overall response rate of about 48%. It is balanced against several census demographic and geographic factors. The resident survey not only allows the City to measure how residents perceive a variety of services but also asks experiential questions, including some about the KC Streetcar.

One year into streetcar operation, 42% of residents report having ridden the streetcar at least once. Of this group, 14% also reported riding a bus within the past year, whereas 28% had only ridden the streetcar and no other form of public transportation. Results vary significantly across each of the City's Council Districts. The fourth district, which is where the streetcar is physically located, saw the highest reported use at 51% of residents indicating that they had used it in the past year. Interestingly, despite its relative geographic proximity to the streetcar, the third district ranked lowest for reported use (25%).

The same survey allows the City to examine ridership from many demographic variables. Income, for example, shows a clear trend where people with higher income were more likely to report using the streetcar. This may be partially due to the streetcar being located downtown, a wealthier portion of the city (Figure 7.12).

A clear pattern also emerges when looking at ridership by age. Younger people were much more likely to report using the streetcar, whereas the city's older residents were least likely to have reported using it (Figure 7.13).

The survey also asks about resident satisfaction with the streetcar. This metric can then be split into two groups: Those who report using the streetcar and those who did not (Figure 7.14).

As expected, satisfaction among streetcar riders was much higher. Interestingly, not only were non-riders more likely to be

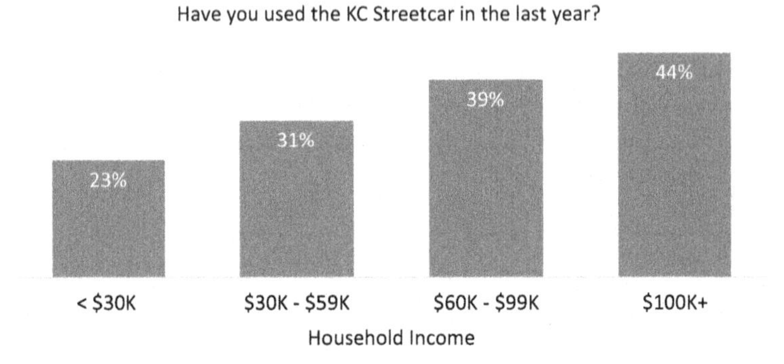

Figure 7.12 Use of KC Streetcar by Income Level (Annual).

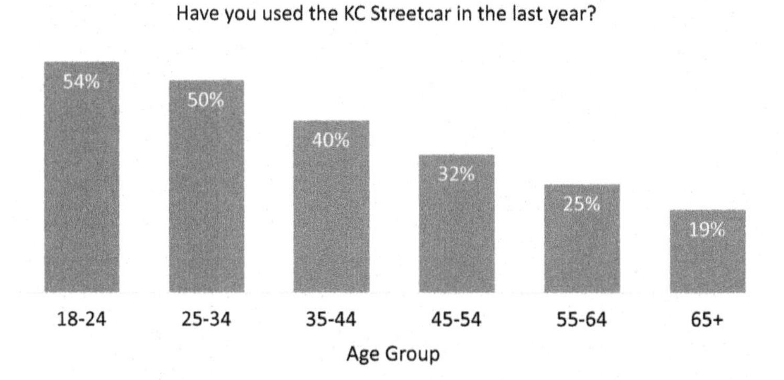

Figure 7.13 Use of KC Streetcar by Age (Annual).

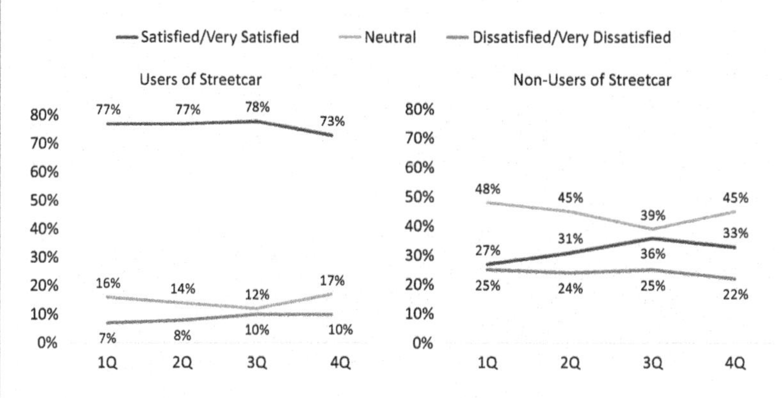

Figure 7.14 Satisfaction by User Groups by Quarter.

neutral (expected) but also more likely to be dissatisfied. Finally, the survey asks residents to rate their satisfaction with public transit (all modes) over time. The streetcar came online in Fiscal Year 2017, which coincides with a relatively large increase in resident satisfaction in public transit in the city. At this time, there were no major changes to the Kansas City Area Transportation Authority's (KCATA) bus system that might explain this significant increase in citizen satisfaction over public transit in the city (Figure 7.15).

Economic Development

The streetcar was set forth from inception not only as a new means of public transit but as a catalytic project for economic development. Following a national trend, the development of the streetcar seeks to bridge larger development goals related to the attraction of

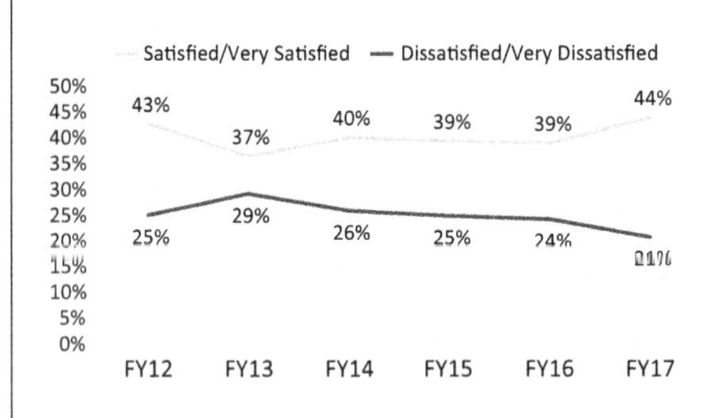

Figure 7.15 Satisfaction with Public Transportation over Time.

investment with smaller goals related to the building of community, the connection of neighborhoods, and improving the walkability of the city's major business centers. The infrastructure put in place during the initial streetcar route has been used to collect data in Kansas City's continuing effort to join the Smart City movement.

The streetcar has been pursued beyond its initial routes and service areas as a means of connecting geographically dispirit areas of the city with mixed success. The mail-in election regarding the southern expansion of the KC Streetcar in early August 2017 was successful in establishing a new TDD to finance the proposed line. This vote for expansion came on the heels of several failed votes to expand the car eastward to some of the more economically distressed parts of the city; reasons cited in these failed votes were that the expansion plan funding for east-west bound routes was not based on financially feasible plans. The proposed TDDs and tax redirections would not sufficiently cover construction and operation, in addition to placing an unwanted tax burden on the properties in the area.

Points of Criticism

The development of the KC Streetcar has shown a great deal of success in its short life span. Public opinion is largely in favor of developments to public transportation options in KC. It is important, however, to acknowledge where there is uncertainty and room for healthy debate. As with all issues involving broad public infrastructure investment and invasive construction, one must be cognizant of all arguments. The issue of investment is a particularly nebulous argument. The estimates put investment within the TDD of the KC Streetcar to be $1.8 billion in a combination of public and private investments. Proponents of the streetcar label this as catalytic investment caused by the city's investment in this area. Opponents argue that this investment is due entirely to the ongoing favoring of the West Crossroads, River Market, and Downtown areas, and has nothing to do with the city's investment in the streetcar. In reality, this increase in investment is likely due to a combination of factors. It is true that a huge proportion of the investment in Kansas City has been in the three aforementioned areas, but many view the streetcar as an essential bridge of connectivity to these areas in which traditional transportation provides a significant barrier for commerce. Some of the $1.8 billion in new investment is sure to have resulted as a catalytic consequence of newly accessible foot traffic and ease of transportation the streetcar provides, and by the same token one must acknowledge that much of the investment in these areas would continue with or without a new public transit system.

Regardless of the available data, focus groups, studies, or financial analyses of the KC Streetcar and streetcars nationwide, there is likely to be no hard and fast conclusion as to whether streetcar infrastructure is "good" or "bad" for a city. The determination of this question is ultimately based on a combination of policy goals, financial outcomes, and ultimately the opinion of the citizen practitioners.

Note

1 Streetcar Business Survey—http://kcstreetcar.org/business/.

References

Akimoto, F. (2009). The birth of 'land use planning' in American urban planning. *Planning Perspectives*, *24*(4), 457–483.

Campbell, S. (1996). Green cities, growing cities, just cities? Urban planning and the contradictions of sustainable development. *Journal of the American Planning Association*, *62*(3), 296–312.

Chapin, T. S. (2012). Introduction: From growth controls, to comprehensive planning, to smart growth: Planning's emerging fourth wave. *Journal of the American Planning Association*, *78*(1), 5–15.

City Planning and Development. (2017). Available at: http://kcmo.gov/planning/kcmo-overview/.

Cronkleton, Robert. (2016). Kansas City area's commutes are among the quickest in the nation. *The Kansas City Star*. January 25, 2016.

Diuguid, Lewis. (March 26, 2014). Streetcar plan in Kansas City is more than 'touristy frou-frou'. *The Kansas City Star*.

Division 4.2, Fort Collins Municipal Code. *Urban estate zoning.* Available at: https://library.municode.com/co/fort_collins/codes/land_use?nodeId=ART4DI_DIV4.2URESDI. Retrieved May 14, 2017.

Dodd, Monroe. (2002). *A splendid ride: The streetcars of Kansas City, 1870*1957.* Kansas City, MO: Kansas City Star Books.

Downs, A. (2003). *Growth management, smart growth, and affordable housing.* Brookings Institute. Available at: www.brookings.edu/on-the-record/growth-management-smart-growth-and-affordable-housing/. Retrieved August 4, 2017.

Duggan, Kevin. (2016). Fort Collins council approves Maple St. housing project. *Fort Collins Coloradoan.* www.coloradoan.com/story/news/2016/07/12/fort-collins-council-approves-maple-st-housing-project/86995650/.

Elliott, D. (2008). *A better way to zone: Ten principles to create more livable cities.* Washington, DC: Island Press.

EPA. (2017). Brownfields. Available at: www.epa.gov/brownfields/overview-brownfields-program.

Feiock, R. C. (2004). Politics, institutions and local land-use regulation. *Urban Studies*, *41*(2), 363–375.

Frieden, B. J. (1983). The exclusionary effect of growth controls. *The ANNALS of the American Academy of Political and Social Science*, *465*(1), 123–135.

Godschalk, D. R. (2004). Land use planning challenges: Coping with conflicts in visions of sustainable development and livable communities. *Journal of the American Planning Association*, *70*(1), 5–13.

Horsley, Lynn. (2013). Kansas City's streetcar glory days hold lessons for today. *The Kansas City Star.* November 22, 2013. Available at: www.kansascity.com/news/local/article332277/Kansas-City%E2%80%99s-streetcar-glory-days-hold-lessons-for-today.html.

Horsley, Lynn. (2015a). Kansas City Streetcar costs are comparable to other cities. *The Kansas City Star.* July 02, 2015.

Horsley, Lynn. (2015b). First KC Streetcar vehicle rolls into town. *The Kansas City Star.* November 02, 2015.

Ingram, G. K., Carbonell, A., Hong, Y. H., & Flint, A. (2009). *Smart growth policies.* Cambridge, MA: Lincoln Institute of Land Policy.

Kaiser, E. J., & Godschalk, D. R. (1995). Twentieth century land use planning: A stalwart family tree. *Journal of the American Planning Association*, *61*(3), 365–385.

Ketcham, Braham Boyce. (2009). The Alexandrian planning process: An alternative to traditional zoning and smart growth. *The Urban Lawyer*, 339–357.

Laporte, T. M., & Opp, S. M. (2016). APSA pracademic fellowship: The third epoch: A pracademic view of the EPA's office of policy. *PS: Political Science & Politics*, *49*(4), 923–926.

Levy, J. M. (2009). *Contemporary urban planning.* Upper Saddle River, NJ: Pearson.

Market Street Railway. (2017). Available at: www.streetcar.org/streetcars/1056-1056-Kansas-City-MO/.

Mazmanian, D. A., & Kraft, M. E. (Eds.). (2009). *Toward sustainable communities: Transition and transformations in environmental policy.* Cambridge, MA: MIT Press.

McDonald, J. F., & McMillen, D. P. (1998). Land values, land use, and the first Chicago zoning ordinance. *The Journal of Real Estate Finance and Economics*, *16*(2), 135–150.

Morgan, D. R., England, R. E., & Pelissero, J. P. (2007). *Managing urban America*. Washington, DC: CQ Press.

Opp, S. M. (2009). Environmental review: Experiences of the States in Brownfield Redevelopment. *Environmental Practice*, *11*(4), 270–284.

Opp, S. M. (2016). The forgotten pillar: A definition for the measurement of social sustainability in American cities. *Local Environment*, *22*(3), 286–305.

Opp, S., & Hollis, S. (2005). *Contaminated properties: History, regulations, and resources for community members practice guide# 9* Spring 2005 Southeast Regional Environmental Finance Center EPA Region 4.

Opp, S. & Mosier, S. (2017). *Counting money: Cities love climate policies if they generate local benefits*. Public Administration Review: Speak your Mind. Available at: https://publicadministrationreview.org/climate-change-symposium-local-climate-change-policy/.

Opp, S. M., & Osgood Jr, J. L. (2013). *Local economic development and the environment: Finding common ground*. Boca Raton, FL: CRC Press.

Opp, S. M., Osgood, J. L., & Rugeley, C. R. (2014). Explaining the adoption and implementation of local environmental policies in the United States. *Journal of Urban Affairs*, *36*(5), 854–875.

Opp, S. M., & Saunders, K. L. (2013). Pillar talk: Local sustainability initiatives and policies in the United States—Finding evidence of the "three E's": Economic development, environmental protection, and social equity. *Urban Affairs Review*, *49*(5), 678–717.

Owens, S., & Cowell, R. (2002). *Land and limits: Interpreting sustainability in the planning process*. London, UK: Routledge.

Pendall, R., Martin, J., & Puentes, R. (2006). *From traditional to reformed: A review of the land use regulations in the nation's 50 largest metropolitan areas*. The Brookings Institution. http://dspace.africaportal.org/jspui/bitstream/123456789/5457/1/From%20Traditional%20to%20Reformed%20A%20Review%20of%20the%20Land%20Use%20Regulations%20in%20the%20Nations%2050%20largest%20Metropolitan%20Areas.pdf?1.

Peterson, P. E. (1981). *City limits*. Chicago, IL: University of Chicago Press.

pLAn. (2015). The sustainable city pLAn. Available at: http://plan.lamayor.org/.

Quigley, J. M., & Raphael, S. (2005). Regulation and the high cost of housing in California. *The American Economic Review*, *95*(2), 323–328.

Reps, J. W. (1955). Control of Land Subdivision by Municipal Planning Boards. *Cornell LQ*, *40*, 258.

Smart Growth America. (2017a). What is smart growth? Available at: https://smartgrowthamerica.org/our-vision/what-is-smart-growth/.

Smart Growth America. (2017b). Rebuilding downtown. Available at: https://smartgrowthamerica.org/work-with-us/workshop-types/rebuilding-downtown/.

Smart Growth Network. (2006). This is smart growth. Available at: www.epa.gov/smartgrowth/smart-growth-publication. Retrieved January 4, 2017.

Stever, D. W. (1986). A brief essay on inclusionary zoning and environmental values. *Pace Environmental Law Review*, 4, 155.

Sustainable Cities Institute. (2013). Available at: www.sustainablecitiesinstitute.org/topics/land-use-and-planning/urban-infill-and-brownfields-redevelopment. Retrieved February 22, 2017.

Tombari, E. (2005). "Smart Growth, Smart Choices Series: Mixed-Use Development". National Association of Home Builders. www.siouxfalls.org/Planning/.../CE42E0F023384CF4991708F2DEC28483.ashx.

8 Social Equity and Social Sustainability

The social equity dimension of sustainability, also known as social sustainability, has not been extensively examined by researchers. To date, no singular definition exists for social sustainability. While most scholars agree that social equity concerns are important to the quest for long-term sustainability, very little effort has been made to fully define or understand the concept. Additionally, few empirical studies that focus on local sustainability efforts have included an examination of social sustainability (Opp, 2017). This lack of a consistent definition coupled with a deficit of research into this important aspect of sustainability has made it exceedingly difficult for interested local officials to pursue public policies and programs in this area.

This chapter provides readers with an in-depth look at the definition of social sustainability, a discussion of why the concept matters for local sustainability goals, and some guidance on how local administrators might be able to engage in this policy area in their own communities. Additionally, this chapter explores some of the ways that the performance of social sustainability programs can be measured to ensure effectiveness and efficiency. Finally, this chapter will conclude with this concept in action as written by an administrator working with local homeless programs in Fort Collins, Colorado.

What Is Social Sustainability? A Multidimensional Concept

Social equity is generally conceived to be one of three central pillars supporting the broader goal of sustainability (Campbell, 1996; Opp, 2017; Opp & Saunders, 2013). By conceptualizing social equity in this way it places it on equal footing with economic development and environmental protection for the achievement of a sustainable future (see Figure 8.1). Even though most researchers recognize that social sustainability is important, little has been done to move the concept into practice in local governments in the United States. Additionally, in the limited research that has been conducted on the topic we see that very few cities adopt policies that explicitly target social sustainability

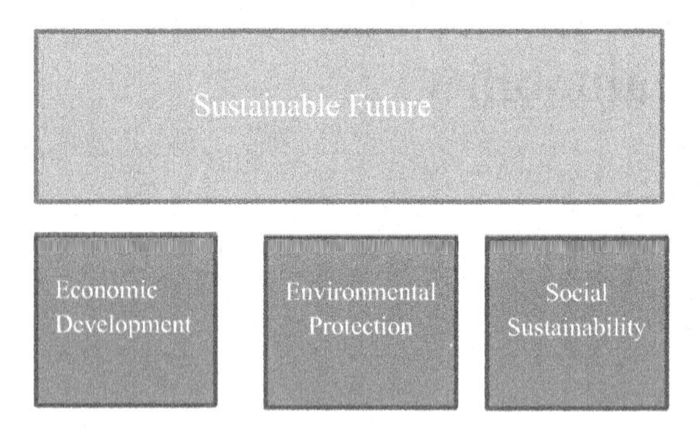

Figure 8.1 Sustainable Future Diagram.

concerns. This is true even in the communities that are labeled as highly sustainable (Opp & Saunders, 2013). Furthermore, when we do see social sustainability policies in a community, they tend to vary widely with no apparent connection to a core definition of social sustainability. In fact, it is often difficult to even determine how social sustainability is defined across this research. For example, in Opp and Saunders (2013), the authors identify a set of nine policies based upon a survey distributed by the International City/County Management Association (ICMA) as ones that represent the social sustainability efforts of the sample of cities. These nine policies range from local community gardens programs to programs meant to provide housing for specific populations within the city. While these policies may reflect elements of social sustainability concerns, the authors do little to explain or justify how these policies work to achieve social sustainability or why they are even able to be labeled as social sustainability policies in the first place. Given the vagueness and lack of consistency in the research on this topic, cities seeking to engage in policy development to achieve social sustainability face a difficult challenge with minimal resources to turn to for assistance.

Ultimately, to date, we have no uniform or consistent definition or common list of social sustainability policies to draw from (Opp & Saunders, 2013; Svara, Watt, & Takai, 2015). In order for communities to approach social sustainability in a way that achieves the underlying goals, it is necessary to have a clearly identified definition as well as a listing of example policies to draw from. In order to fully and appropriately define social sustainability, this chapter will draw from recent research that "...provides a timely review of the interdisciplinary and disjointed literature on social sustainability" (Opp, 2017, p. 1).

The Opp (2017) article defines a socially sustainable city as one where "...all people, regardless of race, ethnicity, gender, or income level must have the ability to enjoy equal access to the fruits of public investment while also being able to satisfy their basic human needs" (p. 6).

Furthermore, "[a] community is not socially sustainable if a subset of the population faces a greater exposure to environmental harms or is less able to enjoy or to access the benefits of public investments" (p. 6). This definition provides a good framework to begin to identify and unpack the complex nature of social sustainability. Drawing from the framework outlined by Opp (2017), it is recognized that social sustainability is a complex and multidimensional concept and includes several interrelated policy dimensions of concern for local governments. These policy dimensions can be loosely sorted into four broad categories: (1) equal access and opportunity, (2) basic human needs, (3) environmental justice, and (4) more abstract concepts related to social cohesion and social capital. Each of these four broad categories is not mutually exclusive, and each also relates to the economic and environmental considerations of sustainability. More will be said on each of these categories in the text that follows.

Dimension 1: Equal Access and Opportunity—The Geography of Opportunity

Equal access and opportunity are both considered important goals for social sustainability in America (Opp, 2017). From a moral and a legal standpoint, equality of access and opportunity are both considered to be foundational goals in the United States. In short, Americans generally expect that everyone should be able to enjoy equal access and equal opportunity to pursue their interests, goals, and achieve upward mobility with hardwork. Any type of discrimination based on race, ethnicity, gender, religion, age, and/or sexual orientation is forbidden in the United States, and a large body of law and policy exists that attempts to prevent discrimination and to promote equal opportunity and access (Mason & Stephenson, 2002). However, even with the presence of decades' worth of laws, court rulings, and policy development, equal access and opportunity are not consistently achieved across the United States. Many policy areas in America show some level of unequal opportunity and unequal access by various subsets of the population (see, for example, Dye, 1971; Ogletree & Robinson, 2015; Welner & Carter, 2013).

Equality of opportunity and access includes a variety of considerations, all of which are important for achieving a sustainable future. A good first step for any community discussing equality concerns is for them to study and document all forms and all types of equal access and opportunity problems that may exist within their jurisdiction. It is probable that each community will face a different set of equal access and opportunity concerns and, as a result, the policies adopted to address this part of social sustainability will vary. Concepts that must be studied include access to public amenities such as parks and open spaces, access to transit options, access to quality public K-12 education, and also access to the government institutions through political voice, participation, and representation.

Opp (2017) highlights four factors that fall under the banner of equal access and opportunity for social sustainability: (1) accessibility of parks, recreation centers, open spaces, jobs, and local services; (2) equal access to transportation; (3) equal opportunities in education; and finally (4) procedural fairness. Each of these four factors has economic, environmental, and also social impacts. A community interested in pursuing social sustainability must be concerned with how equally the fruits of public investment are shared across various subsets of their population. A community with significant inequities in access and opportunity often suffers negative economic and environmental impacts that will jeopardize long-term sustainability (Benner & Pastor, 2012; Burton, 2000; Opp, 2017).

Dimension 2: Basic Human Needs—Housing, Safety, Food, and Income

The second dimension of interest for social sustainability involves whether local residents are able to satisfy their basic human needs with respect to housing, safety, food, and income (Brown, Hanson, Liverman, & Merideth, 1987; Opp, 2017). Housing, sustenance (income and food), and safety are generally identified as three of the primary human needs, and each is important for local social sustainability efforts. Without access to adequate shelter, personal safety, and a basic ability to consume needed items, individuals will be unable to contribute to society and will, instead, likely draw resources away from the community. If a significant subset of the population cannot meet their basic human needs, it is expected that a community will suffer from negative economic and environmental impacts, both of which make sustainability unreachable. Each of the three basic human needs identified as part of social sustainability has relevance to both economic and environmental sustainability and also has a broader impact than just on the people directly affected by the lack of these three needs.

Housing: Homelessness and Affordability Concerns

Housing issues as they relate to social sustainability generally fall into two broad categories: availability of housing and affordable housing. Years of research documents the negative outcomes that cities face when they have problems related to homelessness and/or affordability. To be sure, these two issues are linked in some communities whereby the lack of affordable housing can actually result in an increase in homeless populations. However, at the same time, homeless populations can also be unrelated to the overall affordability concerns. Furthermore, some communities suffer only one of these housing issues, whereas others may suffer from both of these issues.

For many communities, the presence of a local homeless and transient population is the most problematic housing and social issue they face. Although the specific reasons for homelessness vary from person to person, a community that has a homeless population in their jurisdiction will certainly face negative economic, environmental, and social consequences—all which reduce the success of the local sustainability efforts. Most visible for many communities are usually the direct and indirect economic costs associated with the homeless population. Direct costs are expenses that are generally covered by the public through taxes and donations to local nonprofits. These publicly borne costs usually include things like health-care costs, prison/jail expenses, and emergency shelter expenses (National Alliance to End Homelessness, 2017). These direct costs can be quite significant for many communities, with some studies estimating that each homeless person costs the public about $40,000 per year (Moorhead, 2012). At minimum, these direct costs will leave a community with fewer resources to pursue other local policy goals and likely constitute a poor use of scarce resources because these expenditures are not actually focused on fixing the problem in most cities. Indirect costs of the homeless population can be just as problematic for some communities and often include the loss of sales tax revenues and event hosting opportunities in areas plagued by homelessness (see, for example, Roberts, 2016). As revenues decline, a community will have fewer resources available for service provision or for quality of life initiatives—both which detract from the long-term sustainability of a community. These indirect costs can also have a spiraling effect whereby, as the problem emerges, the economic impacts can be magnified through the stigma associated with homelessness.

In addition to the direct and indirect costs associated with homeless populations, this problem also has public health, environmental, and social impacts of concern. Homelessness has been correlated with increases in disease transmission and also to increases in littering. Both outcomes can impact the entire community and can have economic ripple effects (Donovan and Shinseki, 2013). Additionally, homelessness can also be categorized as a significant social problem due to the fact that certain vulnerable populations, such as Armed Forces Veterans and the mentally ill, tend to be overrepresented in the homeless population (Baum & Burnes, 1993; Donovan & Shinseki, 2013).

Although homelessness is a serious problem, a lack of affordable housing can be just as problematic with similarly negative consequences for communities' sustainability efforts. Some of the major consequences that have been identified as resulting from a lack of affordable or accessible housing include environmental degradation through increased commuting (and the greenhouse gas [GHG] emissions that come from that commuting), health-care costs associated with increased stress levels related to those lengthy commute times, educational disparities for children faced with housing insecurity, and residential displacement stemming from gentrification pressures in a tight housing market (Anderson, Charles, Fullilove, Scrimshaw, Fielding, Normand, & Task Force on Community Preventive Services, 2003; Lubell, Crain, & Cohen, 2007). Affordable, accessible, and adequate housing plays an important role in a community's sustainability goals. Sustainability cannot be achieved without a consideration of accessibility and affordability in housing.

Basic Sustenance

Sustenance, as it relates to social sustainability, is concerned with the ability of individuals to meet their basic consumption needs. This usually translates into concerns over income and food. Without adequate income levels, individuals will not be able to meet their needs related to food, clothing, and other necessary consumption items required to maintain a basic standard of living. Healthy food access is also a key component of this dimension of social sustainability. From a broad perspective, a community interested in social sustainability can look to several key indicators in their community to see where problems may exist. First, poverty levels across the various demographic categories can be important indicators of how well these different groups can access needed consumption items. Second, income distribution (in the form of income inequality) across a community can reveal problems with social capital (more on this later) and can also represent a level of residential segregation that might exist in a community. Income inequality has been listed as one of the top 10 global risks of highest concern by the World Economic Forum (2014). A community with significant or increasing income inequality will face substantial economic and social pressure on the local government and on society, which can jeopardize sustainability goals.

From a more narrow perspective, healthy food access is an important part of social sustainability. Food deserts, usually defined as areas without close access to healthy food sources, are a real problem in many communities. Areas with food deserts have been linked to obesity and poor health outcomes (Walker, Keane, & Burke, 2010). Additionally, evidence supports the environmental, economic, and social benefits from locally produced and processed food (Feenstra, 1997). A community that can produce their own food will realize economic benefits through keeping local money in the community, will realize environmental benefits by having fewer trucks transporting food from outside the community, and will have social benefits through the community building that can stem from local food markets.

Safety and Security

Safety and security is also considered a core human need. Without adequate personal safety, residents will be unable to meet any other social needs (Opp, 2017). Additionally, a lack of basic safety and high levels of crime can contribute to environmental and economic problems for a community. For example, locations with increased levels of crime may suffer an economic decline as current development chooses to relocate to a safer community or new development simply decides to not invest in the community at all (Ceccato & Lukyte, 2011). Without a reasonable level of safety in a community, it is impossible to have long-term sustainability. Ongoing crime problems can create a cycle whereby the problem grows in scale as the crime level increases.

Dimension 3: Environmental Justice

Environmental justice is likely the most recognized aspect of social sustainability for observers. Environmental justice is defined by the EPA as the "...fair treatment and meaningful involvement of all people regardless of race, color, national origin, or income with respect to the development, implementation, and enforcement of environmental laws, regulations and policies..." (as cited in Bullard, 2007, p. 26). In simpler terms, environmental justice is concerned with how the environmental *bads*, such as pollution, are distributed across various populations. Additionally, in recent research, environmental justice is also concerned with who gets the environmental *goods*, such as open space access, in life and society (Opp, 2017). For a city to be sustainable, it is necessary to ensure that no subset of the population faces a disproportionate burden of the environmental *bads* and also do not face unequal access to environmental goods.

Dimension 4: Other Hard-to-Measure Concepts—The Value of Place

The final category of interest for social sustainability is a catchall category that deals with more abstract concepts such as social capital and social cohesion. These concepts can be thought of as being broadly part of something we can call "the value of place" (Opp, 2017). "Evidence tells us that where someone lives (their place) influences their lives in ways that are important to understand..." (Opp, 2017, p. 14). Although this factor of social sustainability is more abstract than many of the other factors, there are a few measurable and identifiable components that fall under this category. Specifically, social capital is an important part of this dimension. Social capital generally refers to the ability of people to use high levels of trust, interpersonal relationships, and community networks to come together to achieve a common goal (Paldam, 2001; Putnam, 2001). Communities with high levels of social capital will have residents that participate in the political process, have high levels of health, and will also invest in their community. A quality *place* with increasing social capital stock will have greater successes in long-term sustainability than ones that do not have high social capital stock. Environmental, economic, and social benefits are expected to result from a robust effort at growing social capital.

To say that social sustainability is complex would be an understatement. This part of the quest for sustainability is multidimensional, fragmented, overlapping, and somewhat amorphous. To be sure, moving social sustainability into practice will be a challenge for many cities. The policies that fall under these categories are not easy for most local governments to engage in despite evidence that clearly demonstrates the link between the dimensions of social sustainability described in this chapter and overall sustainability. At this point in the chapter, it is useful to take a step back and consider the broader reasons why cities might struggle with social sustainability and why they should care about pursuing solutions to these difficult problems.

Social Sustainability Matters! The Intersection of Economics, Environment, and Equity

Urban theorists have struggled with questions about how, if at all, a city can engage in policymaking that is redistributive, social equity driven, or even focused on community economic stability as opposed to developmental or allocative policies (Kantor & Judd, 2008; Williamson, Imbroscio, & Alperovitz, 2003). As discussed in the previous two chapters, decades of research has provided a large body of evidence that local governments in America are impacted and constrained by the effects of mobile capital and interjurisdictional competition (see, for example, Peterson, 1981; Opp & Osgood, 2013; Opp, Osgood, & Rugeley, 2014). A primary conclusion of this long history of research is that the interjurisdictional competition for tax revenues, jobs, and wealth can have a perverse effect on a local government's policy choices. It is thought that fundamental limits to local policymaking and revenue raising needs will lead communities to focus on policies that attract and keep mobile capital and wealthier residents in their community (Osgood, Opp, & Bernotsky, 2012). "...[M]unicipalities are constrained in their policy choices by highly mobile capital, interjurisdictional competition, and a need for revenue" (Opp et al., 2014, p. 246).

After the *Great Recession* of the early 2000s, cities report feeling even more constrained by external competition and finite resources than they did in the previously prosperous economic times of the 1990s (Osgood et al., 2012). In an era of increasing demands and scarce resources, it becomes clear to most observers that a rational, although short-sighted, response for many local governments is to adopt policies that will increase local tax revenues, diversify revenue sources, and attract mobile capital. This policy response usually translates into the adoption of policies and programs specifically directed at attracting businesses (and therefore jobs and tax revenues), increasing the proportion of local residents that can contribute to local revenues, and a general shifting of local resources toward the areas that are thought to increase the local revenues and wealth.

It is not hard to find examples from across the country illustrating the significant investment that local governments make in their attempt to attract, retain, or grow businesses and revenues. Tax increment financing (TIF), financial incentives to businesses, and tax credits for development are all common policy tools used to encourage business development and expansion. Even with the large body of evidence that demonstrates these policies do not provide the outcomes desired by communities, these tools still tend to be a city's "go-to" method to try to increase local tax revenues and to provide employment opportunities to local residents. Furthermore, in addition to the lack of benefits derived from these efforts, some observers have cautioned that the quest for mobile capital likely has a negative impact on both the natural environment and on social equity in a community (see, for example, Millimet, 2013; Potoski, 2001; Woods, 2006). It is widely believed and feared that

> ...local governments have incentives to avoid redistributive policies because they offer few benefits and higher costs for those [residents] that cities wish to attract. Jurisdictions deviating from this advice are punished by immigration of lower-income households and emigration of higher-income households and businesses.
>
> (Craw, 2006, p. 361)

Even with this long-standing concern over the negative impacts that competition for economic development can have on local policy choices, some evidence exists that illustrates how economic goals can be effectively merged with environmental goals. As highlighted in Chapters 6 and 7, authors studying economic development have shown that a quality of place, including the presence of environmental amenities, is a powerful economic development tool and need not be viewed as contributing to the decline of economic investment (Koven & Lyons, 2010; Leigh & Blakely, 2013; Opp & Osgood, 2013). Additionally, the author of the best-selling book *The Rise of the Creative Class*, Richard Florida, argued in his books that the quality of a place is actually the key driver of economic development. He goes on to say that people need "...trails or parks close at hand" (p. 289) and a place that is unique and authentic through "...historic buildings, established neighborhoods, a distinctive music scene, or specific cultural attributes" (p. 294). Much of Florida's theory supports the amenity or asset-based economic development strategies that indicate communities should be pursuing a high quality of life through recreational opportunities, lifestyle amenities, and cultural attractions in order to be economically vibrant into the future (Florida, 2012). All of these amenities that Florida calls for in his books work in concert with environmental protection efforts, making this a useful framework for understanding some of the ways that communities can integrate two of the three pillars of sustainability.

While it is generally perceived to be positive to see a connection between environmental protection and economic development, some compelling evidence has emerged that indicates many of these economic development-focused sustainability efforts may actually exacerbate social inequalities across the United States. While this type of effort has undeniably led to some communities enjoying a very high quality of life with desirable environmental amenities, questions emerge about *who* is benefiting from these policies and how these efforts might impact certain populations and overall equity. For example, recent research has expressed a concern that some of the local environmental sustainability efforts are contributing and worsening gentrification and social exclusion problems in communities (Pearsall & Anguelovski, 2016). In fact, as an even clearer example of this concern, in early 2017, Richard Florida announced the release of a new book where he discusses the "urban crisis" of gentrification and inequality in American cities (Florida, 2017). Some might argue that cities rushing to adopt policies meant to attract the *Creative Class* that Richard Florida talked about in his initial books actually created "...a new dimension of urban competition" (Peck, 2005, p. 747) and ultimately contributed to the making or to the expansion of this urban crisis. While the point of this chapter is not to debate the merits of Florida's *Creative Class* theory or to study the interaction between policies seeking to attract the creative class and any social ills that might come from that interaction, it is important to highlight some of what we know about social equity more broadly in American cities and how some of the well-intended policies related to sustainable economic development might have negative side effects that jeopardize long-term sustainability.

A diverse body of evidence highlights the significant range of social equity concerns that exist in American cities—many of which were touched on in the earlier sections of this chapter. These equity concerns vary substantially across the United States and include wicked problems like gentrification, racial or socioeconomic segregation, homelessness, and education inequalities. Some research has explicitly connected social equity problems with efforts that might be labeled under the sustainability umbrella. For example, "...cities that promote economic development by making themselves attractive to the 'creative class'... may be refashioning their cities... in a way that is hostile to some forms of diversity..." (Sullivan & Shaw, 2011, p. 413) and "...smart growth may also result in gentrification" (Pendall, Nelson, Hawkins, & Knaap, 2005, p. 241). By focusing on green space preservation, amenity development, unique public transit options, and other typical sustainable development and smart growth policies, it is possible that communities are losing sight of key equity concerns like affordability, inclusion, and equal access. It is concerning that many of the cities often labeled as the most sustainable in America are also the ones with the highest cost of living in the United States. As Opp (2017) asks, "Given this high cost of living in the cities labeled as sustainable, how does social equity fare? Who is benefitting from these so-called sustainable cities?" (p. 2). Is it possible that many local sustainability efforts are simply creating pockets of concentrated privilege and not actually contributing to long-term sustainability?

While it is clear that many communities struggle with social equity challenges, we do have some evidence that demonstrates that it can be economically advantageous for cities to make explicit efforts to work on improving social equity in their communities. For example, recent research has indicated that "...social equity is correlated with economic growth and the stronger studies have provided evidence of not just correlation, but probably causation..." (Benner & Pastor, 2013, p. 1).

Moving away from the academic studies on this topic, there are also several applied and visible reasons that a lack of social equity is concerning for American cities and the administrators managing them. As described in the earlier section, many social equity problems create environmental or economic problems for a community that can detract from the ability to efficiently manage a city. For example, if a community has a lack of affordable housing, it is likely that the lower income and working-class populations will need to resort to long commutes into the city for employment purposes—the so-called drive until you qualify phenomenon. Ultimately, the sprawl and commuting pattern that come from this issue can have significant environmental and social impacts.

> One can live further away where housing may be less expensive... [but there are] environmental costs resulting from stretching the infrastructure (roads, sewers, water, and power) and the increased pollution from automobiles...[and] there are social costs of having less time with your family and in your community.
>
> (Davis, 2016)

As another visible applied example, residential segregation by race and/or income in a community is often blamed for many of the most difficult social problems facing American cities. It is widely known that concentrated poverty areas have higher crime rates, including homicide

(Lee, 2000). Higher crime rates will lead to an increase in public expenditures on policing efforts. Additionally, poverty and residential segregation can also have significant health impacts, and the costs of these health impacts may end up being borne by the public sector: "...poverty is associated with higher rates of poor health and chronic health conditions in children" (Wood, 2003, p. 709). Next, food deserts are a common reality for lower income areas, which leads to both health and social impacts for these neighborhoods (Cummins, 2014; Walker et al., 2010). As lower income populations face higher health costs, it is not hard to recognize that these health costs will have a larger societal impact and make sustainability very difficult to achieve. Finally, concentrated poverty and residential segregation also lead to disparities in both the funding and the quality of public K-12 education. The disparity in education can have generational impacts on upward mobility and economic opportunity for lower income individuals; this is incompatible with sustainability and will pose significant costs for society (Andrews & Leigh, 2009).

Regardless of whether a community is interested in the moral or ethical reasons that call for them to engage in social sustainability policy development, it is clear that sustainability is not possible without a consideration of these problems. Furthermore, it is clear that there are many self-interested reasons for communities to care about this dimension of sustainability. Unfortunately, based upon survey data, it appears that very few cities are actively engaging in this policy realm.

What Policies Have Cities Adopted in the Pursuit of Social Sustainability?

The most utilized and common data source for researchers studying local sustainability policy in the United States is the 2010 ICMA sustainability survey. Unfortunately, as mentioned already, this survey did an incomplete job at identifying and outlining a full set of social sustainability policies. Nonetheless, this 2010 survey was the first time that any accounting of these types of programs and policies was made. Overall, the responses to this survey showed that most cities do not heavily engage in these types of policies or programs (Opp & Saunders, 2013).

The survey executed for this book project asked cities about a much wider swath of possible social sustainability policies and programs than had been previously documented in the 2010 survey. Table 8.1 lists the policies that were included in the survey as well as the percentage of governments that measure the performance of these policies. As can be seen, the policies fall into four general categories: housing, income programs, local food, and health issues. These four categories capture the areas of social sustainability that cities might be expected to have programs and policies in place for. Altogether, the survey asked about a total of 25 possible policies with room for additional programs and information to be

Table 8.1 Social Sustainability Policies

Policy (Percentage of Cities Reporting)		*Performance Measurement: Percentage of Cities Reporting (Performance Linked to the Budget) (%)*
Housing	Affordability programs (34.1%)	26.6 (3.9)
	Workforce housing (21%)	12 (0)
	Homelessness prevention/ reduction (18.1%)	12 (0)
	Housing for the elderly (25.7%)	21.5 (3.9)
	Housing for the disabled (13%)	6.7 (1.9)
	Housing for veterans (10.9%)	7.9 (2.7)
	Housing for special "at-risk" populations (4.3%)	2.7 (0)
	Foreclosure prevention or assistance (locally provided) (6.9%)	9.5 (0)
	Low-income development incentives (locally funded) (18.5%)	15.8 (5.3)
	Equitable development program (4.0%)	1.4 (0)
	Gentrification prevention policy (2.9%)	2.7 (2.7)
	Other (2.5%)	1.3 (1.3)
Income	Higher than state/federal minimum wage (4.3%)	1.3 (1.3)
	Locally funded income support program (0.7%)	0 (0)
	Other income program (1.4%)	0 (0)
Local food	Local food production policy (15.9%)	10.7 (1.4)
	Local food processing policy (5.4%)	5.4 (0)
	Community supported agriculture program (15.6%)	9.5 (2.7)
	Shared kitchens (4.3%)	4.1 (0)
	Policy on local food use in schools (9.8%)	5.5 (0)
	Policy on healthy food access for citizens (14.9%)	13.2 (0)
	Farmers' market policy (52.9%)	23.8 (9.1)
	Community gardens (47.5%)	25.6 (6.6)
	Publicly supported food cooperative (6.9%)	1.4 (0)
Health issues	Environmental justice program (5.1%)	5.3 (0)
	Special public health concern program (obesity, diabetes, substance abuse, etc.) (19.6%)	19.7 (4.1)

manually typed in by the respondent to ensure we captured all policies considered to be a social sustainability policy. The values in parenthesis in the table indicate the percentage of the cities that report having that policy or program.

Housing Policies

As discussed earlier in this chapter, housing is a central part of social sustainability. The communities responding to this survey demonstrate that a minority of communities have adopted policies related to housing. Across the various types of housing policies and programs asked about in the survey, only a few emerge as being somewhat common. Specifically, programs focusing on housing affordability (as opposed to low income or homelessness) are the most commonly adopted with 34.1% of the cities reporting having an affordability program in place. Moving past the basic affordability programs, the programs designed for specific subsets of a city's population are the second most reported type of policy adopted in this area. Housing for the elderly (25.7%) and workforce housing (21%) represent the next most commonly adopted housing policies.

Policies and programs that focus on homelessness and low-income populations do not fare as well as the broader affordability programs in this group of cities. Only 18% of the cities indicate that they have a homelessness prevention or reduction programs or a locally funded low-income development incentive program. Furthermore, only 2.9% of the cities report having a formal gentrification prevention program. While it is encouraging to see almost one in five cities reporting having some form of a housing program related to lower income populations, much work remains to be done in this area. Across this sample of cities, it appears that moderate-income populations are being focused on for housing assistance while programs to provide for some of the most vulnerable and disadvantaged populations take a secondary position. It is useful to examine a city that has been aggressive in housing policies as a close-up look at how these programs and policies actually work.

Case Example of an Aggressive Housing Program—Nashville

One city emerges from the survey responses as being particularly involved and aggressive in their various housing policies: Nashville, Tennessee. Under the auspices of the Metropolitan Development and Housing Agency (MDHA), Nashville offers residents a variety of housing programs that include programs focused on down payment assistance, foreclosure prevention, affordable housing (rental and homeownership), workforce housing, housing for the elderly/disabled, and also homelessness prevention and reduction programs. While a significant portion of the funding for these programs comes from the federal government and from revenues from agency-owned properties, the city of Nashville also contributes to these programs from their general fund. According to the most recently available financial report for MDHA, the Metro Nashville Government allocated $3.4 million for affordable housing and infrastructure activities in 2016.[1]

MDHA has recently embarked on an ambitious and potentially transformative effort related to housing. As the local newspaper profiled in early 2017,

> If the plan is carried out to fruition, people of all incomes and races will be living side-by-side as neighbors, with the same amenities and opportunities to build a community and prosper in the 'new Nashville'... nothing of this magnitude has ever been accomplished....
>
> (Plazas, 2017)

Under the vision and supervision of the executive director of MDHA, all public housing developments in Nashville will be mixed-income developments in "...prime locations near downtown that will not displace existing residents" (Plazas, 2017). While admitting this lofty goal is ambitious and expensive, MDHA has been very aggressive in seeking out advising and assistance from a nearby university. This university has provided Nashville with guidance and even specific criterion to use to judge the success or failure of these efforts. This judgment criterion list includes both a focus on mixed-income housing provision and also a focus on preventing gentrification—something that is often overlooked in other cities. While it is too early to judge Nashville's success in this ambitious effort, the fact that this city is tackling housing in this way bodes well for social equity in housing for this community.

Income Policies

Access to basic levels of income, living wages, and other income support efforts can be considered part of a community ensuring a basic standard of living for all residents. Not surprisingly, income-focused programs are quite rare in American cities. Less than 5% of the cities in this sample report having a higher-than-required minimum wage and less than 1% of the cities report having any form of a locally funded income support program. Given the very real struggles with service provision, interjurisdictional competition, and scarce resources, adopting policies focused on income provision is likely quite challenging and perhaps considered detrimental to a community's needs. However, one city in this survey emerged as being particularly ambitious in this area, Lewiston, Maine, and warrants a brief overview as an example of an exemplar.

Lewiston is the second largest city in Maine with a population of approximately 36,000 and has seen a significant refugee settlement in recent years. Lewiston's 2010 strategic plan outlines an ambitious and progressive set of goals concerning public involvement, performance measurement, sustainability, and poverty alleviation. The city's strategic plan also calls for a balancing of the three pillars of sustainability in their decision making processes. Of consequence the plan states,

> When undertaking any significant municipal initiatives, consideration will be given to the impact such action will have on Lewiston's poverty level. This would include such areas as economic development, affordable housing, educational attainment, transportation, livable wage jobs, cost-effective health care, childcare, and access to healthy food.
> (Lewiston Strategic Plan, 2010, p. 41)

This strategic plan's goals seem to have resulted in some real programmatic efforts with some early progress to report. In the survey conducted for this book, Lewiston was one of only a few cities to report having a locally funded income support program as part of their social sustainability efforts. Under the direction of the City's Social Services Department, residents are able to apply for and to receive resources under the General Assistance Program to provide for "...basic necessities essential to maintain themselves or their families" (City of Lewiston, 2017a, 2017b). In the city's most recent performance measurement publication, the city's efforts to combat poverty in the non-housing programs served 884 residents. For a community of this size, this is a positive sign for their seriousness of the pursuit of social sustainability.

Local Food Policies

Local food policies and programs have social, economic, and environmental benefits that make them important for sustainability. The responses to the survey indicate that when it comes to food policies and programs only two areas emerge as being common in cities: farmers' markets and community gardens. Slightly over half of the sample of cities report having some sort of farmer's market program and almost half report having a community gardens program. The remaining food policies asked about in the survey were adopted by 15% or less of the communities, with shared kitchens and local food processing representing the least commonly adopted policies.

Health Issues

Some of the food policies and programs in some cities have clear relevance to health; however, the survey also asked about two specific types of health programs: environmental justice programs and any special public health concern program. Only 5% of the cities report having an environmental justice program and approximately 20% report having some form of a special public health program. The most commonly reported public health concern being combatted in this sample of cities is obesity, with diseases like lung cancer or HIV ranking a close second.

Overall, the results of this survey show, even with a wider net of social sustainability policies, most cities are not engaging in this type of policymaking. Furthermore, the policies that are showing higher adoption rates tend to be the ones with a focus on workforce housing and farmers' markets. Policies and programs that are more redistributive or more explicitly focused on lower income populations fall short in this sample.

Performance Measurement in Social Sustainability

Given the complex nature of social sustainability, measuring the performance of social sustainability policies and programs is challenging. Very few cities report that they collect performance data for their social sustainability policies and programs. The survey instrument asked about a number of relevant indicators of the performance of social sustainability and also offered space for communities to add other forms of performance measurement. The major lessons gleaned from this survey with respect to social sustainability will be highlighted in the remaining sections of this chapter.

Performance Measurement Overall Participation Rates

The level of performance measurement occurring in social sustainability policies in this sample is quite low. Table 8.1 shows the percentage of the cities with specific policies that also measure the performance of those policies. The table also shows what percentages of those cities also link the policy or program's performance to the budget. In some cases, such as the local income support programs, no cities report actually measuring the performance of those programs. The areas that see the most performance measurement include the housing affordability programs at 26.6% of cities measuring the performance, the farmer's market programs with 23.8% of cities measuring the performance, and finally the community gardens programs with 25.6% of the cities measuring the performance. It is clear that much remains to be done with respect to measuring the performance of social sustainability programs and policies.

Performance Measurement: Common Metrics

Although most cities do not report measuring the performance of their social sustainability efforts, much can be learned from the cities that do. Table 8.2 lists the performance metrics used by this sample of cities. The table also provides some samples of outcome goals and current

Table 8.2 Performance Measures/Social Sustainability

	Performance Metrics	*Sample Measures/Goals*
Housing	Housing affordability measures	**Lakewood, Colorado Goal:** By 2025, 60% of households in community development block grant (CDBG) qualified neighborhoods will spend less than 45% of income on housing and transportation expenses
	Homeless population counts	**Alexandria, Virginia Goal:** Reduce the number of persons experiencing homelessness to 208. 2017 estimate: 213
	Percentage of low-income housing available	**Seattle, Washington Goal:** Expand the supply of rental units reserved for households earning less than 60% area median income (AMI) each time a measurement is taken
	Housing vacancy rates	**Pittsburgh, Pennsylvania Goal:** 8.7%—based upon the average of comparison regions
	Foreclosure rates	**Pittsburgh, Pennsylvania Goal:** 3.9%—based upon the average of comparison regions
	Housing appreciation rates	**Pittsburgh, Pennsylvania Goal:** 6.3% annually—based upon regional average
	Fair housing compliance annual percentage	**Alexandria, Virginia Goal:** By 2025, 95% or more of housing "tested" passes the federal fair housing act requirements
	Housing segregation index	**Pittsburgh, Pennsylvania Goal:** At or lower than regional average for Duncan Delta Index (measure of how much of the minority population would have to relocate to achieve uniform racial distribution)
Income	Percentage of median household incomes that meet or exceed living wage standard (not specific to a local income program in the survey sample)	**Lakewood, Colorado Goal:** 15% increase in number of households above living wage standard by 2025
Local food	Urban agriculture	**Kansas City, Missouri:** Urban agriculture increased from .75 acres (2005) to 84 acres (2015)
	Number of farmers' markets in the community	**Austin, Texas:** 56% increase in number of farmer's markets from 2011 to 2015
	Acres of community gardens	**Seattle, Washington Goal:** Achieve an annual increase in participation in city gardening program
	Number of food deserts	**Lakewood, Colorado Goal:** Eliminate 100% of USDA-defined food deserts
	Quantity of local food produced	**Denver, Colorado Goal:** Grow and process at least 20% of the food purchased in Denver entirely within Colorado
	Food security	**Baltimore, Maryland Goal:** End food insecurity

Health and safety issues	Average life expectancy	**United States Average (2015):** 78.7 years
	Hospital beds available	**San Francisco, California Goal:** 85% occupancy rate (higher indicates bed shortage risk and lower indicates excess capacity)
	Infant mortality rate	**Baltimore, Maryland Goal:** No more than 6.1 per 1,000 live births
	Nonphysician primary care providers	**Fairfax, Virginia:** 142 per 100,000 in population
	Primary care practitioners per capita	**Fairfax, Virginia:** 8 per 100,000 population
	Suicide rates	**Fairfax, Virginia:** 10 suicides per 100,000 population annually
	Crime rates	**Atlanta, Georgia Goal**: 25% reduction in crime over current Mayor's term
	Time to answer 911 calls	**Atlanta, Georgia Goal:** 100% of all calls answered within 10 seconds (Industry standard)
	Cancer clusters/mortality rates	**Baltimore, Maryland Goal:** No more than 156.1 per 100,000 people
	Asthma cases	**Fairfax, Virginia:** 10.2% of adults with asthma
	Obesity rates	**Pittsburgh, Pennsylvania Goal:** 27.5% or less (based on comparison regions)
	Blood-lead levels in residents	**Kansas City, Missouri 2016 Performance**: 0.06 proportion of children tested with elevated levels
	Air quality at neighborhood level	**Pittsburgh, Pennsylvania Benchmark:** 10 PM2.5 (average of comparison regions)
	Physical activity rates	**Pittsburgh, Pennsylvania Benchmark:** 78% of adults participate in physical activity in the last year (based upon average of comparison regions)
	Participation in recreation programs in the last 12 months	**Alexandria, Virginia Goal:** 50% of households participating each year
	Police response time to serious incidents	**San Francisco, California Goal:** 4 minutes or less
Other	Diversity measures	**Pittsburgh, Pennsylvania Current Measure:** –0.3% change in percent white, non-Hispanic in last year

performance data in cities across the United States. These sample outcome goals and current performance metrics can serve as a starting place for cities interested in setting their own benchmarks for measuring success of their social sustainability efforts.

As discussed in Chapter 1, local performance metrics generally fall into one of four categories: output, efficiency, outcome, and productivity. Most of the metrics cities report collecting for their social sustainability efforts can be categorized as output or outcome measures. However, similar to the other areas of sustainability highlighted throughout this book, cities can also collect and measure performance related more specifically to the output and efficiency of the functioning of the program or policy inside the government structure. For example, a workload (or process) performance measure for social sustainability might be one that measures the city staff time spent on inspecting housing. Furthermore, this workload measure could be combined with an efficiency measure, such as employee cost of housing inspectors, to report a robust productivity measure for this part of the program. This productivity measure could then be reported as a cost *per* housing unit inspected. By reporting this measure in this form, it becomes possible to track changes over time, to understand what the city is spending *in exchange* for some sort of output, and ultimately provide the information to decision-makers, citizens, and program officials in a more user-friendly form.

The cities responding to our survey overwhelmingly agree that lack of resources and lack of political support are the two most significant barriers to achieving successes in their social sustainability efforts. To be sure, many of the programs and policies that fall under the social sustainability umbrella are costly and, as described in this chapter, have stigma that might deter political officials from supporting these efforts. Although the cities that engage in robust social sustainability efforts are still few and far between, the pioneering cities in this area can serve as an example of ways to push forward so that the benefits of sustainability efforts can be realized for all Americans—not just the ones that can afford it.

Conclusions and Concept in Action: Fort Collins, Colorado

Social sustainability is the most complex of the local sustainability areas. Cities pursuing social sustainability will find it necessary to engage in a variety of complex, sensitive, and difficult policy areas. Although the evidence shows that very few cities engage in this policy area, much can be learned from those that do. Using the information in this chapter as a starting point for developing a robust local social sustainability effort is possible, and the evidence supports the benefits of doing so. Furthermore, cities can pursue this area with a deliberate attention to ensuring the performance of these programs is assessed and tracked. The sample benchmarks provided in Table 8.2 provide a good starting place for communities embarking on setting up goals for their own social sustainability efforts.

The following case study, authored by the former Director of Homeward 2020, highlights the case of a coordinated entry program directed at enhancing equity in access to housing. As the case author illustrates, coordinated entry systems can help address the difficult problem of homelessness, but it can also provide a framework to measure and track efficiency and effectiveness of the program.

ENHANCING EQUITY THROUGH EFFICIENT ACCESS TO HOUSING: COORDINATED ENTRY IN NORTHERN COLORADO

By: Vanessa M. Fenley

In Northern Colorado, homelessness has garnered attention from local leaders, businesses, emergency responders, and the community at large. All have voiced increasing concerns with its prevalence and visibility. While conversations can easily migrate toward what resources are lacking, local nonprofit organizations working alongside government agencies have recognized the advantage of reexamining how the resources already existing in the community can be used more effectively and efficiently.

Building off of existing working relationships among nonprofit service providers and by following emerging guidance from the Department of Housing and Urban Development (HUD), a coalition in Northern Colorado—the Northern Colorado Continuum of Care—began developing a coordinated entry system in early February 2016. Coordinated entry is a process that involves using one common assessment tool throughout the community to identify and screen individuals and families in need of housing, storing the information collected from those housing assessments on one community-wide list, and ultimately allocating the housing resources available based on need rather than on a first-come, first-served basis. The first year of implementation of coordinated entry in Northern Colorado focused on veterans and resulted in a total of 103 veteran households obtaining housing. Now, the Northern Colorado Continuum of Care is building out the coordinated entry system to work for adults, unaccompanied youth, and families. Through this process, the way in which the Northern Colorado region addresses homelessness will be completely transformed, creating a more efficient and socially equitable response to homelessness.

The Changing Landscape of Addressing Homelessness

Communities across the country are developing coordinated entry systems, largely because of changes in funding processes, priorities, and requirements from HUD in the past two decades. In the mid-1990s, HUD began requiring communities to submit one consolidated application for homeless services and housing funding for that region. This required communities to analyze system-level data, strategically plan for the best ways to address homelessness, and collectively apply for funding for programs that would have the greatest impact (NAEH, 2010).

In the 2000s, the federal government began promoting "housing first", or the philosophy that individuals experiencing homelessness should be provided housing, with no preconditions, and offered services to then help them retain that housing. Ultimately, housing first became the grounding philosophy for *Opening Doors*, the federal plan to prevent and end homelessness, released in 2010 (USICH, 2010). The housing first approach differs considerably from the previous assumption that individuals needed to reach certain benchmarks, such as remaining sober or obtaining employment, prior to accessing housing. Following this change in emphasis, HUD began directing more funding into permanent housing options and moving funding away from transitional housing, which is antithetical to a housing first approach.

Building on each of these policy and administrative changes, HUD is now requiring communities receiving funding for homeless services and housing to implement coordinated entry systems and report on system-level data. Rather than measuring success by how many people access services, communities need to demonstrate that they can impact homelessness by utilizing new and existing resources to move individuals rapidly out of homelessness and help those currently in homes retain their housing.

What Is Coordinated Entry?

Coordinated entry is an efficient and equitable system for people to access housing. In most communities, several options exist for a homeless household to attempt to gain housing. There are tenant-based housing vouchers to use on the private rental market, there may be units available through nonprofit, public, or private housing providers that are subsidized or dedicated as affordable, there may be temporary rent or deposit assistance available, and there may be a wide range of market-rate housing available to various income levels. In this system, an individual is responsible for accessing each of those resources one by one and completing whatever intake or assessment is necessary to be placed on the waitlist for that housing.

Coordinated entry transforms this existing system in two primary ways. First, it consolidates the process to access each of those resources by using one primary assessment tool and storing households' assessment information on one list, used by a collaborative of service and housing providers to help match households to the housing options available to them. Second, it uses a process of prioritization rather than a first-come, first-served structure. While communities can set some of their own priorities with populations to serve, federal guidelines around coordinated entry clearly state that resources should be used to house those with the greatest needs and who are the most vulnerable (HUD, 2015). By focusing on housing the most vulnerable households, communities can see a reduction in emergency services and resource usage (and their associated costs) (Perlman & Parvensky, 2006) and can be confident that the more expensive and service-intensive housing resources are not being underutilized by housing someone with relatively few needs. With these changes, coordinated entry can create a response to homelessness that is geared toward ending someone's homelessness rather than managing it by creating an effective, efficient, and equitable path into housing.

Coordinated Entry in Northern Colorado

The Northern Colorado Continuum of Care comprises Larimer and Weld Counties, two contiguous counties located about one hour north of Denver. Service and housing providers in the region began implementing coordinated entry in early February 2016, prompted by an opportunity to participate in a two-day workshop facilitated by the nationally recognized nonprofit Community Solutions and supported by the Colorado Governor's Office, the Colorado Office of Behavioral Health, and the Colorado Division of Housing. This workshop focused on establishing coordinated entry specifically for veterans, which was key for several reasons. First, there was increasing pressure on the Northern Colorado veteran service providers from federal funding agencies to be leaders in developing local coordinated entry systems. This aligned with the ongoing emphasis on ending veteran homelessness at the federal level, a goal outlined in the federal plan to prevent and end homelessness (USICH, 2010). This pressure from above created a small and committed group of providers who were able to lead their peers in this effort.

Second, the federal government's emphasis on ending veteran homelessness has been supported by an increase in funding available in the form of long-term housing vouchers, short-term rental assistance, and ongoing case management. As coordinated entry involves a process of matching households in need of housing to appropriate housing resources, having those resources already available to use aided the implementation of coordinated entry. Comparable resources for non-veteran adults, youth, and families do not exist in Northern Colorado. In addition, in the cases in which veterans were renting from private landlords, the appeal of "helping a hero" to gain housing was compelling. This again facilitated the housing process, making the initial implementation of coordinated entry progress easier than without those willing landlords.

Third, the veteran population is limited in size. The experience of homelessness in Northern Colorado is broad, and coordinated entry has to accommodate the unique needs of every population, including needs for different housing resources, different case management models, and even different standards of privacy in the case of households escaping domestic violence. While there was always the intention of expanding out to all other populations, starting with the smaller group of veterans enabled providers to proceed with the major undertaking of developing coordinated entry without being overwhelmed by the breadth of the work.

The current coordinated entry process in Northern Colorado works as follows: a veteran is identified by any number of service providers, including Department of Veteran Affairs (VA) staff, emergency night and daytime shelter staff, street outreach workers, and mental health providers. A trained staff person from one of those agencies conducts a screening on the individual, using the Vulnerability Index—Service Prioritization Decision Assistance Tool (VI-SPDAT), a research-based triage tool developed by Community Solutions and OrgCode. The VI-SPDAT uses information about the individual's housing history, health history, legal history, social connections, and daily functioning to assign each respondent a vulnerability score. Those scoring between zero and three are recommended to receive no housing support as they can likely resolve homelessness on their own. Those scoring between four and seven are recommended to be assessed for rapid rehousing, a form of assistance that can involve short-term rental assistance, housing identification assistance, and case management. Those scoring an eight or above are recommended to be assessed for permanent supportive housing, which provides long-term rental assistance (often in the form of a housing voucher) and supportive services.

Necessary releases of information are completed and all paperwork is submitted to the local Homeless Program Coordinator for the Department of Veteran Affairs. The Homeless Program Coordinator enters selected information about the individual, including their eligibility for veterans' services, their VI-SPDAT score, and any current service provider they are working with onto a community-wide list of veterans that have been screened for housing. This information is brought to a case conference team involving staff from area emergency shelters, mental health providers, housing authorities, the VA, and other veteran service providers, on a biweekly basis. Each case conference involves outlining what housing resources are available and collectively determining which person on the list will be offered that housing resource. In general, resources are offered based on VI-SPDAT score, with those with the highest scores (in other words, those with the most identified risks and vulnerabilities) being offered housing first. Exceptions to this process exist when the most vulnerable individual on the list is not eligible for the available housing program.

The Northern Colorado Continuum of Care has also identified a process for breaking ties of VI-SPDAT scores given local needs and federal priorities. For instance, individuals who are chronically homeless are prioritized above those who are not chronically homeless, based largely on HUD's emphasis on ending chronic homelessness. Once the group decides on the specific individual to be offered a particular housing resource, a lead staff person is identified or confirmed. This person is then charged with locating the individual, offering the housing resource, and following through with the move-in process.

In the first year of implementation, a total of 235 veterans in Northern Colorado were screened for housing using the VI-SPDAT and 103 veterans accessed housing. Those who have not yet obtained housing fall into at least one of several categories. Some may still be homeless and in the process of being matched to housing. Others have a housing resource available to them but may be struggling to find a physical apartment to rent. Almost 40 individuals have gone "inactive" because they left town, are in jail, or are in another facility. When they return to the community, they will automatically be returned to the active list and be considered for the housing resources available at that time.

Improvements in Efficiency and Equity through Coordinated Entry

While housing over 100 veterans in the past year is considered a success for the Northern Colorado coordinated entry process, the fact that as a region this community-level metric is even known and measured is another success. Prior to establishing coordinated entry, each provider may have been able to offer data related to their own program's work, but it was impossible to understand how effectively or efficiently the community as a whole was able to house an individual.

Previously how quickly someone found housing was largely determined by the individual's ability to navigate multiple systems, by their connection to a specific staff person who was willing to help them out more than usual, or by sheer luck. By creating a consistent process that encompasses everyone, those involved in implementing coordinated entry can begin to identify those things within their control that can be adjusted to improve the overall rate at which individuals in the community access housing. For instance, this type of systemic work allows providers to identify where sequential processes can be made parallel or where individuals are being "lost" in the process of trying to gain housing. By improving these steps of the coordinated entry process, the region as a whole can create a more efficient path out of homelessness.

The guidelines for coordinated entry and for addressing homelessness in general that have been released by HUD have prioritized housing chronically homeless individuals. These are all people who have been homeless for a year or more continuously or have had multiple episodes of homelessness totaling at least a year, and who all have long-term disabilities. They are also the people who use the most beds in emergency shelters, as they may return night after night and sleep in a bed that would otherwise be used by someone in a more transitional state of homelessness. Individuals experiencing chronic homelessness also often cost criminal justice and health systems the most. Particularly, once Northern Colorado expands coordinated entry to the chronically homeless population, cost avoidances to these other systems could be tabulated, providing evidence of not only a more efficient housing process but also a more efficient approach to addressing homelessness overall.

Staff members at individual agencies are also able to use their time more efficiently under this program. Currently, a case manager may have to help individual clients gather information on multiple agencies' housing resources, information on the documentation needed for those housing programs, and ways to enroll in each. Once coordinated entry is fully implemented and in operation for everyone, a case manager with a homeless client will have one clear process to follow to ensure their client has access to those resources dedicated for people experiencing homelessness.

In addition to being more efficient, coordinated entry is also a more transparent process. The biweekly case conferencing involves multiple providers using previously outlined, objective criteria. The emotion of providing housing is removed from the process. There are individuals who have had multiple opportunities to obtain housing but may have been evicted or otherwise lost access to that resource. This factor may previously have discouraged a housing provider from offering the person yet another chance. But often the person who has recidivated is the person with the greatest barriers and vulnerabilities. Now, the decisions of to whom housing is offered is not based on past history but on the present need.

Coordinated entry also encourages transparent conversations around eligibility requirements for housing programs. If a referral to a housing provider from the case conference team is rejected, there is now a forum set up for providers to inquire why that rejection happened and establish system rules to ensure any housing provider is not repeatedly rejecting referrals without justification. Previously, decisions regarding who accessed housing and how were not broadly known. Now, it is a community-owned process that all have a stake in and all are accountable to.

All of the components of coordinated entry have ultimately created a process that is more equitable for those experiencing homelessness. Under the old model, each housing provider was concerned with filling vacancies from their own waitlist. If someone did not meet the eligibility requirements of any housing provider, they were left to figure things out on their own, meaning they most likely continued to remain homeless and cycle in and out of shelters, jail, and hospitals. Now, with each provider using the same initial screening tool and putting all names on one single list, the pressure is on the community to ensure every person on that list can obtain housing. If the person is not eligible for any housing resource already available, it is on the community of providers to think creatively about how to provide that needed housing.

No longer is one's ability to find housing dependent on the luck of walking into the right provider. This old model relied on individuals first having the capabilities, capacity, and desire to seek out services. Those dealing with the most severe illnesses or those who had been on the streets the longest would often be the least able to self-navigate even the initial steps of accessing housing.

With coordinated entry, any number of providers could potentially serve as an access point to the system. Street outreach workers who make it their career to build relationships with those living on the streets and disengaged from services could ensure those clients can be screened for housing. It would even be possible for staff in emergency departments or assisting with transitions from jails to help connect people to the coordinated entry process. Coordinated entry moves the Northern Colorado region closer to having complete and equitable access to the housing resources available.

Even the most highly functioning nonprofit service providers cannot significantly impact homelessness on their own. It requires all of those providers working as a system to ensure every person in need of housing can access it. Coordinated entry is the backbone of that community-wide system in Northern Colorado. Already with the veteran population and soon with all other populations of people experiencing homelessness, households can obtain housing through a more efficient process that provides a transparent and streamlined path to follow. In addition, rather than excluding those who are the most vulnerable and the most isolated in the community, coordinated entry will ensure every person has an equitable opportunity to secure housing. It is through these significant improvements to the current standard of providing housing and services that the Northern Colorado Continuum of Care can witness pronounced improvements in how the region supports individuals and families in their effort to escape homelessness.

Note

1 For more information about affordable housing in Nashville, see www.nashville-mdha.org/public-documents/.

References

Anderson, L. M., Charles, J. S., Fullilove, M. T., Scrimshaw, S. C., Fielding, J. E., Normand, J., & Task Force on Community Preventive Services. (2003). Providing affordable family housing and reducing residential segregation by income: A systematic review. *American Journal of Preventive Medicine*, *24*(3), 47–67.

Andrews, D., & Leigh, A. (2009). More inequality, less social mobility. *Applied Economics Letters*, *16*(15), 1489–1492.

Baum, A. S., & Burnes, D. W. (1993). *A nation in denial: The truth about homelessness*. Boulder, CO: Westview Press.

Benner, C., & Pastor, M. (2012). *Just Growth*. New York: Taylor & Francis.

Benner, C., & Pastor, M. (2013). Buddy, can you spare some time? Social inclusion and sustained prosperity in America's metropolitan regions. *MacArthur foundation network on building resilient regions*. http://www.mariselabgomez.com/wp-content/uploads/2013/08/Benner-Pastor-Buddy-Spare-Some-Time.pdf.

Brown, B. J., Hanson, M. E., Liverman, D. M., & Merideth, R. W. (1987). Global sustainability: Toward definition. *Environmental management*, *11*(6), 713–719.

Bullard, R. D. (Ed.). (2007). *Growing smarter: Achieving livable communities, environmental justice, and regional equity*. Cambridge, MA: MIT Press.

Burton, E. (2000). The potential of the compact city for promoting social equity. In K. Williams, E. Burton, & M. Jenks (Eds.), *Achieving sustainable urban form* (pp. 19–29). London, UK: E & FN Spon.

Campbell, S. (1996). Green cities, growing cities, just cities? Urban planning and the contradictions of sustainable development. *Journal of the American Planning Association*, *62*(3), 296–312.

Ceccato, V., & Lukyte, N. (2011). Safety and sustainability in a city in transition: The case of Vilnius, Lithuania. *Cities*, *28*(1), 83–94.

City of Lewiston. 2017a. *Social services*. www.lewistonmaine.gov/index.aspx?nid=293. Retrieved May 20, 2017.

City of Lewiston. 2017b. *Performance and evaluation report*. www.lewistonmaine.gov/documentcenter/view/165. Retrieved May 20, 2017.

Craw, M. (2006). Overcoming city limits: Vertical and horizontal models of local redistributive policy making. *Social Science Quarterly*, *87*(2), 361–379.

Cummins, S. (2014). Food deserts. In W. C. Cockerham, R. Dingwall, & S. R. Quah (Eds.), *The Wiley Blackwell encyclopedia of health, illness, behavior, and society*. New York, NY: John Wiley.

Davis, S. (2016). http://blogs.berkeley.edu/2016/06/27/the-housing-affordability-crisis-can-it-be-solved/.

Donovan, S., & Shinseki, E. K. (2013). Homelessness is a public health issue. *American Journal of Public Health*, *103*(Suppl 2), S180.

Dye, T. R. (1971). *The politics of equality*. Indianapolis, IN: Bobbs-Merrill.

Feenstra, G. W. (1997). Local food systems and sustainable communities. *American Journal of Alternative Agriculture*, *12*(01), 28–36.

Florida, R. L. (2012). *The rise of the creative class: Revisited*. New York, NY: Basic Group.

Florida, R. L. (2017). *The new urban crisis*. New York, NY: Basic Books.

HUD. (2015). *Coordinated entry policy brief*. United States Department of Housing and Urban Development. Retrieved from www.hudexchange.info/resource/4427/coordinated-entry-policy-brief/.

Kantor, P., & Judd, D. (2008). *American urban politics in a global age: The reader*. New York, NY: Pearson.

Koven, S., & Lyons, T. (2010). *Economic development: Strategies for state and local practice*. Washington, DC: ICMA Press.

Lee, M. R. (2000). Concentrated poverty, race, and homicide. *The Sociological Quarterly*, *41*(2), 189–206.

Leigh, N. G., & Blakely, E. J. (2013). *Planning local economic development: Theory and practice*. Los Angeles, CA: SAGE publications.

Lewiston Strategic Plan. (2010). Available at: www.lewistonmaine.gov/index.aspx?NID=150. Retrieved June 2, 2017.

Lubell, J., Crain, R., & Cohen, R. (2007). Framing the issues—The positive impacts of affordable housing on health. *Center for Housing Policy, 34, 1–34.*

Mason, A., & Stephenson, D. G. (2002). *American constitutional law: Introductory essays and selected cases*. Upper Saddle River, NJ: Prentice Hall.

Millimet, D. L. (2013). Environmental federalism: A survey of the empirical literature. *Case Western Reserve Law Review*, *64*, 1669.

Moorhead. 2012. www.politifact.com/truth-o-meter/statements/2012/mar/12/shaun-donovan/hud-secretary-says-homeless-person-costs-taxpayers/. Retrieved February 17, 2017.

NAEH. (2010). *What is a continuum of care? National alliance to end homelessness*. Retrieved from www.endhomelessness.org/page/-/files/Fact%20Sheet%20-%20CoC%202-1-2010.pdf.

National Alliance to End Homelessness. (2017). www.endhomelessness.org/pages/cost_of_homelessness. Retrieved June 5, 2017.

Ogletree Jr, C. J., & Robinson, K. J. (2015). *The enduring legacy of "Rodriguez": Creating new pathways to equal educational opportunity*. Cambridge, MA: Harvard Education Press.

Opp, S. M. (2017). The forgotten pillar: A definition for the measurement of social sustainability in American cities. *Local Environment*, *22*(3), 286–305.

Opp, S. M., & Osgood Jr, J. L. (2013). *Local economic development and the environment: Finding common ground*. Boca Raton, FL: CRC Press.

Opp, S. M., Osgood Jr, J. L., & Rugeley, C. R. (2014). Explaining the adoption and implementation of local environmental policies in the United States. *Journal of Urban Affairs*, *36*(5), 854–875.

Opp, S. M., & Saunders, K. L. (2013). Pillar talk: Local sustainability initiatives and policies in the United States—Finding evidence of the "three E's": Economic development, environmental protection, and social equity. *Urban Affairs Review*, doi:1078087412469344.

Osgood Jr, J. L., Opp, S. M., & Bernotsky, R. L. (2012). Yesterday's gains versus today's realties: Lessons from 10 years of economic development practice. *Economic Development Quarterly*, *26*(4), 334–350.

Paldam, M. (2001, July). Social capital and sustainability. In G. Kochendorfer-Lucius, & B. Pleskovic, *Red: Dynamic development in a sustainable world. Transformation in quality of life, growth and institutions*. Villa Borsig Workshop Series.

Pearsall, H., & Anguelovski, I. (2016). Contesting and resisting environmental gentrification: Responses to new paradoxes and challenges for urban environmental justice. *Sociological Research Online*, *21*(3), 6.

Peck, J. (2005). Struggling with the creative class. *International journal of urban and regional research*, *29*(4), 740–770.

Pendall, R., Nelson A., Hawkins, C., & Knapp, G. (2005). Connecting smart growth, housing affordability, and racial equity. In Xavier de Souza Brigss (Ed.) *The geography of opportunity: Race and housing choice in metropolitan America* (pp. 219–246). Washington, DC: The Brookings Institution.

Perlman, J., & Parvensky, J. (2006). *Denver housing first collaborative: Cost benefit analysis and program outcomes report*. Colorado Coalition for the Homeless. Retrieved from https://shnny.org/uploads/Supportive_Housing_in_Denver.pdf.

Peterson, P. (1981). *City limits*. Chicago, IL: University of Chicago Press.
Plazas, D. (2017). www.tennessean.com/story/opinion/columnists/david-plazas/2017/03/26/how-public-housing-ease-nashvilles-housing-crunch/99507326/. Retrieved June 20, 2017.
Potoski, M. (2001). Clean air federalism: Do states race to the bottom? *Public Administration Review*, *61*(3), 335–343.
Putnam, R. D. (2001). *Bowling alone: The collapse and revival of American community*. New York: Simon and Schuster.
Roberts, M. (2016). www.westword.com/news/16th-street-mall-are-homelessness-drugs-crime-on-mall-costing-denver-8113379. Retrieved January 11, 2017.
Sullivan, D., & Shaw, S. C. (2011). Retail gentrification and race: The case of Alberta Street in Portland, Oregon. *Urban Affairs Review*, *47*(3), 413–432.
Svara, J., Watt, T., & Takai, K. (2015). Advancing social equity as an integral dimension of sustainability in local communities. *Cityscape*, *17*(2), 139.
USICH. (2010). *Opening doors: Federal strategic plan to prevent and end homelessness*. Washington, DC: United States Interagency Council on Homelessness.
Walker, R. E., Keane, C. R., & Burke, J. G. (2010). Disparities and access to healthy food in the United States: A review of food deserts literature. *Health & Place*, *16*(5), 876–884.
Welner, K. G., & Carter, P. L. (2013). Achievement gaps arise from opportunity gaps. In P. L. Carter & K. G. Welner (Eds.), *Closing the opportunity gap: What America must do to give every child an even chance* (pp. 1–10). New York, NY: Oxford University Press.
Williamson, T., Imbroscio, D., & Alperovitz, G. (2003). *Making a place for community: Local democracy in a global era*. New York, NY: Routledge.
Wood, D. (2003). Effect of child and family poverty on child health in the United States. *Pediatrics*, *112*(Suppl 3), 707–711.
Woods, N. D. (2006). Interstate competition and environmental regulation: A test of the race-to-the-bottom thesis. *Social Science Quarterly*, *87*(1), 174–189.
World Economic Forum. 2014. http://reports.weforum.org/global-risks-2014/. Retrieved January 13, 2017.

9 City Organizational Sustainability Efforts

One of the more challenging considerations for community sustainability is to green city operations itself. As Chicago Mayor Richard Daley told his future Chief Environmental Officer, Sadhu Aufochs Johnston, "We can't ask our residents or our businesses to do something that we haven't already done ourselves" (Johnston, Nicholas, & Parzen, 2013). If a city is to push for sustainability, city governments should practice what they preach. This feat may be easier said than done. Greening of city operations can include a variety of activities such as the development of formal sustainability policies, plans, and departments that incorporate waste, pollution, and energy conservation measures into city operations. In essence, local governments would need to adopt and pursue many of the same efforts documented in previous chapters of this book to achieve conservation, waste reduction, and wise energy use, and create more sustainable operation practices for their own organization.

This chapter provides an introduction for how cities *go green* in their operations by highlighting some of the major methods that cities use to incorporate sustainability into their policies, programs, and departments. This chapter starts with an overview of what a sustainable city organization encompasses and then details how city governments seek sustainably grounded operations. Specific attention is devoted to the adoption of overarching sustainability policies and initiatives that drive organizational management decisions. Next, performance measurement for the sustainable city organization is discussed. This chapter concludes with a case study on city operations in Silver City, New Mexico, a community that embodies efforts to become sustainable and more resilient.

What Makes a City Organization Sustainable?

Defining a sustainable city requires attention to questions of if and how city governments embed sustainability practices into policy development, organizational design, and routine management and operational decisions (see Figure 9.1). Creating a sustainable city organization

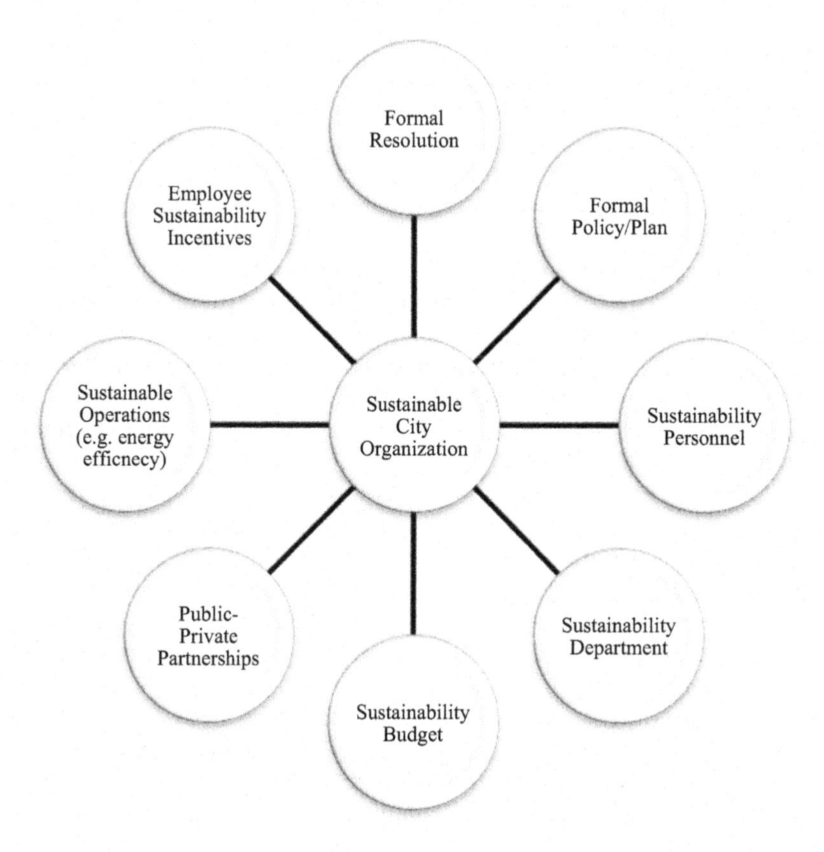

Figure 9.1 Components to the Sustainable City Organization.

mandates a balance of both broad visionary goal statements, such as those expressed in resolutions and plans, and the enactment of operational procedures that impact day-to-day operations. The evidence presented in previous chapters demonstrates a range of policies enacted by local governments to achieve sustainability goals through external means. Reliance on policies and programs to alter citizen and private sector behavior is but one aspect to a sustainable community. Greening of city operations and organizational design is a secondary, but equally as important, avenue for pursuing and achieving sustainability goals within a community. This component specifically focuses on the institution of local government itself.

One of the primary and overarching components to a sustainable city is the adoption of a resolution or formal policy and plan highlighting sustainability goals and intentions. A resolution, usually adopted by an elected governing body, may be relatively short but generally commits a city to a set of sustainability goals. A formal sustainability plan or policy, formulated primarily by civil servants or appointed officials, is usually a more comprehensive document that highlights specific goals, objectives, and criteria over a set time period. Both a resolution and a plan serve as a guiding framework for how a city seeks to become sustainable. Each is a key document and first-order measure to determine how sustainability is achievable at the local level. Resolutions and formal plans identify a set of goals to be achieved and, if pursued, methods for measuring performance on stated goals. The goals can include both policies aimed at the entire community and policies that integrate sustainability into existing city operations. Moreover, the measurement of performance is key, as this book demonstrates, for assessing if and how cities are achieving their sustainability goals. Plans and resolutions for sustainability may be adopted under several other umbrella concepts including climate change, environment or environmental, and resiliency.

Resiliency is the latest catchphrase or buzzword to be used by cities to signify a commitment to sustainable practices. Resiliency planning is a growing phenomenon among cities that is complementary and aids sustainability planning (Portney, 2013). In part, the political tension surrounding such concepts and terminology like climate change and sustainability is bypassed by adopting resiliency-based action plans, which encompass connotations of being prepared to bounce back from natural disasters and anthropogenic hazards. The concept signifies a beyond-sustainability practice that addresses the inevitable need to respond to disasters ranging from hurricanes and wildfires to contaminated drinking water. Often dubbed the *new sustainability*, local resilience policies are intended to provide the local community, including vulnerable populations, with the tools necessary "to survive, adapt, and grow in the face of unforeseen changes" (OSU Center for Resilience, ND). While there has been some debate regarding the interpretation of the term (see Shaw & Maythorne, 2013), the most common application of the concept involves an expansion and incorporation of emergency service agencies into sustainability efforts including the ability to respond to extreme weather events or public health crises. Moreover, education of the community is also essential to prepare individuals for uncertainties associated with climate change.

If focusing on the internal dynamics of the sustainable city organization, administrative organization and management are key drivers. Portney (2013, 207) discusses the challenges of implementing sustainability policies by noting, "In many ways, implementation information fills gaps in assessing how seriously cities seem to take sustainability". Once resolutions and plans are adopted, true enactment requires that a city make concrete actions toward making policies a reality. This effort requires attention to the organizational departments and the people held responsible for implementing sustainability programs and tracking performance.

Organizationally, cities can pursue one of several avenues for structuring bureaucratic operability. One option is to integrate and to mandate a sustainability function to be carried out by existing departments. A singular department, such as planning or an environmental services department like public health, may take the lead or primary responsibility for implementation with other departments serving supplementary and supporting roles. A second option is to create a stand-alone sustainability office or department in charge of leading implementation efforts. This office or department would be responsible for leading sustainability efforts in the city and, similar to using an existing department, could rely on other administrative units for support. Because sustainability is a concept and a practice that can be integrated across all departmental functions, a stand-alone department would presumably ensure coordinated interdepartmental and programmatic coordination. Finally, a third organizational implementation strategy is the public-private partnership. A city may choose to reach out to community partners and anchor institutions, like hospitals, universities, or other major employers in the area, for help and collaboration in the development and implementation of sustainability policies. The public-private partnership can be executed as a stand-alone measure with a particular programmatic focus or in tandem with the other two organizational strategies. Partnerships offer significant benefits that permit cost savings in implementation, spur innovation, and build community capacity and support for environmental sustainability efforts.

It is important to note that no singular strategy is proven to be the most effective, and there are trade-offs to each administrative implementation design. Even Portney suggests that there is no particular pattern of administrative organization for sustainability efforts among cities and there are inherent trade-offs (Portney, 2013). Variability in organizational design may be attributed to the level of resources dedicated to the policy. Some cities may opt for a dedicated sustainability budget and staff members, whereas other communities fuse financial and staff resources into existing departments and staff responsibilities. Variability in administrative design does vary among cities and may be largely dependent on available resources and capacity.

As a final consideration, the operations of the city itself can be greened. Achieving sustainability throughout a city demands that government-owned and -operated facilities adhere to sustainability practices, too. Previous chapters demonstrate the wide variety of policies that can be instituted within government facilities to encourage certain behaviors and outcomes. One of the first ways many cities may opt to achieving sustainable operations is through examining construction methods and energy use in city buildings and facilities. Heating, cooling, lighting, and water use in a singular building can be very energy intensive and costly. According to the U.S. Energy Information

Administration (2016), heating, lighting, and ventilation, refrigeration and cooling constitute 64% of energy demand in commercial buildings, which include government office buildings.[1] Government office buildings represent 10% of all office buildings and consume less energy per person but more energy per building compared to other office building types (EIA, 2010, 2015). The average size of a government office building is 18,400 ft^2 with buildings operation on average 50 hours per week (EIA, 2010). Government workers have significantly less space per worker with a 383 ft^2 mean, which is 9.3%–23% less space compared to workers in other commercial buildings. Since 2003, total energy consumed among all commercial buildings has decreased, but government facilities still have room for improvement. To date, improvements to building energy performance are attributed to better construction practices (e.g. insulation and materials) and small adjustments to existing practices (e.g. using energy-efficient light fixtures). Some cities have even pursued LEED accreditation, entered the Living Building Challenge, or sought to develop net zero energy buildings. All three programs are developed for the sole purpose of creating more sustainable buildings and demonstrate high levels of building performance achievement goals.

Similar to improving building performance, cities may also extend energy-use reduction policies to other infrastructure projects and physical assets. Cities can opt to use permeable pavement on public roadways, opt for energy efficiency streetlights, and mandate green purchasing requirements for supplies and fleet vehicles. Chapter 3 highlights how cities can use permeable pavement on public roadways and opt for energy-efficient streetlights. In addition to these transportation measures, cities may also choose to purchase fuel-efficient or compressed natural gas vehicles and create idling restrictions for city-owned and -operated vehicles. These measures are also discussed in Chapter 5 as part of a discussion on energy and resource conservation efforts. Likewise, efforts by cities can also seek to reduce waste generated by engaging in recycling and reuse behaviors outlined in Chapter 4.

Finally, cities may also seek to alter the behavior of employees. City employee policies can reduce the overall carbon footprint by offering alternative work scheduling and commuting incentives. Cities could adopt a compressed work week (e.g. a four-day work week) or offer flexible hours, telecommuting, and incentivize employees to use public transit or avoid singular passenger vehicle commuting. Of note, the federal government has been particularly active in making use of teleworking options for federal employees. See, for example, www.telework.gov/guidance-legislation/telework-guidance/telework-guide for more information on the teleworking processes in the federal government. Collectively, each measure meant to offer alternative working arrangements works to reduce traffic congestion, pollution, and stress associated with daily travel. The National League of Cities Sustainable Cities Institute (ND) provides how-to guides for city officials interested in adopting an alternative work schedule or providing alternative commuting incentives.[2] The guide outlines strategies and tips for transitioning and maintaining sustainability policies for employee management.

A sustainable city organization is a multifaceted effort that may include various components for a greening city. The broad, visionary component to the sustainable city organization can be manifested in either a city resolution or formal policy and plan. Yet, true achievement of stated goals is only achievable through appropriate managerial channels and enactment of operational policies. The benefits to creating a sustainable city organization are numerous. Investments in sustainable facilities and operations can lead to long-term savings by reducing material consumption, water use, and energy use. In addition, sustainable organizational operations may also lead to healthier employees and integrative communities.

What Have Cities Done to Achieve Sustainability within the Organization?

In our survey, cities were asked a number of questions about how their own operations were becoming more sustainable. As previous chapters demonstrate, the creation of a sustainable city organization intersects many other policy areas from transportation, resource and energy conservation, and pollution prevention. In that respect, cities were asked to identify broader efforts to become sustainable, such as the adoption of a formal resolution or creation of a sustainability department. Next, cities were asked to specify if they had adopted specific employee policies, pollution prevention, or energy and resource conservation policies that would green city operations. These questions were incorporated throughout the survey. To dissect how city operations are greening, overarching organizational policy efforts will be discussed first and then followed by an analysis of specific policy adoptions by cities to create sustainable operations.

Overarching City Sustainability Policies and Organizational Management Design

Approximately half of all the cities surveyed have adopted some policy or initiative that demonstrates an organizational commitment to sustainability. Table 9.1 outlines different components to city sustainability policies and organizational management design. Adoption of a formal sustainability resolution is the most common visionary engagement among cities at a 47.83% adoption rate. However, not all sustainability resolutions contained the same targets for how to achieve local-level

Table 9.1 City Sustainability Policies and Organizational Management Design

Policies and Programs	*Cities Reporting (%)*
Adopted a formal resolution regarding sustainability	47.83
Formal sustainability policy or plan	28.62
Formal sustainability department	10.14
Formal social sustainability department	2.17
Formal partnerships with community sustainability groups	29.71
Providing a budget or dedicated sustainability staff or staff for sustainability efforts	23.91

Table 9.2 City Sustainability Resolution Target Areas

Policies and Programs	*Percentage of Cities Reporting (%)*
The environment	28.26
The economy	21.01
Social justice/sustainability	11.23
Climate change	13.04
Energy conservation	28.62
Green jobs	4.71
Housing for all income groups	27.17
Public transit	18.84

sustainability (Table 9.2). Resolution targets for the environment, energy conversation, housing, and the economy are the most frequently reported with an average of 26% adoption rate. As expected, social justice or equity received far less attention in sustainability resolutions compared to the other two pillars of sustainability (i.e. economy and the environment) with only 11.23% of cities reporting specific resolution targets. Yet, the area of housing for all income groups, one of the top four resolution target areas connected to equity consideration, did receive equal and considerable attention, with 6% more cities concerned with the issue compared to the economy. One potential explanation for high degree of concern with affordable housing is the 2007 financial crisis and continual stagnation of wages amidst rising home prices. To date, the housing market has recovered and exceeded prefinancial crisis pricing, but average household income has remained steady, and new homebuyers, primarily those adults identified as part of the Millennial generation, have not or do not have the capacity to enter the market. Inability to find affordable housing in some markets may impact economic performance and create long-term challenges with growing local economies.

Resolutions are but one glimpse for how cities are approaching sustainability and, while very important, may not demonstrate an action-based commitment to sustainability like other efforts outlined in Table 9.1 that require more time and resources to accomplish. For example, the development of a sustainability plan, establishing a sustainability department or dedicating staff and a budget to sustainability, creates more meaningful action toward stated goals. Yet, these policies received far fewer adoptions by cities compared to resolutions. The creation of a formal sustainability plan or policy occurred in 28.62% of cities. This is at a similar adoption rate to developing partnerships with community groups (29.71%). However, only 10% of cities established a sustainability department, and 2.71% of cities created a social sustainability department in addition to a primary sustainability department. This indicates, once again, how social equity and inclusion is often the forgotten pillar of sustainability (see Chapter 8). As for dedicating resources to sustainability implementation, about a quarter of all cities report providing a dedicated budget or staff for their sustainability efforts. This suggests that many cities have adopted plans and resolutions but are not providing dedicated resources for achieving successes in this policy area.

The rate of adoption of broader sustainability policies and initiatives among cities is not ideal, but it is promising. The 2010 ICMA survey showed only 28.7% of cities adopting a resolution and only 18.1% of cities establishing a sustainability plan or policy. The expansion of local-level policy action in these areas suggests strengthening commitment toward sustainability and the environment. While performance measurement across policy areas remains significantly low, there is room to improve how cities remain accountable to sustainability goals that are established and provide funding for such endeavors.

Operational Policies to Create Sustainable City Organization

Our survey included a number of specific questions that examined how cities integrated sustainability into organizational operations. Table 9.3 outlines various organizational policies that have been adopted by cities in the areas of facilities and energy consumption, public fleet decisions, purchasing requirements, and employee practices. The survey also elected to ask cities to identify any other additional operational policies that created sustainability within the city organization. In addition, Table 9.3 identifies what percentage of cities measure performance and link performance outcomes to the budget for most policies.

Of all the operational policies adopted, cities most frequently pursue those that address energy consumption of government facilities; 82.6% of all communities in the survey have policies or a program in place to upgrade lighting within public facilities, nearly 62% conduct energy audits of government buildings, 28.62% of cities installed solar panels

Table 9.3 Specific City Organizational and Operation Policies

Policy Area	*Policies and Programs*	*Percentage of Cities Reporting Policy/ Program[a] (%)*	*Percentage of Cities Reporting Performance Measurement (%)[a]*	*Percentage of Cities Reporting Performance Linked to Budget (%)[a]*
Facilities and energy	Energy audits of government buildings	61.96	27.49 (17.03)	8.77 (5.43)
	Installed energy management systems in government buildings	44.93	29.03 (13.04)	0.48 (4.71)
	Installed solar panels on government property	28.62	37.97 (10.87)	6.33 (1.81)
	Upgraded lighting in public buildings or spaces for higher efficiency	82.61	22.37 (18.48)	0.96 (9.06)
Fleet	Purchased fuel-efficient or hybrid vehicles	41.67	26.96 (11.23)	9.57 (3.99)
	Purchased compressed natural gas vehicles	13.8	31.58 (4.35)	5.26 (<1)
	Idling rules for city-operated fleet	4.7	7.69 (<1)	—
Purchasing	City purchasing/contracting decisions based on sustainability goals	31.16	N/A	N/A
	Established green purchasing requirements	18.12	30 (5.43)	[illegible] (1.45)
Employee policies	Incentives for public employees to use multimodal/ alternative transport methods	11.59	18.75 (2.17)	3.13 (<1)
	Free or reduced passes for public transit for public employees	10.14	42.86 (4.35)	—
	Parking policies to reduce single-occupancy commuting	3.62	40 (1.45)	—
	Telecommuting option for city employees	10.87	23.33 (2.54)	—
	Compressed work week option for city employees	17.39	20.83 (3.62	4.17 (<1)
Other policies	Other	5.07	—	—

[a]Reported as the following: % of cities with reported policy (% of all cities surveyed).

on government facilities, and almost 45% of cities have installed energy management systems. A total of 4.17% of all cities adopted all four facility and energy savings policies. Of those cities that upgraded lighting, only 22.36% of those same cities track performance and approximately 11% connect performance to the budget. Measuring the performance of public building energy audits and energy management systems occurred slightly more frequently and nearly 38% of cities tracked the performance of solar panels. Other facility and energy policies adopted by cities including recycling goals, building competitions for energy use reduction, and adoption of green building and infrastructure of policies. These policies were reported through the "other" policy category provided in the survey.

Cities were also ambitious in pursuing more efficient options for the city fleet. Purchasing fuel-efficient or hybrid vehicles for city use was reported by 41.67% of cities surveyed. Of those cities, almost 27% measure performance of that policy, but only 9.57% link performance to the budget. Purchasing compressed natural gas vehicles was a less popular policy (13.8% of cities), but performance measurement was on par with that of fuel efficiency or hybrid vehicles policies. City survey participants indicated efforts to both increase the efficiency of public transit vehicles and vehicles used for official city business by public employees. However, policies regarding idling of city fleet vehicles are significantly less popular. Only 4.7% of cities reported policies regarding idling rules and restrictions for city-operated vehicles. Comparatively, fewer cities place explicit restrictions on city-operated vehicles compared to policies established for restricting idling within the broader community (see Chapter 3, Table 3.1).

Organizational policies for purchasing decisions and public employee commutes received far less support among cities compared to other sustainable organizational policy areas. While 31.16% of cities claimed to base purchasing and contracting decisions on sustainability goals, only 18.12% reported establishing green purchasing requirements with a third tracking performance and only 8% of those same cities linking performance to the budget. Even fewer cities engage employee policies that compress the work week (17.39%), encourage alternative transportation (11.59%) or public transit usage (10.14%), or offer telecommuting options (10.87%). In some communities, these sorts of policies may not be a feasible option. Most survey respondents that adopted employee-commuting policies were larger to midsize communities, which are more likely to employ a wider range of employees and have public transit commuting options available.

In sum, cities appear to be engaging in a wide variety of organizational policies to increase the operational sustainability. Facilities and energy-based policies are the most popular perhaps because of the co-benefit of cost savings. Moreover, transitioning energy management systems and lighting structures is likely an easier and more feasible goal to accomplish compared to purchasing requirements, fleet upgrades, or employee commuting options. Engaging in energy savings among public facilities is good first step toward creating a sustainable organization, but it cannot be the only step. Adoption of other policies would greatly benefit the overall impact of government operations on the environment. The list of policies in Table 9.4 is not an exhaustive list of all policies that could be adopted by a city to green operations. Indeed, many cities can customize and adopt a variety of policies to increase participation in city-led sustainability initiatives and promote sustainable behaviors among city employees. For example, the City of Denton, Texas, has developed educational and participation goals to promote sustainability initiatives within the community.[3] As stated in the city's *Simple Sustainable* 2012 strategic plan, "The success of this plan depends on the active involvement of city residents, business, and institutions". As such, the active participation and support of community members is vital to achieving policy success for greening city operations and behavior.

Performance Measurement for Sustainable City Organization Efforts

A number of performance measurements are used by cities to assess sustainable operations. Table 9.4 identifies some common metrics used in assessing the sustainable city organization. A combination of output- and outcome-based metrics was reported. For example, most cities that adopted one facility or energy management policy also track the total energy consumption in public buildings and tracked the cost changes or energy savings for public facilities. One measure is a simple output while the other can adequately assess how certain policies, once enacted, influence energy usage. Other cited performance measurement examples include tracking the number of energy-efficient vehicles purchased, accounting for the number or percentage of streetlights converted to energy-efficient bulbs, tracking recyclables and waste diversion, accounting for the number of green-certified buildings, and community support for city sustainability initiatives.

Challenges and Barriers in Sustainable City Organization Policy Success

Policy success for sustainable city operations is challenged by a number of barriers. Most frequently, cities indicate a lack of resources as being the number one barrier to policy success (see Chapter 2, Table 2.6). A total of 23.3% of cities claim lack of resources as a first rank ordered barrier and an additional 12.8% rank ordered the barrier as second. Upgrading and investment into energy-efficient systems and equipment can

Table 9.4 Sustainable City Organization Performance Metrics Examples

Example Performance Metrics	*Sample Benchmark*
Energy consumption of public buildings	**Austin, Texas, Goal:** (1) Reduce annual building energy usage at City buildings by 5% each year through 2020
	Lakewood, Colorado: Reduce city facility energy use by 30% by 2025
	Santa Monica, California: Reduce total municipal energy use by 10% by 2020
	Silver City, New Mexico: Overall town reduction of GHG emissions by 15% by 2015 (2009 plan)
Energy savings/cost changes in public sector	**Silver City, New Mexico:** Adopt and execute green building standards for an annual cost savings of $15,400
Green purchase audit	**Palo Alto, California:** Conducts an annual "green purchasing practices" audit as a part of the city's annual audit work plan. Audit presents annual recommendations
City fleet GHG reduction	**Boulder, Colorado:** City met its city fleet vehicle goal to meet the 2012 Kyoto goals to reduce GHG emissions to 7% below 1990 usage levels. The fleet continues its efforts to reduce GHG emissions by purchasing alternative fuel and hybrid vehicles
Number of energy-efficient vehicles purchased	**Santa Monica, California:** Achieve 80% of city fleet vehicles using alternative fuels
Number or percentage of streetlights converted to LED/energy-efficient bulbs	**Lakewood, Colorado:** 100% conversion of streetlights to LED/high efficiency lighting by 2025
LEED Certification/green building standards	**Austin, Texas:** Maintain 100% compliance with minimum LEED Silver Certification for city capital improvement projects
Reduction in water use	**Lakewood, Colorado:** Reduce city water use by 20% by 2025
Increase community engagement and support	**Denton, Texas:** Have an average attendance of 25 or more people to monthly workshops and education sessions
	Silver City, New Mexico: Train a minimum of two neighbor volunteers (per identified neighborhood) on climate, conservation, protection, adaptation, and preparedness

lead to higher up-front costs with savings realized after several years or decades after implementation. Some communities may not be able to invest so much in up-front costs to infrastructure and capital upgrades. Moreover, the sheer cost of creating new departments and dedicating staff to new policies can be cumbersome. As noted by the case study of Silver City, New Mexico, at the end of this chapter, grant funding was instrumental in the establishment of a sustainability department and the creation of a town sustainability plan. Low rates of creating sustainability department or adopting sustainability plans may be directly related to allocation of already scarce financial resources of towns and cities.

Human capital is a secondary barrier to organizational initiatives with roughly 30% of all cities ranking as a top-three constraint. Lack of talent or knowledge can impede organizational efforts to be more sustainable. Staff may lack proper or adequate skills and experience to identify critical areas and needs for sustainability efforts. Finally, political support was a barrier cited by a fifth of cities as a reason for not achieving policy success. Climate change, sustainability, and environmental policy discussion can be particularly tense subjects and politically tainted by misinformation and skepticism. Conservative or Republican-majority communities may face higher barriers in adopting sustainability policies particularly in tough economic conditions, where jobs and economic growth may be emphasized as more important than environmental quality and social equity.

Concept in Action: The Sustainable City Organization in Silver City, New Mexico

Creating a sustainability city organization is a true commitment to local-level sustainability efforts. In where the rubber meets the road, city policies not only are developed for the broader community, but the city transforms public facilities and operations to also be more sustainable. Evidence from this chapter suggests many city governments are pursuing sustainability policies and organizational strategies to reduce energy consumption, improve the performance of public facilities, and redirect resources that reduce overall environmental burdens.

The following case study highlights how one community, Silver City, New Mexico, began to address sustainability by initially developing a citizen's advisory committee to develop a sustainability plan. Denise Smith, Director of the Office of Sustainability for the Town of Silver City, provides a road map for how the community identified the needs of the town and translated those needs to tangible actions. The case study is truly unique, as it highlights how one town justified not just climate change or sustainability planning but planning for resiliency. Portney (2013) identifies resiliency planning as a new direction for city sustainability efforts. It is complementary and extends beyond current sustainability planning efforts. In addition to resiliency planning, the case demonstrates the power derived from involving community stakeholders in the planning for sustainability initiatives. Involvement of the local population can lead to a deeper buy-in and effort to promote sustainable city operations. As a result, the Town of Silver City, New Mexico, has operationally sought to manage sustainability goals through a Department of Sustainability, which now leads the city's sustainability initiatives and coordinates resiliency planning, and adopted a long-term sustainability plan.

A RURAL SOUTHWEST TOWN LEADS BY EXAMPLE: SUSTAINABILITY AND RESILIENCY PLANNING IN SILVER CITY, NEW MEXICO

By: Denise Smith

Silver City, New Mexico, is a small, rural community nestled against the 3.3 million acre Gila National Forest in the southwestern corner of the state. This high-desert town of 10,000 people was founded in the summer of 1878, and soon became known for silver mining, and later, copper. Today, health care, tourism, the cultural economy, and Western New Mexico University supplement mining and ranching as the primary economic drivers.

Changing weather patterns worldwide have increased awareness of possible effects at the local level. Silver City officials were proactive in seeking information about how the Silver City area may be affected in order to anticipate changes and increase preparedness. Valuable sources of information on climate patterns are state universities that provide predictions of seasonal weather patterns to agricultural producers. New Mexico State University climatologist David DuBois has been helpful in providing predictions specific to southwest New Mexico based on analysis of data from the National Oceanic and Atmospheric Administration, National Climate Data Center (NCDC). According to DuBois, temperatures are projected to rise approximately 2°F (geographic average) between 2013 and 2050 in the area, though overall precipitation is not likely to change (DuBois, 2013). DuBois predicts less frequent but heavier precipitation events, a possible delay in monsoon rains, and reduced mountain snowpack with earlier runoff. Additional impacts may include more frequent drought (increasing heat and aridity) resulting in increased evaporation and reduction in soil moisture. Increased energy demand during extreme weather events could lead to blackouts.

A Community Approach

In 2007, the mayor of the Town of Silver City appointed concerned citizens to form the Mayor's Climate Protection Agreement

Citizen's Advisory Committee (the Climate Committee). The Committee's initial research showed that reduction of greenhouse gas (GHG) emissions was a common goal in many places worldwide, and the resultant Climate Action Plan presented to the mayor and the town council in January 2009 laid out a pathway to accomplish this on a local level. The strategy addressed climate change at its source: in the daily operations of the municipality and surrounding communities. It was recognized that reducing GHG emissions would also save Town and taxpayer dollars, improve quality of life for area residents, and help maintain a healthy local economy.

One of the plan's key recommendations was to form an Office of Sustainability within the Town of Silver City's Community Development Department, which was accomplished in 2010 through the American Recovery and Reinvestment Act (ARRA) grant funding. Some of the most notable achievements, realized in the first three years of the office and made possible through ARRA funds, include the following:

- Installation of a five-acre solar array to run the Town's wastewater treatment plant;
- A solar-covered parking structure that powers the Silver City Visitors Center; and
- Low-cost energy efficiency retrofits in over 800 homes within Grant County.

In May 2012, the Second International Conference on Climate Change was held at the University of Arizona in Tucson, providing a timely and accessible educational opportunity on the subject. Nineteen community members attended the conference, including the mayor, many members of the Climate Committee, and staff of the Office of Sustainability (OoS). This event inspired the year-long effort to develop the *Town of Silver City Sustainability Plan 2030*.[4]

Many of the presenters at the conference focused on adaptation to climate changes and how to remain resilient in the face of these changes, rather than relying on a worldwide reduction in GHG emissions that would halt climate change. This shifted our local approach from developing baseline measurements of emissions and tracking the decrease in emissions over time as a way to determine progress, to adopting best practices in municipal operations and maintenance actions that would help us protect our citizens, conserve our resources, and prepare for the future.

Developing a Sustainability Plan

In the fall of 2012, a public/private task force was formed to develop and present these best practices in a sustainability plan. The task force included key municipal departments, leaders from nonprofit organizations, and local citizens with expertise in key elements such as public health risks, the environment, and energy systems. The task force looked at how changes in climate could affect a variety of Town government functions.

The task force first identified planning areas and functions of the Town's municipal operations and of the community that could be impacted by changes in climate, grouped the elements into categories, systems, and key planning areas (see Table 9.5), and performed vulnerability and risk assessments for each area.

The vulnerability and risk assessment was performed to identify areas where the Town may be vulnerable to climate variability and projected weather impacts, and to provide a foundation for the sustainability plan. The task force considered the sensitivity of the Town to climate variability, and identified non-climate factors such as population, public safety, and the local economy. They then determined the degree of impacts to each area, and considered the

Table 9.5 Categories, Systems, and Key Planning Areas in Silver City

Category	*System*	*Key Planning Area*
Community	Emergency services	Police and fire services, disaster response, emergency medical services
	Food	Local agriculture, food delivery/ distribution, people
	Public health	Public health personnel and support People and public services
	Transportation	Transportation infrastructure, petroleum costs, public transit, alternative modes of transportation
	Waste	Solid waste, wastewater
Environment	Energy	Energy assurance and delivery, energy demand and cost
	Land and urban forest health	Land management, urban forest management, wildlife and vegetation
	Storm water	Storm water infrastructure, floodplain management
	Water	Water quantity, water quality, water delivery infrastructure

Source: Town of Silver City Sustainability Plan 2030.

Table 9.6 Combined Vulnerability and Risk Assessment—Planning Areas for Action Priority in Silver City

		Risk (Likelihood of Occurrence by 2030)		
		High	*Medium-high*	*Medium*
Vulnerability (sensitivity and adaptive capacity)	HIGH	Emergency services:– Police and fire– Disaster response		Emergency services: EMS
	MEDIUM-HIGH		Public health: People and public services	Storm water: Infrastructure
	MEDIUM		Public health: Personnel and support	Storm water: Floodplain management Land/ urban forest health:– Land management– Urban forest management Transportation: Infrastructure

Source: Town of Silver City Sustainability Plan 2030.

resources currently available to adapt and respond to the associated impacts of climate change. Adaptive capacity is the capacity to accommodate change with minimal disruption or additional cost. This determination of vulnerability used a five-stage vulnerability ranking from low to high. Table 9.6 shows those planning areas deemed most at risk, providing a platform for priority actions.

After seven months, the task force completed the *Town of Silver City Sustainability Plan 2030, Protect, Conserve, Prepare, An Approach to Community Resiliency.* The plan sets forth recommendations for policy and priority actions to reduce the Town's vulnerability to impacts from increasing heat, drought, and other climate variability, such as larger and more intense wildfires and increased stress on emergency services personnel and equipment from intense weather events.

The Rationale for Resilience

As deBuys (2011) states about the changing climate in the American Southwest, the curious thing about adapting to climate change in the North American Southwest (and indeed in most places) is that the adaptations commanding highest priority are tasks that have needed doing for a long time, irrespective of climate. They are the difficult, postponed chores that never went away. None should come as a surprise; all involve the pursuit of resilience.

Resilience may be defined as "the ability of a community to absorb a disturbance while retaining its essential functions" (Longstaff, Armstrong, Perrin, Parker, & Hidek, 2010). As increasing disturbances are expected as a result of climate change, building resiliency effectively becomes preparation for the future. Therefore, Silver City officials prepared a resiliency approach as a practical strategic option for several reasons:

1 *The climate has already changed and future changes are highly likely.* In the Silver City area, annual average temperature has increased and projections indicate a rise in the rate of warming, according to climatologist DuBois.
2 Climate variability poses a threat to existing community priorities and affects local government's ability to deliver on its existing commitments. Existing priorities and commitments may shift as projected impacts (power outages, fire) increase over time.
3 *Local officials' choices today will shape tomorrow's vulnerabilities.* It is important to build the capacity to adapt to unforeseen circumstances by increasing diversity, redundancy, and network overlaps within municipal operations, as well as commercial, retail, and residential.
4 *Planning now can save money, while inaction will lead to higher costs in the future.* Paying for prevention up-front can avoid more significant costs in the future. On average, a dollar spent by FEMA on hazard mitigation (actions to reduce disaster losses) provides the nation about $4 in future benefits (Multihazard Mitigation Council, 2005). Indeed, the goal of the 2012 *New Mexico Energy Assurance Plan*[5] is to "...transition from response and recovery [reaction] to energy assurance [prevention and preparation] planning. This requires a significant change in local government thinking".
5 Planning for uncertainty and future variability is not a new process and can be integrated into current planning frameworks. Key elements of the approved Sustainability Plan 2030 have been incorporated into the Town's recent Comprehensive Plan update.

A commitment to resilience means a continual process of monitoring, reevaluation, and updating. Building resiliency in the community to deal with disruption from climate variability also develops resiliency in social and economic disturbances that may not be directly related to climate change.

Successes and Ongoing Challenges

Through the process of developing and creating a sustainability plan, the ground work was laid to carry the Town forward toward making sustainability and resiliency a part of the Town's organizational fabric. The Town now takes these principles into consideration in short- and long-term decisions concerning maintenance and operations. Many new partnerships were made and existing partnerships strengthened that make it possible to accomplish so much more than the municipality could do on its own. Private nonprofit groups and other public entities help secure grant funding. The knowledge and energy provided by our citizen volunteers, including retirees and youth organizations, help make this a strong and vibrant community. Building, sustaining, and leveraging local and regional partnerships is key to success.

Municipalities are in need of a holistic set of standards, indicators, targets, or explicit sustainability goals against which they can measure impacts, performance, and progress toward agreed upon outcomes. Benchmarks and performance measurements can be used to help assess goal and priority area achievements. In Silver City, benchmarks and performance measures are currently sector specific. For example, annual water reports from the Utility Department document decreases in water production over the last 10 years due to conservation efforts including semiannual leak detection and repair in the main service lines, and the recent installation of new residential and commercial water meters with automatic meter-reading technology that helps identify leaks through real-time water use data. Energy usage in all of the Town buildings is documented, tracking how energy efficiency upgrades have decreased energy use. Documenting the dollars saved from using solar energy to power the wastewater treatment plant and the visitor center is another way to measure sustainability performance in the public sector, because every dollar saved contributes to a more resilient economy.

Grant funds from federal, state, and nonprofit sources have helped move us toward our goals and will likely be the main source of funding in the future. Competition for these funds is rigorous, but having a written sustainability plan and other relevant plans help increase competitiveness. In addition to the solar panels installed to run the wastewater treatment plant and the visitor center, various grant funds have helped the Town increase the recycling rate from 11% to 33%, distribute hundreds of trees on private property through tree giveaways, and expand bicycle lanes and multiuse trails. Savings in operation and maintenance costs from implementing sustainability goals provide more working capital for the Town. These savings contributed to the Town's ability to purchase two new rescue units that were needed to increase our emergency response capabilities, a vulnerability that was identified in the risk analysis.

Local governments and organizations have collaborated to install a reverse 911 call system to provide emergency alerts, develop a wildfire protection plan, coordinate on Critical Incident Management, improve communication during disasters, conduct joint exercises, and update the All Hazards Plan. A Symposium on Preparedness was conducted in 2013 to help organize community response.

Local authorities and municipalities across the southwest are facing unprecedented socioeconomic challenges in the context of budget cuts and increasing demand for services. Silver City is constantly looking for innovative approaches and practical instruments to support our ability to meet the needs and ongoing responsibilities while also planning for an unknown future of climate variability. The proactive response to climate change seems to attract more like-minded people who are interested in living in and contributing to a progressive community, further increasing our ability to remain resilient in a world of change and uncertainty.

Notes

1 The EIA has not released water consumption data for smaller office buildings citing quality checks on the data set for commercial building water consumption (EIA, 2017). The median government facility is 6,000 ft^2.
2 See www.sustainablecitiesinstitute.org/topics/transportation/ridesharing/telecommuting.
3 www.cityofdenton.com/CoD/media/City-of-Denton/Simply_Sustainable_Plan_2012.pdf.
4 The plan can be found on the Town's website at www.townofsilvercity.org/r/town_of_silver_city_NM.php?r=75,9w8qm.
5 The town's plan can be found at www.emnrd.state.nm.us/ECMD/Multimedia/documents/NMENERGYASSURANCEPLANREPORTDECEMBER2012.pdf.

References

deBuys, W. (2011). *A great aridness: Climate change and the future of the American southwest.* New York, NY: Oxford University Press.

Dubois, D. (2013). Changing weather in the SW New Mexico mountain range: Heat, drought, precipitation and extreme weather [Lecture Presentation]. WNMU Global Resource Center Auditorium.

Energy Information Administration [EIA]. (2010). Office buildings: Full report. Available at: www.eia.gov/consumption/commercial/data/archive/cbecs/cbecs2003/officereport/office_print.pdf.

Energy Information Administration [EIA]. (2015). 2012 commercial buildings energy consumption survey data. Available at: www.eia.gov/consumption/commercial/data/2012/index.php#b22-b33.

Energy Information Administration [EIA]. (2016). Commercial buildings energy consumption survey: By usage summary. Available at: www.eia.gov/consumption/commercial/reports/2012/energyusage/.

Energy Information Administration [EIA]. (2017). How was water usage information collected for commercial buildings? Available at: www.eia.gov/consumption/commercial/reports/2012/water/methodology.php.

Johnston, S. A., Nicholas, S. S., & Parzen, J. (2013). *The Guide to Greening Cities.* Washington, DC: Island Press.

Longstaff, P. H., Armstrong, N. J., Perrin, K., Parker, W. M., & Hidek, M. A. (2010). Building resilient communities: A preliminary framework for assessment. *Homeland Security Affairs*, *6*(3), 1–24.

Multihazard Mitigation Council [National Institute of Building Sciences]. (2005). Natural hazard mitigation saves: An independent study to assess future savings from mitigation activities, Volume 2—Study documentation. Available at: https://c.ymcdn.com/sites/www.nibs.org/resource/resmgr/MMC/hms_vol2_ch1-7.pdf.

OSU Center for Resilience. (ND). Concepts. http://resilience.osu.edu/CFR-site/concepts.htm.

Portney, K. E. (2013). *Taking sustainable cities seriously* (2nd ed.). Cambridge, MA: MIT Press.

Shaw, K., & Maythorne, L. (2013). Managing for local resilience: Towards a strategic approach. *Public Policy and Adminsitation*, *28*(1), 43–65.

The National League of Cities Sustainable Cities Institute. (ND). Telecommuting. Available at: www.sustainablecitiesinstitute.org/topics/transportation/ridesharing/telecommuting.

10 Conclusions of Local Sustainability and Performance Measurement

In these final few days of editing of this book, several news articles have been published across the United States that provide a clear signal of the importance of sustainability efforts for all Americans. First, as the September 21, 2017, article titled "Flint's lead-poisoned water had a 'horrifying large' effect on fetal deaths, study finds" in the *Washington Post* demonstrates, environmental problems are not just about regulation, or economic competitiveness, or even about green spaces; it truly is a life-or-death issue (Ingraham, 2017). Although all the facts are not yet public record on this case, it seems that a catastrophic combination of old water infrastructure, local revenue shortages, and a significant policy failure of the state environmental agency are to blame for deaths, permanent cognitive impairment, and various other health problems across the population of the community (CNN, 2017). Second, in addition to the ongoing Flint news, the coverage of two major hurricanes, Irma and Harvey, has also raised some questions about resilience, local development, social equity, and sustainability. As one NBC news story says, "...61 percent of households in Miami-Dade County, and 44 percent in Broward County, were either poor or working poor, meaning they struggled to pay basic bills – let alone survive for a disaster" (Schuppe, 2017). You only have to look as far as Hurricane Katrina's impact on the poor in New Orleans to begin to see a relationship between income levels and survival of major disasters. Furthermore, these catastrophic events beg the question about a continual development of vulnerable coastal areas.

Would a higher level or *better* engagement in local sustainability efforts have prevented the problems seen with Flint or Hurricane Irma? Prevention may be a bit too strong of a word. However, what is certain is that a city that engages in a robust sustainability program that also engages in critical self-assessment through performance measurement will have explored questions about poverty and environmental events, will have created policies and programs to guide development in ways to minimize environmental degradation, and will have pursued policies and programs to improve the overall quality of life in their communities. All of these sustainability efforts could provide important indicators and methods to avoid problems like Flint where possible and also rebound faster from events like hurricanes Harvey and Irma.

It should be clear at this point in this book that the pursuit of sustainability is an important but challenging policy endeavor for any government. The absence of significant federal or state action on sustainability has meant that local governments in the United States must take the lead on adopting sustainability policies and initiatives. A number of studies document the depth and growing commitment among U.S. cities to sustainability principles (Conroy, 2006; ICMA, 2016; Jepson, 2001, Opp & Osgood, 2013; Opp & Saunders, 2013; Portney, 2013; Saha & Paterson, 2008). For some American cities, the pursuit of sustainability initiatives coincides with economic development goals and, in turn, is more appropriately labeled sustainable development. For others, as this book demonstrates, the pursuit of local sustainability policies is part of a larger plan dedicated toward a delicate marriage of environmental concerns to both social equity and economic considerations.

This book serves a key role in reassessing the current state of local sustainability policies and programs but also moving toward a comprehensive and deeper understanding for how cities track outcomes and policy performance. As Portney (2013, p. 333) states, "What has largely been missing from research on sustainable cities is a systematic effort to relate the programs and policies, and their implementation approaches, to actual results…" Research on the local sustainability efforts must address both the frequency of adoption and the performance of the policies. The survey results outlined in this book track the performance measurement and assessment activities of local sustainability initiatives in the United States with a mixture of both optimism and concerned reservation. While local governments in the United States have made significant strides in adopting sustainability policies, there is still a need to systematically or deliberately assess the implementation successes of such policies. Furthermore, given the very real concern with unintended consequences that may stem from many of these sustainability efforts, a lack of critical assessment is concerning for the future of American cities and for the successes of these efforts to lead to sustainability.

Local sustainability initiatives can reap many benefits for the community at large while also addressing larger global concerns about climate change and a rapidly growing population that strains natural resources. Sustainability, at its core, seeks to improve the quality of life for all Americans, not just a select few. Communities can enhance the overall quality of life by enacting policies that address key economic concerns, such as income and jobs, while simultaneously addressing environmental quality and equity concerns that impact public health, resource management, and the ability to respond effectively to natural disasters. However, as this and previous research has shown, cities seem to overwhelmingly pursue policies with clear economic co-benefits as opposed to other sustainability initiatives. Overcoming the limitations of local resources and the long-standing emphasis on economic growth is the key to moving local sustainability initiatives in a better direction. Moreover, tracking the performance of local sustainability policies proves a key challenge to improve the overall quality and outcomes of local sustainability initiatives.

Assessing and Measuring Local Sustainability Policies

The aggressive push for sustainability policies at the local level emerged after the publication of *Our Common Future*, a 1987 Brundtland Commission Report that defined and made the argument for sustainable development. However, sustainable development is a different concept and applicable measure as compared to sustainability. Sustainable development focuses on the ability to continually grow and manage a healthy economy in balance with protecting environmental quality. Much has been written on sustainable development efforts across the world (Heberle & Opp, 2008; Opp & Osgood, 2013). At the same time, we know that there is an inherent tension between economic development goals and environmental protection efforts, and finding a balance can be challenging—but not impossible (Heberle & Opp, 2008; Opp & Osgood, 2013). Unfortunately, equity is not often integrated into discussions of sustainable development, but it is, however, a part of the broader conception of just *sustainability*. Sustainability is meant to balance and depend upon the trifecta of the "three E's"—economic development, environmental protection, and social equity. In order to achieve local sustainability, a community must fulfill all three pillars to achieve both short- and long-term sustainability goals (see Opp & Saunders, 2013; Portney, 2013). Across American cities, we often see evidence that policies related to sustainability emerge under several umbrella concepts including climate change, environment, sustainable planning, and resiliency. Regardless of what framing concept a city elects to use, all of these policies are important to understand and to assess if these policies are the front line for sustainability efforts in the United States.

We know that sustainability efforts in the United States lag behind many other countries, particularly other industrialized and economically advanced countries in Europe (Slavin, 2011). Policies at the federal and state level have generally stagnated and, in some cases, regressed to earlier eras of policymaking with a reduction of emphasis on sustainability principles. Failure to bridge consensus within Congress, increasing pressures to use the courts to resolve environmental disputes, and lack of state government involvement have left U.S. municipalities with the primary responsibility for pursuing sustainability efforts (Fischer, 2010; Klyza & Sousa, 2013; Mazmanian & Kraft, 2009). Of the American cities pursuing sustainability, several trends have emerged through previous studies. We know that wealthier centralized cities located in the Western region of the United States are more likely to adopt sustainability policies. Yet, research also demonstrated that cities are failing to adequately engage with the pillar of equity and pursue policies that have clear co-benefits (Opp & Mosier, 2017; Opp & Saunders, 2013; Saha, 2009). Moreover, little is known about the nature of how cities are implementing and measuring the performance of sustainability policies and initiatives (Portney, 2013).

Performance measurement is an important and necessary task for governments for improving the efficiency and effectiveness of government policies, programs, and processes (Radin, 2006). Tracking performance creates an accountability mechanism to ensure governments are working toward stated policy goals. Generating accountability for sustainability policies ensures that valuable resources are well spent and the government can maintain needed political support for such policies. Given current political environment within the United States, it is imperative to prove that protecting the environment and promoting equity within a community can be achieved while simultaneously improving economic conditions. The future of our society and our overall quality of life is largely dependent on clearly identifying how sustainability policies are performing and demonstrating the benefits received from implementation.

Local Sustainability Experiences and Lessons

The chapters throughout this volume have outlined what cities are doing for sustainability and how they are measuring the performance of such policies. For scholars and practitioners alike, this book provides further evidence that cities are continuing to pursue sustainability policies. However, the survey results also demonstrate significant shortcomings for measuring and assessing policy performance. Each chapter provides an overview and depth to understanding the various dimensions related to sustainability efforts and how cities are working toward performance assessment. Chapter 2 provides a broad overview of local sustainability policies and Chapters 3–9, or Part II of this book, provide further depth to particular dimensions of those policies with case examples for how cities can actively measure and improve policy performance.

Chapter 2 provides a broad overview of the three key questions the authors seek to answer:

1. Using a comprehensive definition of the "Three E's" framework of sustainability, what policies are cities adopting?
2. What are the policy goals for the three E's of sustainability policy across cities (what are cities trying to accomplish)?
3. What methods do these cities employ to measure the effectiveness and efficiency of these policies (what information do they collect)?

The results of the 2016 survey show that American cities, including smaller to midsize communities that are an understudied population, are pursuing sustainability policies that include components related to transportation, pollution prevention, social equity, greening of city operations, and energy, water, and resource conservation. One caveat is that policies that are easy to implement and are low cost are more likely to be adopted because of potential co-benefits.

While this is not surprising given financial and other resource restrictions facing most local governments, it is very concerning trend. It begs the question of how can cities be pushed or enticed to adopt policies that are more difficult or costly to implement? To claim that cities are taking sustainability seriously requires local governments to pursue those policies that may not result in clear co-benefits or immediate and short-term financial savings. The nature of sustainability clearly indicates an intergenerational demand for current generations to curb their own resource needs so life and the environment can be sustained at a quality level suitable for future generations to thrive.

Another concerning policy trend discovered by the survey is that social equity is still a pillar largely ignored by most cities. Social equity is an integral component to sustainability initiatives and is as equally important as economic development and environmental protection for policy outcomes. Economic and environmental considerations may encompass certain equity concerns, but those policies may not directly include marginalized groups into local sustainability efforts. How then can cities begin to directly address this pillar of sustainability? Equity is a sensitive subject for most and requires the adoption of complex and difficult-to-implement policies. Reconceptualization or reframing of equity-based concerns to directly address economic or environmental concerns may only go so far to improving political acceptance and would likely not fulfill demands for co-benefits. Instead, cultural shifts may be necessary to create a sense of value of policies that lead to self-sufficiency of all while simultaneously creating policies that create individual responsibility and duty to community goals. This could largely depart from current cultural and political paradigms that emphasize economic rationalism or individualistic cultures found in liberal democracies.

In addition to reconfirming previous research findings on local sustainability efforts, the results of this survey study also demonstrate that performance measurement is lacking. Of those cities that are pursuing sustainability policies and plans, only a fraction of cities are actually measuring performance. This is particularly disheartening and concerning. No policy or program can claim to be efficient or effective if it is unknown where progression toward an end goal or set of goals currently stands.

A silver lining from our survey demonstrates that some communities are able to serve as models for how others can seek to integrate performance assessment practices into implementing sustainability policies and programs. Chapters 3–9 outline common performance measurements in various areas of sustainability planning. Indeed, the basis of the survey itself served to capture the variety of potential performance metrics that cities could use. While freely available census data may serve as a basis for many communities measuring performance, each chapter also highlights a variety of output- and outcome-based measurements used by cities that are not freely available from outside sources and would be more useful in assessing overall performance. Capturing current greenhouse gas (GHG) emissions or carbon footprint, tracking the number of improved walking or biking pathways, or calculating the cost savings by switching to energy-efficient lighting or appliances are just a few of many potential performance metrics that have been used and are more helpful in assessing over performance compared to freely available census data. Identifying strategies for how cities may integrate performance assessment into current administrative processes is a key step for cities to truly take sustainability seriously.

Strategies for Local Sustainability Performance Measurement Engagement

Performance measurement is a tool and task that any level of government can utilize to assess the overall efficiency and effectiveness of policies. For the issue of sustainability, identifying sets of indicators that aid in performance assessment should be seen as a necessary step for executing and evaluating policies and programs. Without the use of indicators, how could any government assess overall performance or seek to improve current programmatic offerings? It would be an insurmountable task and could result in biased and inaccurate results. However, the use of indicators and performance measurement assessment should be used with caution. The utility of indicators, particularly for the issue of sustainability, and benchmarking activities may not be well suited for all types of potential assessments or as education tools (see, for example, Brugmann, 2007), and performance measurement is a process that can be tainted with good intentions gone awry or misinterpretation of results (Radin, 2006). So how can local governments in the United States appropriately integrate indicators and performance assessment into current and future sustainability initiatives? Plan accordingly.

Research on sustainability indicators and benchmarking has identified a number of steps to fully utilizing indictors and benchmarking into local sustainability performance measurement. First, effectively incorporating performance measurement into the implementation process requires early and methodical planning. Indicators should ideally be directly associated and linked to existing policies and programs or identified during the development of a new policy and program. For example,

Bell and Morse (2003) developed a 12-step process for measuring sustainable development efforts in Malta. The authors' systemic and prospective sustainability analysis (SPSA) offers a step-by-step process for any government official to use when identifying and constructing indicators to measure the performance of a new or existing policy or program. Selecting indicators haphazardly could result in very inaccurate or misleading evaluations. Instead, indicators should be selected based on their ability to clearly demonstrate some desired outcome or output related to a policy goal or objective. In this respect, merely collecting data that is easy to assess or free will not lead to an accurate assessment unless it is clear that the free or easily assessed data serves an overarching policy or programmatic purpose.

Second, sustainability indicators, and by extension benchmarking, may only truly be useful in performance measurement at the local level. Sustainability indicators can be used in a variety of local governmental activities including public education and performance measurement. Yet in case evaluations of Seattle, WA, and Santa Monica, CA, Brugmann (2007) found that indicators were most successfully used to assess performance rather than used for public education or technical assessment. Brugmann notes,

> ...indicators are a tool that can be used for diverse purposes – to educate residents, to assess existing conditions, to guide planning decisions, or to focus and evaluate actions. However, each use implies different methods of development and standards of use, and it cannot be assumed that the indicators used for one purpose can be effectively applied for another purpose.
>
> (p. 70)

This is not to say indicators cannot be used for other purposes beyond performance assessment, but it does indicate caution when multipurposing indicators for different uses. Some researchers argue for indicators to be used in public education because of the inclusion of community stakeholders in local government efforts (for example, see Shields, Solar, & Martin, 2002; Pupphachai & Zuidema, 2017). Bell and Morse's 12-step SPSA process includes steps that incorporate stakeholder perspectives. Inclusion of community stakeholders may help to reinforce pre-identified indicators and the nature of local sustainability initiatives; however, the process of community inclusion may also fail to be more imaginative or accurate in the identification of indicators. The broader community may lack the capacity to truly understand the problem of sustainability or how indicators connect to policy assessment and communication. As a result, it may be possible to use indicators to achieve both public education and performance measurement processes, but city officials would be wise to clearly denote how indicators would best be used and err on the side of caution if intending multiuse indicators. Some indicators and benchmarks may only be useful in performance assessment and would be stretched to effectively communicate to community stakeholders about the intentions and quality of local sustainability programs and policies.

Finally, it is never too late to start tracking the performance of sustainability policies. The nature of sustainability policies leaves little wiggle room for assessment inaction. For the city official reading this book, a wide range of potential indicators and benchmarks are identified for how to measure local sustainability initiatives. Not all measured indicators are difficult to collect or freely available. Dedication of staff and resources to collection of indicator data and performance assessment would be necessary. For the cash-strapped city, it may be difficult to allocate resources for performance measurement activities, but the long-term benefits received can outweigh short-term costs. Proving sustainability policies create sustainable cities is the only definitive way to demonstrate the proof is in the pudding. If sustainability policies are demonstrated to create a better society, communities will face an easier battle in dedicating resources to such efforts.

Key Challenges for Local Sustainability in the Future

The concept and practice of "think globally but act locally" has taken on a more significant meaning the United States as more pressure is exerted upon local governments to answer the call for developing and implementing sustainability policies. A number of assessments on the adoption of local sustainability policies are promising because more cities are now in pursuit of sustainability initiatives. However, the results of our 2016 survey paint a bleak picture for if and how cities are tracking the performance of their sustainability policies. Adoption of sustainability-based policies is only one step in the effort to address the effects of climate change and to promote a healthier and more equitable society. Measuring the performance and outcomes of local sustainability policies is an equally important second step to actually addressing environmental, economic, and equity goals.

Performance measurement is a practice that embeds accountability in local government actions. Information obtained through the collection of measurement activities suggests if particular programs and policies are effective and efficient in achieving desired goals. It is imperative for cities to track performance of local sustainability efforts. Scarce resources and potential political hostility can manifest if cities are not accurately assessing the programs and policies enacted. Sustainability-based policies must deliver promised benefits to the community, and failure to know if benefits are received can undermine even the best-designed and executed policies. The information and lessons derived from this book demonstrate a range of sustainability initiatives undertaken by local governments in the United States. Moreover, the book demonstrates how cities can track the performance of such policies. Tracking the performance of sustainability policies can be as easy as tracking the number of miles of improved roadways to as complex as GHG inventory assessment. Yet, no matter the complexity, the ability to prove that sustainability can lead to better communities is key for current and future societies.

References

Bell, S., & Morse, S. (2003). *Measuring sustainability: Learning from doing.* London: Earthscan.

Brugmann, J. (2007). Is there a method in our measurement? The use of indicators in local sustainable development planning. *The International Journal of Justice and Sustainability*, 2(1), 59–72.

Conroy, M. (2006). Moving the middle ahead: Challenges and opportunities of sustainability Indiana, Kentucky, and Ohio. *Journal of Planning Education and Research*, 26, 18–27.

CNN. (2017). *Flint water crisis fast facts.* Available at: www.cnn.com/2016/03/04/us/flint-water-crisis-fast-facts/index.html.

ICMA. (2016). https://icma.org/articles/nearly-third-local-governments-have-adopted-sustainability-plans.

Ingraham, C. (2017). Flint's lead-poisoned water had a 'horrifyingly large' effect on fetal deaths, study finds. *The Washington Post*, September 21, 2017. Available at: www.washingtonpost.com/news/wonk/wp/2017/09/21/flints-lead-poisoned-water-had-a-horrifyingly-large-effect-on-fetal-deaths-study-finds/?utm_term=.e5e4b3df63c4.

Fischer, D. (2010). Local governments lead efforts to combat climate change. *Scientific American*. Available at: www.scientificamerican.com/article/local-governments-lead-efforts-to-combat-climate-change/.

Heberle, L. C., & Opp, S. M. (2008). *Local sustainable urban development in a globalized world.* Aldershot, UK: Ashgate.

Jepson, E. (2004). The adoption of sustainable development policies and techniques in U.S. cities: How wide, how deep, and what role for planners? *Journal of Planning Education and Research*, 23(2): 229–241.

Klyza, C. M., & Sousa, D. J. (2013). *American environmental policy, beyond gridlock.* Cambridge, MA: MIT Press.

Mazmanian, D. A., & Kraft, M. E. (2009). *Towards sustainable communities: Transition and transformations in environmental policy.* Cambridge, MA: MIT Press.

Opp, S. M., & Mosier, S. L. (2017). Counting money: Cities love climate policies if they generate local benefits. *Public Administration Review Speak your Mind.* Available at: https://publicadministrationreview.org/climate-change-symposium-local-climate-change-policy/.

Opp, S. M., & Osgood Jr, J. L. (2013). *Local economic development and the environment: Finding common ground.* Boca Raton, FL: CRC Press.

Opp, S. M., & Saunders, K. L. (2013). Pillar talk: Local sustainability initiatives and policies in the United States—Finding evidence of the "three E's":

Economic development, environmental protection, and social equity. *Urban Affairs Review*, doi:1078087412469344.

Portney, K. E. (2013). *Taking sustainable cities seriously* (2nd ed.). Cambridge, MA: MIT Press.

Pupphachai, U., & Zuidema, C. (2017). Sustainability indicators: A tool to generate learning and adaptation in sustainable urban development. *Ecological Indicators*, 72(1), 784–793.

Radin, B. (2006). *Challenging the performance movement: Accountability, complexity, and democratic values*. Washington, DC: Georgetown University Press.

Saha, D. (2009). Empirical research on local government sustainability efforts in the USA: gaps in the current literature. *Local Environment*, *14*(1), 17–30.

Saha, D., & Paterson, R. G. (2008). Local government efforts to promote the "three E's" of sustainable development: Survey in medium to large cities in the United States. *Journal of Planning Education and Research*, *28*(21), 21–37.

Schuppe, J. (2017). Hurricane Irma will test South Florida's breakneck development. *NBC News*. Available at: www.nbcnews.com/storyline/hurricane-irma/hurricane-irma-will-test-south-florida-s-breakneck-development-n799886.

Shields, D. J., Solar, S. V., & Martin, W. E. (2002). The role of values and objectives in communicating indicators of sustainability. *Ecological Indicators*, 2(1–2), 149–160.

Slavin, M. (2011). *Sustainability in America's Cities: Creating the Green Metropolis*. Washington, DC: Island Press.

Index

Page numbers in italic indicate figures and in bold indicate tables on the corresponding page.